Creating
Small Gardens

Roy Hay

Galley Press

Contents

This edition published 1979 by
Galley Press
In association with Cathay Books
59 Grosvenor Street, London W1

© 1975, Hennerwood Publications Limited

ISBN 0 904644 70 7

Produced by Mandarin Publishers Limited
22a Westlands Road
Quarry Bay, Hong Kong

Printed in Hong Kong

Growing
Plants
Indoors

Conditions

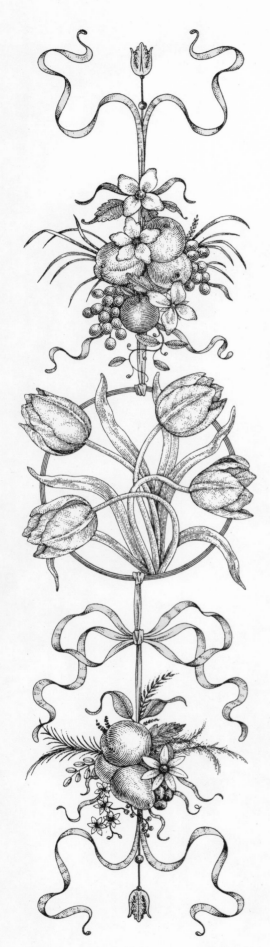

It is only comparatively recently that house plants have become as popular as they now are in city dwellings. At the beginning of this century the potted palm – a *Kentia*, now to be correctly known as *Howea* – was to be seen in many homes, largely among the more affluent, and in most public places. The less affluent contented themselves with a green or gold or silver-striped aspidistra and truly enormous specimens were grown and handed down from generation to generation.

Despite the fact that it is a lovely plant, the aspidistra seems to have taken a back seat in the resurgence of interest in house plants generally. We seldom see one in a florist's shop today or, for that matter, in a home. Its place has been taken by a range of foliage plants all of which require more warmth and few of which will withstand any frost.

While the use of central heating has greatly widened the range of plants that may be grown, it has also brought its problems. The main one, of course, is that the humidity in the air in a centrally heated room is too low for the comfort of many plants. Some, such as the mother-in-law's tongue, *Sansevieria*, the ivies, and the rubber plant, *Ficus elastica*, are not unduly perturbed by the fairly dry atmosphere. Others not so amenable to dry air can be made more comfortable if they are stood on pebbles in shallow trays which are kept filled with water. The moisture evaporating constantly from the water creates a slightly more humid atmosphere – a more congenial microclimate – just around the plants.

Again, several plants may be placed close together in a large container of some kind – an old copper coal bucket or preserving pan, a modern fibre-glass or exfoliated polystyrene 'jardinière' type of container. The pots are plunged in peat which is always kept moist and the evaporating moisture round the plants creates a more favourable atmosphere. If the plants are close enough for the leaves to form a canopy over the container, so much the better – it traps the moist air and stops it rising into the room so fast.

The worst places for plants that need a humid atmosphere, such as the African violets, or saintpaulias, are on a window sill above a radiator or hanging from a bracket on a wall. The warm air rising as it does causes the plant to dry out even more quickly than it would if it were standing on a side table in a room away from the source of heat.

Because we cannot see our plants 'sweating', that is, transpiring moisture through their leaves, we have no idea of how much water they lose in this way. I have not seen any estimates of moisture loss through transpiration of house plants, but to give you some idea of water loss through leaves, a fully grown maize plant in the open can transpire 2 lbs. (0·91 kg.) of water in a day.

Another problem that often arises with central heating is the considerable drop in temperature if, as in many homes, the heating is automatically turned off at night. The heat may be cut off from, say, midnight until 6 in the morning to economize on fuel. This may mean a drop in temperature from something between 21–27°C. (70–80°F.) to something like 13–15°C. (55–60°F), and many plants resent such drastic fluctuations. Even more violent fluctuations of temperature can, of course, occur in houses or apartments that have no central heating.

Then, too, the atmosphere in a living room in the evening may be over-heated and fuggy with tobacco smoke. Flowering plants especially do not like these conditions and it is prudent before a party to remove them to cooler and fresher surroundings. This will help to prolong their flowering.

It must be remembered that the coldest spot in a room on a frosty night is on a window sill between the glass and the curtains. If the curtains in your room shut the plants off from the warmth of the room, bring the pot plants inside the curtains on a cold night.

Then again, there are plants that do not like temperatures much above 15 to 18°C. (60 to 65°F.). The cyclamen is one of these plants, and indeed it reacts strongly and quickly to an over heated and over dry atmosphere. The plant is best – and longest – kept if placed in a cool part of the house, such as the hallway. I grieve to think how many cyclamen, or other pot plants, die within two or three months of being brought into a living room.

More will be said later about the care of cyclamen, but they are plants that do not readily adapt themselves to different growing conditions. It is not only a failure to adapt quickly enough to changed atmospheric conditions that may cause a cyclamen to languish, turn yellow, and drop its buds; it can also be caused by failure on the part of its owner to provide adequate water for the plant to 'live in the style to which it has been accustomed'.

Many pot plants today are grown in greenhouses on sub-irrigation benches. That is, the pots are stood on sand which is always kept moist automatically or they are watered by automatic tubing systems, and the plants draw up just as much water as they require. When you get the plant home from the florist's and you give it whatever amount of water you may think it needs, you may not be giving it as much as it was used to absorbing from its irrigation bench. It will usually soon tell you it is thirsty by drooping, or by losing its fresh bright green colour.

Light is not so great a problem in modern apartments or houses. If anything, you have to be on your guard against certain types of plant receiving too much hot sunlight during the day. Such plants should be kept further back in the room, away from direct sunlight, in summer, and moved nearer the windows in winter. Modern slatted blinds are excellent for windows that receive full sun. They may be adjusted to admit the right amount of sunlight to suit the type of plant being grown.

In old houses, especially in rooms with a north or east aspect, most plants will need to be kept as near the windows as possible.

It is, of course, possible to overcome adverse conditions – of heat, humidity, and even light, by growing plants in containers of one kind or another. Special growing cabinets with heating and lighting are available. Old glass fish tanks – aquaria – glass carboys, even large glass sweet jars may be used to grow various house plants. This aspect of modern cultivation is dealt with in more detail on page 17.

❧ Supplementary Lighting ❧

Some plants, particularly African violets and their many relatives, benefit from some supplementary lighting, either to highlight the plants by means of special spot lights, or to improve their growing conditions. For this purpose, ordinary fluorescent tubes are suitable except in a conservatory or somewhere with a moist atmosphere where waterproof fittings for tubular lighting are essential. Growing cabinets and units fitted with fluorescent tubular lights are also obtainable.

The tubes are usually hung, in reflector housings, about 20 inches (50 cm.) above the base upon which the plants stand, the latter being raised on inverted pots if necessary to be closer for more light. For foliage plants any regular fluorescent tube will do. Flowering plants, however, need more light. For these, use one tube each of wide-spectrum and cool white types or one warm white and one cool white, the latter combination being the less expensive. Usually they are governed by automatic timers to provide light 14 to 16 hours per day.

9

This attractive plant arrangement includes
Philodendron erubescens, Hibiscus rosa-sinensis
hybrid, *Scindapsus aureus, Neoregelia carolinae*
'Tricolor'

Choice of Plants

The choice of pot plants is obviously dictated by a number of factors – the heating arrangements, the amount of daylight available and, very important, the amount of space available. There is also the human factor. Some people have so-called 'green fingers' and grow a wide range of plants indoors with conspicuous success. Yet there are other people who are really best described as 'plant killers'. I know several who admit it quite cheerfully – you would almost think they take a pride in it.

I have never been very convinced by the 'green finger' theory. I am sure that people who have the reputation of being green-fingered have only earned it by years of patient observation and developing a feeling for plants. After all, it is usually 'old Mrs So and So', or 'my old grandmother' who is referred to as having green fingers. You do not often hear people referring to some young person as having the magic touch.

Success with growing anything depends on keen observation, anticipating a plant's needs and devoting sufficient time to the plants. They need to be looked at every day – not that it will be necessary to do something to them every day, but you must get to know and recognize any sign that a plant is not happy, needs more or less water, should be fed or repotted.

Then the amount of space available can to some extent influence the choice of plants. Some of the flowering plants – bulbs such as amaryllis (*Hippeastrum*), fuchsias and others – while charming in flower, are not attractive at other times. One really needs space to accommodate such plants during their off season, where they will not detract from the effect of more attractive plants.

Some plants too, like azaleas, the calamondin orange, *Citrus mitis*, benefit from being stood outdoors in a garden for some weeks in the summer. If you do not have a garden then a balcony or even a window box may be available to accommodate these plants for a time.

Another problem is the care of your plants when you go away for a holiday. Unless you have somebody whom you can trust to water and generally look after the plants intelligently in your absence, it is best to keep to those plants whose needs are simple and which will not suffer greatly from some neglect and maybe erratic watering. There are, of course, automatic watering devices and various techniques which you can adopt to keep plants adequately supplied with water for two or three weeks if necessary, and these are discussed on page 91.

Pot plants roughly fall into two main categories: those which can be grown happily for years in a living room, given favourable conditions and those which will put up with living room conditions for a few months and will then fade away. If a small heated greenhouse or conservatory is available they may be transferred there before they have deteriorated too much. Then, after a period of convalescence, they may return to do another spell of duty in the living room. Indeed, a small greenhouse, even the smallest lean-to, is a splendid investment, and if a lean-to can be constructed so that a window or French doors communicate with it, a delightful feature is added to the home.

A profusion of colour provided by sinningias (gloxinias) and begonias

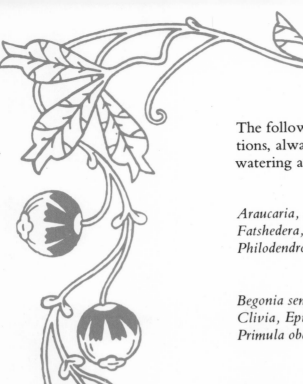

❧ Easy Plants ❧

The following are fairly easy plants to grow in normal living room conditions, always provided their likes and dislikes as regards warmth, light and watering are looked after.

Foliage Plants

Araucaria, Aspidistra, Begonia rex, Chlorophytum, Cissus, Cyperus, Fatshedera, Fatsia, Ferns, *Ficus elastica, Ficus pumila, Hedera* (ivies), *Philodendron, Rhoicissus, Sansevieria, Saxifraga, Scindapsus, Tradescantia.*

Flowering Plants

Begonia semperflorens, Beloperone, Billbergia, Cacti, *Campanula isophylla, Clivia, Epiphyllum, Fuchsia, Hippeastrum, Impatiens, Pelargonium, Primula obconica, Schlumbergera, Streptocarpus.*

❧ Foliage Plants ❧

Broadly speaking the foliage plants are the easiest to keep growing happily in the home. They fall into three main categories, those which make shapely plants like *Sansevieria, Fatshedera* and the like; the climbing plants like ivies, *Cissus, Philodendron* and *Scindapsus,* and the trailing plants suitable for hanging baskets and for hanging down over the side of large containers, such as *Tradescantia, Ficus pumila* and *Gynura sarmentosa.* The latter two may be considered together because several, like the ivies, *Ficus pumila* and *Cissus,* can be grown either up a supporting framework or hanging down.

❧ Climbing and Trailing Plants ❧

There is a good range of climbers which can be grown up a trellis to form a natural division to a room. The plants are best grown in pots plunged in peat within the container rather than being planted direct in the containers.

Climbers too may be grown around a wigwam of canes or a wire framework in a variety of shapes. This type of support is very popular with climbing flowers such as *Hoya carnosa.*

Climbing Plants

Cissus, Ficus, Hedera, Hoya, Monstera, Philodendron, Rhoicissus, Scindapsus, Thunbergia alata.

Trailing Plants

Trailing plants play an important part in any plant arrangement and, indeed, a single trailer can be most attractive on its own. Most of the trailers are easily propagated by cuttings and so one can use them fairly generously to hide, or in many cases to enhance, a container.
Asparagus, Cissus, Ficus, Gynura, Tradescantia, Zebrina.

❧ Flowering and Fruiting Plants ❧

Flowering plants and those grown for their ornamental fruits are generally regarded as more difficult to accommodate happily in the home than foliage plants. Some like hydrangeas really need a period standing outdoors in semi-shade after flowering. Others like saintpaulias do not like temperatures that fall below 10°C (50°F.) at night and cyclamen are really happiest when this temperature is kept between 10–13°C. (50–55°F.); it can rise higher but the plants will not last so long in flower. The flowering plants described on pp. 31–34 may be reasonably expected to last a year or two, some for many years. Of the fruiting plants mentioned, *Citrus mitis*, the calamondin orange, will probably last longest in the home. It will make a bush about 2 feet (60 cm.) high and wide. It produces small, rather bitter, oranges about the size of a plum. The capsicums are usually grown as annuals and discarded after they have fruited; the winter cherry, *Solanum capsicastrum* is usually treated likewise. It can be trimmed back in March however, repotted and kept for another year.

Bulbs

Bulbs are among the most rewarding of plants to grow indoors, and of course outdoors as well. Nature has done 90 per cent of the work for us because a bulb contains in embryo the already formed leaves, stem and flower, and all we have to do is provide the right conditions for the bulb to grow and blossom.

Bulbs indoors fall into two categories – those that may be grown in pots for years, like the *Hippeastrum* or amaryllis, and those which we grow in pots or bowls to flower indoors once and then to be planted out in the garden or discarded.

Of the bulbs that we grow in bowls or pots there is the possibility of growing prepared bulbs that will flower for Christmas or very early in the new year. Daffodils and tulips are given special pre-cooling treatment by the bulb growers to encourage them to flower earlier than normal and hyacinths are also treated – they are given heat treatment in fact – to flower easily by Christmas. Then of course there is a great range of bulbs beside the daffodils, hyacinths and tulips, which can be grown in pots indoors – scillas, muscari, ranunculus, crocuses, tritonias, ixias, sparaxis, and even chionodoxas.

Bulbs such as those of hippeastrums which are to be grown in the same pot for years need to be potted originally in a fairly good loam-based potting soil. If this is not available, one of the peat-based mixtures may be used.

For those bulbs to be grown only for flowering once indoors and then to be planted out in the garden a special bulb fibre based on peat with charcoal and crushed shell added to keep the mixture sweet, is the best type of medium to use. These bulbs may be grown in pots with a drainage hole, or in bowls without drainage. Obviously watering is more tricky in bowls without drainage. It is necessary to water regularly to keep the peat fibre always moist as it is very difficult to wet again if it is allowed to dry out. Do make sure that there is no surplus water lying at the bottom of the bowl. Put your hand over the bulbs and the fibre to keep them in place, and tip the bowl gently on its side to allow surplus water to drain out.

It is also important never to allow water to touch the developing bud of a hyacinth because if this happens it is quite likely that a number of the little florets on the spike will turn brown and fail to develop.

Planting Bulbs

See that the potting mix is just moist but not too wet – a little moisture should escape between your fingers if you squeeze a handful. Spread a layer of the mix on the bottom of the bowl or pot and then gently place the bulbs in contact with the fibre, but do not firm them down too much. Fill up the container with more fibre so that the noses of the bulbs are just visible above the top of the mix.

A most imposing display can be obtained by planting 2 layers of tulips, or daffodils, in an 8–10 inch (20–25 cm.) pot. The technique here is to half-fill the pot with the fibre or peat-based mixture and then place 5 double-nosed daffodil bulbs, or 8–10 tulips on the mixture half way up the pot. Add more mix and place another layer of daffodils, say 7 daffodil bulbs, or another 8 or 9 tulip bulbs, on top. The lower bulbs will grow up between the uppermost ones and a massive display of blooms is the result.

It is important to keep bulbs in pots or bowls as cool as possible. It is preferable also to keep them in the dark until they are well rooted, but this is not necessary. You can place them in black plastic bags in a cupboard or somewhere until they are showing signs of growth. They may then be brought out into the warmth and light gradually. The essential is to try and keep them at a temperature of about 4–7°C. (40–45°F.) for 8 to 10 weeks after planting to encourage good root development.

When the daffodils or tulips have made about 2 inches (5 cm.) of growth they should be ready to be brought into a warm room. Do not bring hyacinths into the warmth until the bud is well clear of the neck of the bulb.

When you do bring bulbs into the warmth accustom them to the light gradually. Put them fairly well back in the room for a few days until they become green because the stems will be rather pale and yellow after being brought out of the dark, and gradually move them towards the light. Turn the bowl every day so the plants do not draw too much towards the light.

Remember that the window sill can be the coldest place in the house at night. All pot plants, and especially bulbs, should be brought into the room before the curtains are drawn on a cold night.

When bulbs have finished flowering place them in some odd corner if possible, or even outside on a balcony or in the garden if the weather is warm enough. Continue to water them until the foliage dies down if it is not possible to plant them out. Alternatively, if they can be planted in the ground, tip them out of their bowl and plant as soon as flowering is over.

Bulbs that have once been forced in pots or bowls cannot be used a second time for this purpose. With the probable exception of tulips which must be looked upon as expendable, most bulbs will flower again in the garden, but they may take a year or more to recover from their forcing.

❧ Cacti ☙

Cacti and other succulent plants are excellent for growing in the home as most of them will survive short periods of neglect better than most house plants. Those described on page 34 are fairly easy to grow in the home and should flower regularly.

❧ Herbs ☙

If there is room for a box or a few pots in a sunny window it is possible to grow an interesting range of herbs indoors. Some, such as sage and rosemary, need frequent pinching to stop them from becoming too large. They need to be replaced by young plants every year or so. Normal snipping or pinching of leaves or shoots as required for culinary use is usually sufficient to keep the plants bushy and compact. It is of course easily possible to clip them too hard and this temptation must be avoided. It is probably best to grow the different herbs in separate pots and plunge them in peat in a box or container. If planted direct in a box or trough some of the more invasive herbs like mint may be too rampant for the others.

Grow them in any normal potting mixture and feed with liquid fertilizer as directed by the manufacturers. The following are worth growing indoors:

Balm, a perennial which may be kept to a low bush by frequent pinching of the shoots. Propagate by division.

Basil, an annual raised from seed sown in March. Pinch shoots regularly to keep the plant to about 12 inches (30 cm.) high.

Cactus dish garden

Bay, a small bay tree may be grown in a pot for a number of years until it becomes too big. Propagate by cuttings.

Chives, which grow well in containers in sun or partial shade if given a rest before forcing. Propagate by division.

Marjoram, a dwarf bushy hardy perennial much used in 'bouquets garnis', stuffings and stews. The common marjoram and the sweet marjoram prefer a sunny aspect. Propagate by seed or cuttings.

Mint, best kept in a box on its own as it is very invasive. There are several kinds of mint but spearmint is probably the best for a window box. Mint will grow in sun or partial shade. Cut the plants down in October. Some pieces of root may be placed in a box or pot of soil and brought indoors to provide fresh leaves in winter. Propagate by division.

Parsley, this also will grow in sun or partial shade. Seeds are sown in March or April. Thin the seedlings as soon as they are large enough to handle, leaving the plants 6 inches (15 cm.) apart. Cover them with a glass or plastic cloche in the winter.

Rosemary, like sage will make a large bush but can be kept small and bushy by regularly pinching the young shoots. Propagate by cuttings.

Sage, must be trimmed frequently to keep it bushy and about 2 feet (60 cm.) high. It will grow in sun or partial shade. Propagate by cuttings.

Tarragon, pinch growth regularly to keep the plant to about 12–18 inches (30–45 cm.) high. Propagate by division.

Thyme, there are several types of thyme, including varieties with gold or silver variegated foliage. Propagate by cuttings.

Mustard and cress, while they cannot be classified as herbs, may be grown very easily indoors in full light on pads of cotton wool, flannel or old sacking or in a seed sowing mixture. Sow cress 3 days before the mustard or rape seed. They will both be ready 11–14 days after sowing the cress.

Plants from Pips

You can have a certain amount of fun by growing plants from kitchen scraps such as date, peach or avocado stones, orange and lemon pips, and tops of pineapples. Many of these plants can eventually grow too big for an indoor situation but will meanwhile, however, give much pleasure.

An amusing and cheap way of obtaining greenery is to slice off the top of root vegetables such as carrots, beetroot and turnips. Remove any old or broken leaves, and stand the flat base of the sliced off part in a tray with an inch or two of pebbles and fill with water. Keep the tray full of water and new growths will appear giving fresh foliage for months.

There are several ways of germinating seeds from orange, grapefruit, lemons, apples and pears. One is to sow them in a pot of peat kept moist in a plastic bag. Another is to put them between two thick paper napkins and keep these always moist. The seeds should germinate in about a month, and the seedlings can then be potted singly in small pots.

To germinate an avocado stone, pierce it with several toothpicks or cocktail sticks, and suspend it over a jar or tumbler of water. The pointed end should be uppermost, the other end constantly in the water. When roots appear, pot the stone in an 8 inch pot. The growths need to be pinched to promote side shoots, and these too are pinched or stopped in turn to promote bushy growth.

Peach, apricot or plum stones should be cracked and sown in sand or peat, and kept moist. They may take several months to germinate.

The trick with a pineapple top, after cutting off the leaves and a slice of the fruit, is to run a hot iron over the flesh very quickly to seal it. Otherwise the flesh will rot. Plant it in a pot of gritty soil and water it very sparingly.

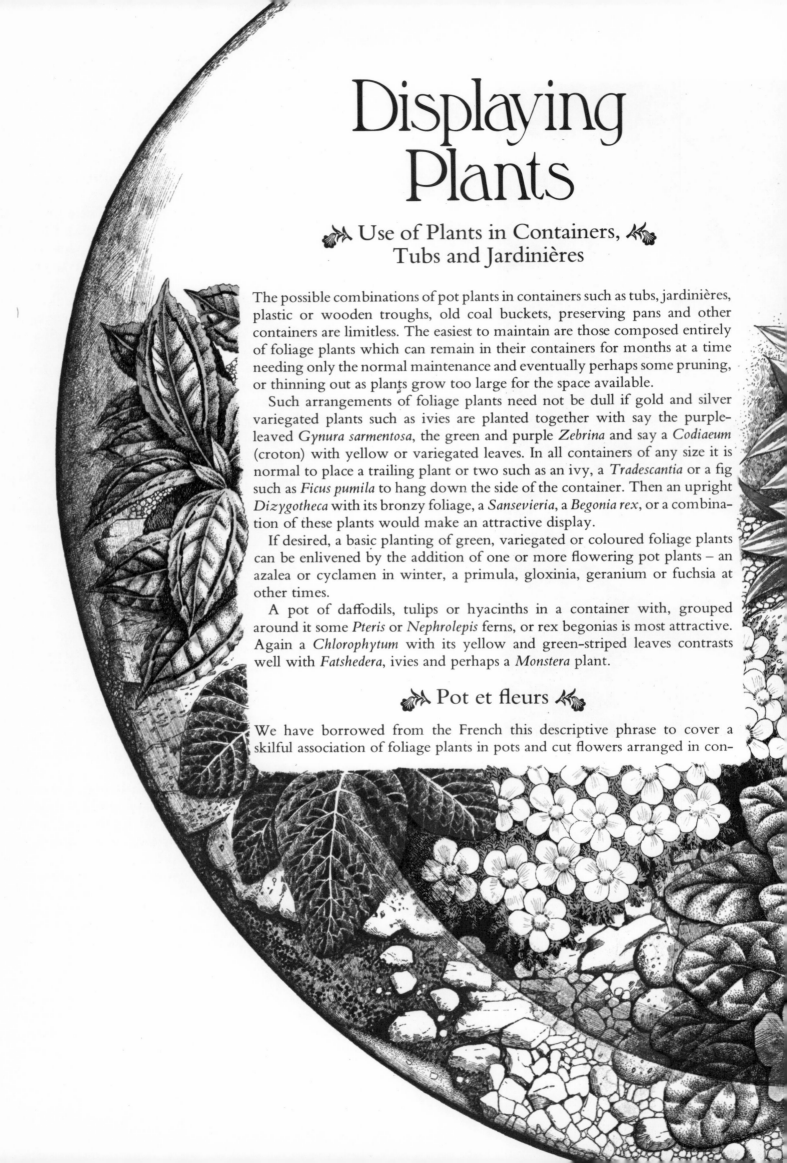

Displaying Plants

❧ Use of Plants in Containers, ❧ Tubs and Jardinières

The possible combinations of pot plants in containers such as tubs, jardinières, plastic or wooden troughs, old coal buckets, preserving pans and other containers are limitless. The easiest to maintain are those composed entirely of foliage plants which can remain in their containers for months at a time needing only the normal maintenance and eventually perhaps some pruning, or thinning out as plants grow too large for the space available.

Such arrangements of foliage plants need not be dull if gold and silver variegated plants such as ivies are planted together with say the purple-leaved *Gynura sarmentosa*, the green and purple *Zebrina* and say a *Codiaeum* (croton) with yellow or variegated leaves. In all containers of any size it is normal to place a trailing plant or two such as an ivy, a *Tradescantia* or a fig such as *Ficus pumila* to hang down the side of the container. Then an upright *Dizygotheca* with its bronzy foliage, a *Sansevieria*, a *Begonia rex*, or a combination of these plants would make an attractive display.

If desired, a basic planting of green, variegated or coloured foliage plants can be enlivened by the addition of one or more flowering pot plants – an azalea or cyclamen in winter, a primula, gloxinia, geranium or fuchsia at other times.

A pot of daffodils, tulips or hyacinths in a container with, grouped around it some *Pteris* or *Nephrolepis* ferns, or rex begonias is most attractive. Again a *Chlorophytum* with its yellow and green-striped leaves contrasts well with *Fatshedera*, ivies and perhaps a *Monstera* plant.

❧ Pot et fleurs ❧

We have borrowed from the French this descriptive phrase to cover a skilful association of foliage plants in pots and cut flowers arranged in concealed vases or jars of water.

There is much to be said for this technique. The foliage plants form the basis of the arrangement which is enlivened by the cut flowers – different flowers in the different seasons – and you do not become bored with the foliage plants.

It is also economical of flowers as, say, 5 daffodils or tulips or 3 or 4 chrysanthemums make a colourful contrast with the foliage plants.

Bottle Gardens

A terrarium is basically a glass container that is planted with a carefully chosen selection of plants to achieve a balanced environment. The plants absorb moisture from the soil, transpire it through their leaves and after it has condensed take it in again from the soil. Naturally this calls for careful management – seeing that the soil is kept only moist, not wet and that the top of the container is kept in position unless water condenses and fogs the inside of the glass. When this happens it is left partially open at night to allow some ventilation.

With bottles of varying sizes up to the large glass carboys that were used for transporting chemicals, now alas almost collector's items, begin by depositing a layer of an inch or so (a few cm.) of pea gravel on the bottom. This is then covered with 3–4 inches of potting mix. This has to be poured in dry and it is important that the inside of the glass is dry as if by chance soil sticks to wet glass as you are pouring it in it is difficult to clean it off.

Unless the bottle, carboy or other glass container – old fish tank or specially made glass case – is open at the top or has an opening through which a small hand can pass, you have to make a few primitive tools. An old kitchen fork with the prongs bent at right angles to the handles or an old tea spoon may be tied to a cane. These implements enable you to dig a little hole in the planting mixture and after placing a plant in it to draw the soil up to cover the roots. It is possible to lower the plant into place by holding it between 2 pieces of cane. A thread reel on the end of a cane is useful for tamping or firming the soil gently. When the plants are all in place spread a layer of small gravel or stone chippings over the planting mixture after watering it well.

Depending on the size of the bottle or other receptacle a choice of plants for terrariums may be made from the following:
Cryptanthus, Fittonia, Ferns, *Hedera* (ivies), Mosses, *Peperomia, Pilea, Saintpaulia, Saxifraga, Sedum, Tradescantia, Zebrina.* Cacti

❧ Hanging Baskets ❧

The different types of hanging baskets and pots and how to plant in them are described on page 36 where we are considering these containers for use outdoors.

Indoors the plastic pot with a 'built-in' saucer at the base is convenient as with care you can water it without having to take it out and stand it over a basin or sink. Failing this type, or if the plastic bowl is considered unsightly even when partially hidden by trailing plants you may use an open wire or metal type of basket.

A layer of sphagnum moss is packed round the inside of the basket and the pots are bedded in more moss. This type of basket of course needs more careful and frequent watering than the solid plastic bowl type.

Many lovely combinations of plants may be arranged in a hanging pot or basket. Quite a simple display may be made from 4–5 different varieties of ivy – say one of the crested leaf types, a small green variety and both a silver and gold variegated form. One could be trained to grow up over one or two short sticks and the others allowed to hang down.

Alternatively you could combine a bush-type fuchsia with some trailing plants; an ivy-leaved geranium hanging down with an upright begonia and one or two trailing ivies or tradescantias form a colourful basket.

Plants for Hanging Baskets

Asparagus, Begonia, Campanula isophylla, Chlorophytum, Cissus, Ficus pumila, Ficus repens, Fuchsia, Gynura, Hedera (ivy), *Impatiens, Pelargonium* (geranium), *Saxifraga stolonifera* (syn. *S. sarmentosa*), *Streptocarpus, Schlumbergera, Tradescantia, Zebrina.*

❧ Miniature Gardens ❧

Great pleasure may be had from miniature gardens indoors and of course outdoors too.

Almost any kind of bowl, tray, trough or similar container is suitable for making a miniature garden provided it has at least one drainage hole in the base. It means of course that the garden must be on a tray of some kind to protect furniture from moisture draining out from the container.

The round or square earthenware pans or 'half pots' as they are known in the flower pot business are excellent as they have adequate drainage holes. Some people do not like the 'flower pot red' or terracotta colouring but you can always paint the outside with a stone-coloured cement wash if desired.

Cover the drainage hole or holes with one or two pieces of broken flower pot or china, then cover the base of the container with a layer of an inch or so of pebbles or broken flower pot. On top of the pebbles place a layer of peat and then fill the container to about two-thirds of its depth with preferably a loam-based potting mix. If this is not available fill it with a peat-based compost, in which case it is not necessary to put the layer of peat over the pebbles. Place one or two pieces of rock so that they are partially submerged and then 'landscape' the surface soil so that it undulates gently.

One or two true dwarf conifers, *Saxifraga stolonifera* or other low growing house plants may then be placed in position.

Alternatively a small garden may be made entirely of cacti – a desert garden. For this a sandy soil and plenty of drainage material in the bottom of the container are necessary. Garden shops often sell a soil mixture especially for cacti.

All the plants mentioned on page 17 for bottle gardens may of course be grown in miniature gardens.

Various ferns and ivy have been used to great
effect in these hanging baskets

Propagation

There are several ways of raising house plants, or of increasing your stock. The most commonly practised is rooting cuttings, usually, but not exclusively, of the foliage plants. Propagation by leaf cuttings is an easy way of increasing some plants like begonias and African violets.

Plants like sansevierias, aspidistras and clivias may be increased by division of the root when it has made a sufficient number of growths.

Many house plants grown for their flowers, and also a number of foliage plants are raised from seed.

A fourth way of increasing your stock is to detach and plant the small plantlets which are produced on the parent plants. The thousand mothers, or pig-a-back plant, *Tolmiea menziesii*, and *Chlorophytum elatum* are propagated in this way.

Air layering is sometimes practised for rooting a shoot of a large shrubby plant like a *Ficus* or rubber plant.

Cuttings

Cuttings may be taken from either the stem or the leaf of the plant. Many cuttings will not root unless grown in a warm and humid atmosphere. This may be artificially provided by using a propagating case.

You can buy plastic seed trays which have dome-like covers. Some of the plastic covers have adjustable ventilators set in the top of the cover. You can also buy propagating cases with electric heating capable of maintaining temperatures of 21–27°C. (70–80°F.) which are desirable for raising seeds of certain types of tropical plants. For most cuttings, however, ordinary room temperatures of around 21°C (70°F) are satisfactory.

An improvised propagator can be made by filling either a box or a large flower pot with the cutting medium and then bending 4 pieces of wire into a rough half circle and pushing the ends into the pot. After the cuttings have been inserted in the potting mix, drape thin clear plastic over the wires and tie it round the pot just below the rim.

Most stem cuttings consist of young unflowered shoots about 3–4 inches (7·5–10 cm.) long. The lowest pair of leaves is removed and a clean cut is made with a sharp knife or a razor blade just below the node or joint where the lower leaves were removed. This is the type of cutting made from plants of *Pelargonium* (geranium), *Hydrangea*, *Fuchsia*, *Tradescantia*, *Cissus* and similar plants.

The prepared shoots are inserted in a mixture of peat and really coarse sand or, as some call it, grit. The fine sticky yellow sand is not good for this purpose as the object of mixing the sand with the peat is to help drainage and to keep the mixture sweet. For most cuttings equal parts by bulk of moist peat and sand is a suitable mixture. Or you can buy proprietary peat-based cuttings mixtures. There are also peat-based mixtures which are suitable for seed sowing, rooting cuttings and for potting.

Some people use a 'hormone' type of rooting compound to hasten rooting. The base of the cutting is dipped in the powder before it is inserted in the rooting medium. Some rooting compounds contain a fungicide such as captan which helps to prevent the cutting from rotting at the base. Bruising of the base of the cutting, as often happens if they are cut with secateurs, may encourage rotting. For this reason always use a sharp knife or a razor blade.

Make sure the cutting mixture is nicely moist. Insert the cuttings around the inner edge of the flower pot, making a hole with a pencil deep enough to

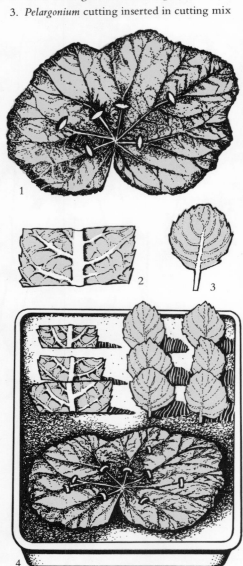

1. Stem cutting of a *Hydrangea*
2. Stem cutting of a zonal *Pelargonium*
3. *Pelargonium* cutting inserted in cutting mix

1. A *Begonia* leaf with cuts made through the veins
2. Sections of a *Streptocarpus* leaf
3. A *Saintpaulia* leaf
4. The leaves appropriately placed in the cutting medium

20

take the bottom 2 inches (5 cm.) or so of the cutting. Do not make the hole too deep – the base of the cutting should rest on the soil at the bottom of the hole.

When the cuttings have been inserted, and the plastic cover put in place, stand the pot in a light place but out of direct sunshine.

A pot is really the best receptacle for rooting a small number of cuttings. If a large number is required use a seed box, but do not cram the cuttings in too close together – they should not touch each other. As soon as the cuttings have rooted, put them singly in small pots – 3 inch (7·5 cm.) diameter is a good size for the first potting.

Short shoots, about 4 inches (10 cm.) long, of some foliage plants such as ivy and *Impatiens* (busy lizzie) will produce roots if the stems are inserted for about 2 inches (5 cm.) of their length in water. When they have produced roots an inch (about 2·5 cm.) or so in length they may be inserted carefully in a small pot – 3 inch (7·5 cm.) diameter – of potting soil.

🌿 Leaf Cuttings 🌿

A number of plants, notably *Saintpaulia*, *Streptocarpus* and *Begonia* may be propagated by leaf cuttings. With *Saintpaulia*, the African violet, a leaf with a length of stem is used, and the bottom inch or so of stem is inserted in the cutting medium. African violet leaves will also make roots if the bottom inch or so of stem is inserted in water. *Streptocarpus* leaves are cut right across horizontally in sections about 1–2 inches (2·5–5 cm.) wide. These are inserted in the soil vertically.

Leaves of *Begonia rex* and similar foliage forms may be treated in different ways. A whole leaf may be laid on the surface of the cutting medium, and cuts made through the veins at a distance of about 2 inches (5 cm.) apart with a razor blade or a sharp knife. Small stones are placed at intervals on the leaf, or pegs of bent wire are used, to keep the cut surfaces in contact with the soil.

Alternatively small pieces of leaf about the size of a large postage stamp, each piece containing a section of a vein, may be laid on the rooting medium or inserted in it to half their depth vertically. The cuttings, leaves or leaf sections must be kept moist and in a temperature of 18–24°C. (65–75°F.). They will root best if kept in a propagating case or in a box covered with a sheet of glass or plastic film.

🌿 Air Layering 🌿

This is a favourite method of propagating certain types of plant with a woody stem, such as the rubber plant, *Ficus elastica*, or cordylines.

At a point, say 2 feet (60 cm.) below the top of the shoot, make an upward slit in the stem about 1–1½ inches (2·5–4 cm.) long. Wedge the slit open with a sliver of wood. Additionally, if desired, remove a narrow circle of bark about ½ an inch (1·3 cm.) wide round the stem just above the slit. Dust this area liberally with rooting compound. Then wrap thin plastic film round the stem, tying it below the slit. The film should be wide enough and over-lapping so that it forms a kind of cylindrical 'bag' over the cut part. Fill this container with moist sphagnum moss or peat, and then tie it to the stem above the cut. In about 10 weeks roots should grow from the wounded area, and the stem may then be severed from the parent plant and the new plant potted carefully, taking care not to damage the roots.

🌿 Plantlets 🌿

Several plants we may grow in the home produce tiny plantlets on their leaves, or on stems or stolons. These little plantlets may be detached carefully

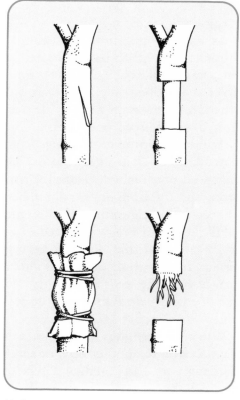

Air layering

21

and rooted in a pot or box of cutting medium. Some plantlets, such as those that appear on stems produced on plants of *Chlorophytum elatum*, may be left until they are say 2 inches (5 cm.) high before they are detached. Those produced at the top of the leaf stalk on *Tolmiea menziesii* are detached as soon as they are large enough to handle.

Another plant that produces small plantlets is *Saxifraga stolonifera* (*S. sarmentosa*), commonly known as mother of thousands, Aaron's beard, roving sailor or strawberry geranium. The red creeping stems or stolons are produced from the heart of the plant, and these bear the young plantlets which root easily.

A succulent plant easy to grow in the home is *Bryophyllum daigremontianum*. It produces many tiny plantlets around the edges of the leaves. These may be detached when they are quite small – ¼–½ inch (0·64–1·3 cm.) across, and 'sown' or scattered on the cutting or seed sowing mix in a pot, and kept warm and moist. They root very easily.

Division

A few plants are propagated by division of the crowns, or by separating 'offset' shoots as in sansevierias. Prise the soil away from the ball of soil and loosen the roots as much as possible. Then with a sharp knife separate and sever where necessary young well rooted pieces of the old plant. Pot these separately.

Seeds

Many flowering plants such as *Cyclamen*, *Clivia*, *Impatiens* and *Begonia* are easily raised from seed provided one has the space on a window sill or on a bench near a window. Many foliage plants too may be raised from seeds – *Coleus*, *Ficus*, *Pilea* and *Grevillea* among them.

It is also possible to raise young plants from date and peach stones, orange and lemon pips, and the seed of the avocado pear (see page 15). This gives a certain amount of interest and pleasure, but eventually the plants become too large for a living room and have to be discarded.

As with propagation by cuttings, no elaborate equipment is necessary although it helps to have a heated propagating case that can be kept at a temperature of 21–27°C. (70–80°F.). Failing this, a pot or box with a plastic cover as described on p. 20 may be stood near a radiator or in another warm situation to maintain a steady degree of heat. It is not necessary to exclude light from the seed pot or box. The only seed I know which must have darkness for germination is *Nigella*, the love in a mist, which is never germinated indoors or in a greenhouse. The reason why gardeners used to cover their seed pots or boxes with brown paper was to keep them shaded from strong sun and from drying out unnecessarily. Naturally, as soon as the seeds are seen to have germinated, they must be brought into the light.

Fill the pot or box with a seed sowing mixture, either one based on loam, or a peat-based mix. Level it very gently by pressing a flat board on the surface, but on no account consolidate the mixture – just make an even level surface. Sow the seeds very thinly. With fine seeds it helps to mix them with fine dry sand before sowing. Just cover the seed with fine sifted soil or fine sand.

When the seedlings have opened 2 leaves, prick them off – that is, transplant them into another box, or singly into very small 1–2 inch (2·5–5 cm.) diameter pots. Later on they will be transferred to 3–3½ inch (7·5–9 cm.) pots in which they should pass their first year or 18 months. After seedlings have been pricked off shade them from strong light, and of course see that they

This effective room-divider uses *Neoregelia carolinae* 'Tricolor', *Philodendron erubescens*, *Sansevieria trifasciata* 'Laurentii', *Dracaena deremensis*, *Vriesea splendens*, *Cyperus alternifolius*, *Ficus elastica* 'Doescheri', *Schefflera actinophylla*, *Scindapsus aureus*

never dry out.

Cactus seeds are often sold as a mixture of as many as a dozen species or varieties. These often germinate over a long period – months even. So, as the seedlings appear, carefully remove them, using the tip of a penknife blade, as they become large enough, and pot them singly in small pots.

The flat seeds of the attractive foliage plant *Grevillea robusta* germinate best if they are inserted in the soil edgewise.

23

Care of Plants

Success with house plants depends on several factors. One is the maintenance of temperatures within the upper and lower ranges that the plants being grown will tolerate. We must accept that if we cannot do this, some plants will sulk and dwindle away and we end up, as we should probably have begun, by trying to find plants to fit their surroundings rather than by trying to make the surroundings fit the plants.

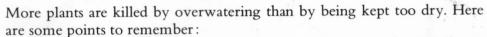

Watering

More plants are killed by overwatering than by being kept too dry. Here are some points to remember:

The larger the leaf area the more water the plant will transpire through the leaves.

The warmer the atmosphere the more water the leaves will transpire. Plants will use more water in spring and summer when they are in active growth than in winter when growth is not so active.

Plants standing on their own with dry warm air circulating freely around them will dry out more quickly than several plunged together in a container filled with moist peat.

Plants in clay pots will need watering more often than those in plastic pots as water evaporates through the sides of a clay pot but not through plastic. If, therefore, you have several plants in a jardinière or other container, do not mix clay and plastic pots. Watering will be easier if you have all clay or all plastic pots.

Many plants today are grown in peat-based mixes. If these are allowed to dry out it is very difficult to wet the mix again by pouring water into the top of the pot. This applies, but to a lesser extent, to loam-based mixtures. The soil ball shrinks, leaving a small gap between it and the pot wall. You pour in water, but most of it runs down through this gap and out at the bottom. With either type of mix, but essentially with the peat-based ones, it is best to plunge the pot in a basin or bucket of tepid water. When bubbles stop coming to the surface the soil will have absorbed enough water.

It is not possible to say that you should apply water once a week, every 2 or 3 days, or according to any preconceived programme. You should apply water when the plants need it, and just before they tell you they are thirsty by allowing their leaves to droop. It does not matter very much if the leaves do flag a little now and then, but it is better to see that plants do not suffer from want of water.

If you have plants in a container or a cache-pot, there should be a layer of peat, sand or pebbles at the bottom so that if surplus water drains through the pot it will not be standing in a pool of water. Individual pots are often stood in a saucer or some kind of deepish tray to protect the surface of furniture or a window sill. Again, do not let such trays fill with water. It is better to fill the tray with pebbles so that the base of the pot is not standing in a pool of water.

If you look at your plants frequently – every day or two – you will soon get to know when they need water. Simply by lifting a pot you will be able to tell whether it feels light and therefore needs water. If you tap a clay pot with

To retain moisture, group several pots together in a container filled with moist peat.

Stand the pot on pebbles and not directly in water

your knuckle it will ring hollow if the soil mixture is dry, but there will be a dull thud if it is wet.

As a general rule it is best to wait until a plant needs a good watering, and to give it plenty, allowing surplus water to drain away.

Some plants need more careful watering than others. Begonias, for example, do not like water on their leaves in hot sunshine – the little globules of water act as a lens and scorching of the leaves can occur. Cyclamen, when flower buds are present, should be watered from below, by standing the pot in water so that it comes half way up the pot. The soil mix will eventually soak up water until it is wet again. If you do water from above take care not to allow water to come into contact with the small flower buds on top of the corm since they may rot.

As I said before, a plant will tell you if it is thirsty by flagging, and no great harm will be done. But by the time a plant tells you it has had too much water for too long, by rotting at the base or by its leaves turning yellow, becoming spotted, or by buds or leaves dropping off, it is often too late to do much about it. Obviously a much drier regime is indicated, and on no account should a sickly plant be fed with liquid fertilizer.

It can happen, especially in winter and if plants are being kept in rather low temperatures, that the leaves may droop causing you to think the plants are dry. But they may flag because they are too wet, and if you give them more water you only make them more unhappy.

❧ Feeding ❦

To keep pot plants growing happily the roots obviously must be able to absorb adequate supplies of food. This they do by absorbing the plant nutrients in solution – they cannot take in solid food. Hence another reason for seeing that plants get all the water they need.

When you buy a pot plant, or if you propagate your own using, usually, a 3–4 inch (7·5–10 cm.) diameter pot for their first potting, they can generally be kept in this size pot for a year. Then if the ball of soil mix is permeated by roots and these are wrapped thickly round the outside of the ball, the plant needs repotting. This is explained in more detail on page 26.

When a plant has rooted nicely into its mix, no matter what size of pot, after 2–3 months it responds to regular feeding. Plants are fed during their growing season – spring to autumn, March to October, and not during the winter when growth is not active.

There are many proprietary fertilizers specially formulated for pot plants, and these should be applied according to the maker's instructions. With some concentrated liquid fertilizers it is usual to add a few drops to the can of water each time you water your plants. With others, you see that the soil is moist, not saturated, and then you apply a dose of the diluted plant food. Never apply fertilizer to dry soil.

With some fertilizers it often pays to apply the liquid at half the recommended strength and twice as often as the makers suggest. Many plants seem to appreciate this 'little and often' treatment.

There are also solid fertilizers which can be sprinkled on the surface of the soil, but these have to be watered in anyway, so it is really more convenient to apply a liquid fertilizer in the first place.

Foliar feeding – that is, applying the fertilizers by spraying it on the leaves of plants is becoming very popular. There are several foliar feeds containing the basic plant foods as well as a number of trace elements which plants need. A fine spraying with a foliar feed now and then stimulates root action and improves the colour of the foliage. Do not, however, apply foliar feeds to plants standing in full sun.

Newly repotted plant showing original soil ball in larger pot of fresh potting mix, see following page.

❧ Repotting ❦

When a plant has made a large amount of root growth it needs moving into a larger pot. To find out if a plant needs repotting, put your hand over the top of the ball of soil with your fingers either side of the plant, invert the pot, and tap the edge smartly on the top of a table or shelf. The plant should come cleanly out of the pot. If the roots are virtually covering the outside of the ball then the plant needs repotting.

Usually when a plant needs repotting it is moved into a pot an inch or so larger all round – from a 3½ inch (9 cm.) pot to a 5 inch (13 cm) pot, and so on. Do not 'overpot' – that is, do not put a plant in a pot unnecessarily large. If there is too great a volume of soil it may become sour before the plant roots have penetrated it thoroughly.

Once you have decided that a plant needs repotting, and which size pot you are going to use, remove the top inch or so (a few cm.) of soil from the top of the soil ball. If the ball is very thickly encased in roots, press the sides of the ball firmly to loosen some of the roots. If the plant has been in a clay pot there will probably be embedded in the base of the soil ball, one or more pieces of 'crock' or broken pot which were put in to ensure good drainage. Remove these and tease out the roots at the base.

If you are going to put the plant into another clay pot then 'crock' it by placing a large piece of broken pot over the drainage hole and one or two small pieces on top of this. It is not necessary to crock plastic pots as the drainage holes are usually more numerous and smaller so that there is no danger of soil washing out through the bottom of the pot.

Whether you use clay or plastic pots, make sure that they are scrupulously clean. Soak them in water with household detergent and brush off all dirt. Soak new clay pots thoroughly in clear water before use.

After placing the crocks if a clay pot is used, put a layer of potting mix in the bottom of the pot. Make the layer thick enough so that the top of the ball of soil is about an inch below the level of the pot rim. Then fill the space between the old soil ball and the new pot with potting mix, working it in with a wooden label or with fingers. Cover the top of the old ball with mix, but allow about ½–¾ inch (1·3–2 cm.) between the top of the mix and the pot rim to make watering easy. Usually if you fill the pot with water this is all the plant requires at that particular watering.

Firm loam-based mixes gently, but do not firm peat-based composts. Just tap the pot smartly on the bench to settle the mix; the necessary watering in will consolidate the mix sufficiently. If peat composts are firmed they will become waterlogged and plants will rot.

Always water newly potted or repotted plants and keep them in a warm spot, but shaded from the sun for a few days until they have settled into the new mix.

❧ Diseases and Pests ❦

In many cases diseases are caused, or aggravated by unsatisfactory conditions. Be vigilant for the first signs of trouble, and check for possible causes – watering, irregular temperatures, draughts, too dry an atmosphere, fumes, poor light conditions, starvation or actual presence of pests.

It is very difficult to cure a disease. The most one can do is to try to provide conditions which will not encourage the incidence and spread of disease, see pages 8–9. In most cases rotting of leaves and stems, especially at the base of the plant, indicates that the plants have been consistently overwatered.

Immediately you see a yellowing, mottled, mouldy or mildewed leaf, or rotting stems or foliage, cut out the affected parts.

If you see any of the signs of pest damage indicated below, then examine the plant carefully. Turn the leaves over, as many pests feed on the underside of the leaves. If there are young tender leaves, say at the end of a shoot, look carefully among these for aphis (greenfly) and other pests. Naturally they tend to congregate and feed on tender young tissue.

As part of the general care of pot plants, clean the foliage regularly to remove dust. This can be a killer if plants are left too long with a layer of dust preventing the leaves from breathing. Wipe large leaves with a damp cloth. Plants with large numbers of small leaves may be stood out in the rain on warm days, or, holding your fingers firmly over the top of the pot to prevent the plant from falling out, draw the foliage to and fro several times in a sink filled with tepid water.

There are plenty of effective insecticides on the market – derris is a very safe control for aphis and most of the other pests likely to infest house plants. One of the easiest and most effective ways of destroying pests is by means of an aerosol spray. These are rather expensive but so little is used that the convenience outweighs the cost. With an aerosol the fine misty liquid penetrates between young leaves and under the foliage. Some insecticides, particularly any containing derris, are poisonous to fish, so if you have a fish bowl keep it covered when spraying your plants.

Symptoms of Trouble

Leaves turning yellow – dropping off.
> Faulty watering – usually overwatering. Unsuitable temperature – too cold in winter, wide fluctuations or draughty conditions.

Leaves yellowing or becoming streaked, spotted or mottled, brown at the edges.
> Mechanical damage (breaks, cuts and abrasions), draughts.

Leaves covered with white or grey mould.
> Mildew or *Botrytis* mould.

Leaves drooping or dropping off.
> Drought, usually in summer; overwatering, usually in winter.

Leaves or stems rotting.
> Usually caused by overwatering, sometimes as a result of physical injury.

Flowers and buds dropping off.
> Overwatering, too dry an atmosphere.

Leaves or buds eaten at edges, distorted.
> Caused by pests – aphis (greenfly), white fly, thrips, mealy bugs, or vine weevils.

Leaves tunnelled.
> Leaf miner.

Leaves pale, brittle and minutely spotted.
> Red spider or spider mite; worst in too dry conditions.

Plant pale, weak and spindly.
> Lack of plant food. Too high temperatures. Too little light.

Sinningia, (Gloxinia), special hybrids

A-Z of Plants

Foliage House Plants

Aphelandra squarrosa
Distinctive pointed, white-veined leaves; flowers like bright yellow pineapples composed of overlapping bracts. Best in warm room in bright but not direct sunlight. Keep away from draughts.
Water freely in summer, feeding weekly until flowers form. Water sparingly in winter and hardly at all for about 10 weeks after the flowers fade. Raise new plants from shoot tip cuttings in gritty potting mixture in gentle heat.

Araucaria excelsa (Norfolk Island pine)
Christmas tree shape with slightly pendent branches clad with needle-like leaves. Thrives in full sun or semi-shade in normal room temperature. Water freely in spring and summer, less so when growth slows down in autumn and winter. Feed fortnightly in growing season with liquid fertilizer if growth poor.
Prevent it from becoming pot-bound and suffering, by repotting each spring, in a size larger pot. Raise new plants from seed.

Asparagus
Two kinds generally grown: *A. plumosus* with ferny fronds and *A. sprengeri* with leaves like pine needles. Grows well in sun or semi-shade; good for hanging baskets, draughty halls or ill-lit windowsills. Normal room temperature.
Keep soil moist throughout growing season or leaves inclined to yellow and fall. Let soil remain drier in winter. Feed weekly from spring to late summer.

Propagate from seeds sown in gentle heat or division of the rootstock.

Aspidistra (cast iron plant)
Broad, glossy spear-shaped leaves, green or striped creamy white. Does well in semi-shade and does not object to gas fumes. Will stay healthy even if neglected for many weeks. Normal room temperature. Freshen leaves by sponging them or spraying them occasionally with clear water.
Give ample water in spring and summer but less in winter.
Increase it by dividing the rootstock.

Begonia rex
Large heart-shaped leaves with irregular edges, patterned with cream, red or purple.
Develops most handsome foliage in moist, semi-shade conditions in normal room temperature.
Keep the soil moist in summer, but drier in winter. Feed fortnightly with dilute liquid fertilizer throughout the growing season.
Set pots inside larger ones, packing gaps with peat which is kept moist to encourage strong healthy growth. Dry air can cause leaves to wither and fall. Propagate from leaf cuttings pegged flat on to sandy surface in gentle heat or cut into sections, each containing a main vein.

Bryophyllum
Spear-shaped leaves edged with baby plantlets. *B. daigremontianum* has leaves which are purplish red in colour and distinctly toothed. Pinkish yellow flowers borne in winter.
Set plants in good light at normal room temperature, watering frequently in summer, but less so in winter. No

28

feeding necessary.

Get new plants from the babies which are easily detached from the leaf margin, often complete with roots, and grow them on in small pots of potting mix.

Chlorophytum (spider plant)

Rosette of green, white-striped leaves. Pendent stems of creamy white flowers appear from the centre, often with plantlets at their tips. Established plants have a cascade of rosettes which look most effective from the top of a pedestal.

Tolerates light shade or bright hot conditions in which many other house plants would fail. Normal room temperature best.

Give plenty of water in summer, less in winter.

No feeding necessary if plant is set in good potting mix to start with. Root plantlets that form at ends of stems.

Cissus (kangaroo vine)

Two forms commonly grown: *C. antarctica* with shining spear-shaped leaves and *C. discolor* with triangular green leaves patterned silvery white and purple. Thrive in semi-shade or full sun.

Keep the soil moist during the growing season, but less so in autumn and winter. Feed once a fortnight if growth slow.

Normal room temperature.

Raise plants from stem cuttings.

Codiaeum (croton)

Broad or narrow glossy leaves variously patterned, flecked or striped with yellow or orange.

Needs evenly warm and moist atmosphere in good light. Bathroom or kitchen ideal. Keep the soil moist throughout the year and feed every ten days during the growing season. Sponge leaves to keep them bright and shining and spray them frequently with clear water in summer.

Good plan to set pot inside larger one, packing space with peat, keeping this moist. This lessens risk of leaf drop. Raise new plants from stem cuttings.

Coleus

Magnificent foliage plant. Leaves splashed or patterned red, green, yellow, purple, brown or black; heart-shaped with toothed or frilled edges. Grows well in good light position at normal room temperature.

Keep roots well watered in summer but drier in winter. Spray leaves with clear water during growing season but not in winter.

Propagate from stem cuttings or seeds sown in gentle heat.

Cyperus alternifolia (Madagascar umbrella plant)

Long thin stems topped by umbrella of leaves.

Set plants in good light in humid atmosphere. Keep out of full sun. Normal room temperature. Water freely in summer but keep soil drier in autumn and winter. Feed every 10–14 days throughout the growing season. Cut away fading leaves to make way for new growth.

Propagate from stem cuttings rooted in water, or by dividing the stock.

Dieffenbachia (dumb cane)

Large paddle-like leaves mottled green and white.

Light shade or good light, but not direct sunlight or leaves may shrivel. Normal room temperature, humid atmosphere.

Feed weekly throughout spring and summer and keep soil moist during the growing season, and in winter.

Raise new plants from suckers from base of plant or by rooting sections of the stem.

Dizygotheca elegantissima

Graceful long stemmed palmate leaves composed of narrow toothed 'fingers'. Green or reddish brown in colour.

Semi-shade in summer but have plants in good light in winter. Humid atmosphere necessary for strong growth, so ideally fit pots into larger ones, filling intervening space with peat which is kept moist.

Keep the soil moist in summer, dryish in winter. Normal room

temperature. Encourage handsome leaves by feeding every 10 days during the growing season.

Raise plants from stem cuttings.

Fatshedera lizei

Result of crossing an ivy (*Hedera*) with a *Fatsia*. Trailing habit. Leaves large, glossy, palmate.

Normal room temperature. Water freely throughout the year. Feed weekly and freshen leaves by sponging regularly. Keep plants shapely by nipping out growing point if they become too tall. Support growth with canes, wires or trellis-work.

Increase plants from stem cuttings.

Fatsia japonica (aralia, fig-leaved palm)

Dark green, shiny fingered leaves. Does well in semi-shade or good light. Normal room temperature. Water freely in spring and summer, less in autumn and winter.

Feed every 10 days and sponge leaves or spray them with clear water to keep them bright and fresh.

Increase from stem cuttings.

Ficus elastica (rubber plant)

Central stem set with broad, pointed leathery leaves that take a high gloss; there is a variegated form.

Best in good light but tolerates light shade. Normal room temperature. Water thoroughly, then leave until soil becomes dry on top. Keep soil fairly dry in winter.

Feed fortnightly from April to September. Either sponge leaves with water to keep them glossy and bright, or use proprietary leaf-cleaning substance.

Air layer top of plant if lower stem loses its leaves. Alternatively, raise new plants from stem or leaf cuttings.

Ficus pumila (creeping fig)

Creeping rubber plant with tiny heart-shaped leaves.

Grows well in light shade or full sun, in warm or cold room.

Give ample water in summer, less in winter. Feed weekly only if growth slow. Spray leaves with clear water if the air is hot and dry to prevent leaves curling.

Grow new plants from stem cuttings.

Gynura sarmentosa

Spreading plant with long nettle-like leaves with a silky purple sheen.

Grows well in baking sun; ideal for conservatories or sun lounges where few other plants can stand the dry heat. Normal room temperature. Water freely in summer, less in winter. Feed fortnightly from March to September.
Raise new plants from shoot tip cuttings.

Hedera helix (English ivy)
Glossy, green or variegated lobed and pointed leaves. Trailing plant for semi-shade, or good but not bright conditions. Looks well in hanging basket. Can be grown outdoors throughout the year. Spray leaves with clear water once a week if plants grown in warm dry room. This will prevent leaf drop and red spider attacks. Water freely in summer, less in winter. Feed weekly throughout the growing season.
Remove any green leaves which sprout up in variegated foliage varieties. Increase plants from stem cuttings. 'Glacier', 'Gloire de Marengo' and 'Chicago' are 3 of the brightest varieties.

Howea belmoreana (Kentia)
Graceful palm for warm conservatories or greenhouses. Fronds consist of central midribs set with numerous long and narrow leaflets about 12 to 15 inches (30–38 cm.) in length. Height of plant 10 feet (3 m.).

Frond stems around 18 inches (45 cm.) long.
Sun or shade, good rich soil to encourage luxuriant growth. Spray leaves frequently with warm water in spring and summer. Feed fortnightly with dilute liquid fertilizer. Normal room temperature.
Prune away dead leaves as they fade.
Raise new plants from seeds.

Monstera deliciosa (Swiss cheese plant, hurricane plant)
Handsome climber with large sliced or perforated leaves. Occasionally a pine cone-like flower appears followed by a fruit which is edible and has a pineapple flavour. Prefers semi-shade in warm moist conditions at around normal room temperature. Keep the soil moist in summer and drier in winter.
Sponge the leaves frequently to keep them shining bright. Provide some form of support for the trailing stems which often grow attractive white aerial roots. Feed weekly throughout the growing season.
Raise new plants from cuttings.

Peperomia
Low growing plant with deep green crinkled and ribbed, heart-shaped leaves; creamy white-striped or mottled creamy yellowish leaves. White rat's tail flower spikes.
P. caperata, P. sandersii and *P.*

magnoliaefolia most commonly grown for their striking foliage.
All do well in normal room temperature in good light or semi-shade. Water freely in summer, less in winter. Feed fortnightly if growth poor. Syringe leaves to freshen them and keep them free from dust.
Raise new plants from division of the parent plant or from cuttings.

Philodendron
Leaves glossy and of various shapes, as: *P. bipinnatifidum*, deeply fingered; *P. scandens*, heart-shaped; *P. melanochrysum*, large and narrowly shield-shaped. All thrive in good but not bright light or semi-shade, in a humid atmosphere at normal room temperature.
Give plenty of water in summer, but let soil dry so that it is just moist in winter. Feed weekly throughout spring and summer. Sponge and syringe the leaves frequently to enhance their appearance and keep down red spider mite. Provide support for the climbing stems.
Increase from stem and leaf cuttings.

Pilea cadierei
Oval leaves patterned with silver. Spreading plant for sunny windowsill; tolerates light shade.
Grows well in dry air conditions at normal room temperature. Water freely in spring and summer, slightly less in autumn and winter.
Feed weekly during growing season.
Increase from shoot tip cuttings.

Rhoicissus rhomboidea
Climber with tripartite diamond-shaped leaves. Good for hanging baskets, trailing from pedestals. Thrives in light shade or good but not direct light in normal room temperature. Give plenty of water in spring and summer, keeping soil just moist in winter. Feed fortnightly during the growing season if progress slow.
Raise new plants from stem cuttings.

Sansevieria (mother-in-law's tongue, snake plant)
Erect sword-shaped leaves. Three kinds usually grown: *S. trifasciata* has greyish white banded leaves, *S. trifasciata laurentii* has tall yellow-

Exacum affine

Impatiens sultanii (Busy Lizzie)

edged leaves, while *S. trifasciata hahnii* is much smaller with greenish grey banded leaves. Best at normal room temperature. Water very carefully at all times making sure not to over-wet the soil. Keep fairly dry in winter, just moist in summer.
Feed fortnightly throughout the spring and summer. Enjoys good light position though will tolerate semi-shade. Raise new plants from division or stem sections.

Scindapsus aureus

Climbing or trailing plant with fleshy, flecked and mottled creamy yellow variegated leaves.
Does well in good but not bright sunlight. Tends to lose its variegation in semi-shade. Normal room temperature.
Water freely in summer, less in winter. The soil should never be waterlogged. Encourage strong growth by feeding weekly throughout the spring and summer. Pinch out shoot tips of straggly shoots to encourage them to bush out.
Increase plants from stem cuttings.

Tradescantia (wandering Jew)

Two widely grown are *T. fluminensis*, with silver and green-striped leaves and *T. blossfeldiana*, with boat-shaped leaves dark purple beneath. Normal room temperature. Best in good but not bright sunlight. In semi-shade, leaves lose their colouring and remain pale grass-green.

Water to keep soil moist in summer but dryish in winter when growth slows down. Finest leaves in warm humid atmosphere of bathroom or steamy kitchen. Raise new plants from cuttings of shoot tips. Feed fortnightly throughout the growing season, from April to September.

Vriesea splendens (flaming sword)

Rosette of thick, narrow, dark green banded leaves from centre of which appears an ear-of-corn-like flower in red and yellow. Prefers semi-shade but tolerates bright but not direct sunlight. Normal room temperature. Water well in spring and summer, less so during winter. Fill funnel-shaped centre of leaf rosette with water to help flower spike form. After flower fades, the plant dies, to be followed by sucker growths around the edge. Detach these with roots and plant them out singly in small pots of peaty potting mix. Feed fortnightly while growing strongly and flowering.

Zebrina (wandering Jew)

Effective trailer with mauve, green and silver striped leaves, the undersides of which are shining purple.
Best in semi-shade or good light – not direct sunlight. Normal room temperature.
Water freely while plants growing strongly in spring and summer. Keep soil just moist in autumn and winter. Feed fortnightly throughout the growing season.

Raise new plants from shoot tip cuttings which strike easily.

Ferns

Adiantum (maidenhair fern)
Asplenium (bird's nest fern)
Nephrolepis (ladder fern)
Pteris (ribbon fern)
The above need similar treatment and thrive in light shade; they object to hot sunny conditions. Normal room temperature.
Water freely in both summer and winter, feeding weekly in spring and summer. Syringe fronds with water to keep them fresh in dry air.
Raise plants by dividing the rootstock; sowing spores.
Asplenium needs very warm moist conditions and thrives if set in larger pots packed with sphagnum moss which is kept watered.

Flowering House Plants

Azalea see **Rhododendron**

Begonia semperflorens

Splendid as a summer bedding plant or house plant for semi-shade or full sun. Red, white, or pink flowers massed on short stems clad with bright glossy green or bronzy foliage. Normal room temperature. Give plenty of water in summer, just

keeping soil moist in winter.
Feed every 7 days in summer and early autumn. Remove faded flowers to help others form.
Raise new plants from stem cuttings or division of the rootstock.

Beloperone guttata (shrimp plant)
Small arching stems with 'shrimp' or 'prawn' shaped flowers of brownish red overlapping bracts. In flower for many weeks at a time.
Needs position in full sun or shoots become leggy and flowerless. Normal room temperature, humid atmosphere. Water freely in spring and summer, less in winter. Feed weekly throughout the growing season. Shorten straggly shoots after flowering.
Raise new plants from cuttings.

Billbergia nutans (angel's tears, queen's tears)
Rosette of thin strap-shaped leaves and hanging carmine flowers with yellow centres.
Best in semi-shade or good but not direct sunlight. Water freely throughout the summer, less so in winter. Normal room temperature; able to withstand dry air of central heating. Feed fortnightly from April to September. After flowering the plant dies, but sucker shoots from the base can be planted out singly in small pots of gritty potting mix.

Campanula isophylla (star of Bethlehem)
Perfect for hanging baskets in light airy conditions. Starry blue or white bellflowers form freely on trailing stems. Normal room temperature; may be set outdoors in summer. Water freely in summer, but less so from late August onwards until fresh shoots appear. Feed fortnightly from mid-summer until fresh growth forms. Cut back fading flowers to encourage new shoots. Keep soil dryish and plant cool during resting period from early autumn to mid-winter. Increase plants from stem cuttings.

Capsicum (pepper)
Glossy red or yellow cone-shaped peppers; highly decorative. Best in bright sunshine at normal room temperature. Water freely in summer, spraying the leaves with clear water from time to time. Feed fortnightly throughout the spring and up until flowers form.

Raise new plants from seed each year. Old plants discarded after flowering.

Citrus mitis (Calamondin orange)
Scented white flowers followed by small golf ball-sized oranges. Leaves narrow, pointed, quite striking. Fruits form early in the life of this plant. Grows well in pots.
Living-room conditions in good light but not direct sun. Water freely in summer, syringing leaves occasionally, but keeping soil drier in winter.
Feed fortnightly to encourage lustrous leaves.
Raise new plants from seed or cuttings.

Clivia (Kaffir lily)
Rosy red flowers born in umbels on top of stout fleshy stems. Strap-like leaves.
Best in good light in airy conditions at normal room temperature. Give ample water in summer, less in winter. Avoid saturating potting mixture. Encourage growth by feeding fortnightly throughout the spring and summer. Let soil become fairly dry and set plant in coolish spot from September to late December. Return to warmer conditions in spring and replace top inch of pot soil with fresh potting mix.
Increase from suckers at base of plant, or division of the rootstock.

Cyclamen persicum
Frilled or smooth pink, red purple or white flowers. Blooms borne on tubular fleshy stems from among handsome patterned and marbled leaves. Best in good light in airy conditions. Temperature critical: 13–16°C. (55–60°F.) ideal. If too hot and dry leaves rapidly yellow and wither.

Plunge pot rim deep outdoors in sunny position for the summer. No special watering needed throughout the summer. Bring indoors in August and repot in rich potting mixture. Water carefully in autumn and winter, making sure that the corm does not get too wet. Feed fortnightly throughout the autumn and winter period.
Raise new plants from seed.

Exacum affine
Small yellow-centred, blue-flowered plant with bright green leaves. Prefers semi-shade. Thrives at normal room temperature.
Give plenty of water in summer and feed fortnightly throughout the growing season.
This is grown as an annual and plants are raised from seed or cuttings.

Fuchsia
Fat or slender bell-shaped flowers like ballet skirts. Colours range from deep purple through scarlet, rosy red, pink, orange and white; there are even some with bluish tints.
Grows best in good light in airy conditions but will tolerate semi-shade. Water freely throughout the summer but keep soil dryish in winter when plants resting. Feed fortnightly during the spring and summer.
Prune back shoots in late winter, early spring and repot in fresh soil, watering well to encourage new growth.
Raise new plants from stem cuttings.

Geranium see **Pelargonium**

Gloxinia see **Sinningia**

Hippeastrum (amaryllis)
Flared trumpet-shaped flowers in vivid colours; sword-like leaves. Does well in good light position at normal room temperature.
Keep soil moist in spring and summer, but drier from August onwards until the leaves die back and the bulb rests until December.
When planting, set the bulb only halfway in the soil. Feed fortnightly from late winter to early autumn.
The flowers are produced after Christmas and specially prepared bulbs will flower a few weeks earlier than unprepared bulbs.

Hoya carnosa (Japanese wax or honey flower)

Climbing evergreen whose broad leathery leaves offset rounded clusters of starry, pale pink flowers. Rich fragrance. Light, sunny position best; ideal for hanging baskets. Normal room temperature in summer, cooler in winter. Water freely throughout the growing season but less so in winter. Feed every 10 days with dilute liquid fertilizer, from late winter to September. Train stems round a wire support up canes.
Raise new plants from stem cuttings.

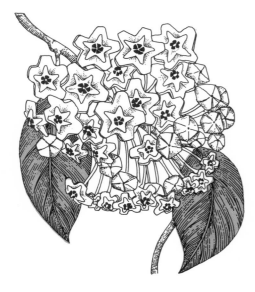

Hydrangea hortensis (H. macrophylla)
The florist's hydrangea has very large, usually single or occasionally double ball-headed blooms on short stems around 9 inches (23 cm.) high. Colours: shades of blue, red, pink and white. Give it a cool light airy position when in flower and feed weekly with dilute liquid fertilizer to prolong the display. Blooms appear over the winter period. Change pink varieties to a deep, ultramarine-blue by adding a teaspoonful of alum to the pot soil and watering this in.
After flowering, shorten the shoots to leave one or two pairs of leaves above the older wood. Continue to feed and water to sustain new growth.
Set the plant outdoors in a lightly shaded spot for the summer and bring indoors in September for plant to flower again.
Raise new plants from stem cuttings in early summer.

Impatiens sultanii (busy lizzie)
Popular flowering house plant that almost thrives on neglect. Fleshy stems set with myriads of pinkish rose, scarlet, carmine, orange or violet flowers.

Set in full sun to encourage free flowering. Normal room temperature, humid atmosphere. Pinch out growing tips to encourage branching. Feed weekly throughout the growing season from March to September. Water freely throughout the summer, less in winter or stems may rot. Increase from seeds or stem cuttings.

Pelargonium (geranium)
Geranium is the common misnomer for *Pelargonium*. There are three distinct kinds: ivy-leaved; zonal, with banded leaves; and regal, with more irregularly shaped leaves. The latter is tender and is best grown indoors in light airy conditions at normal room temperature. Both the zonal and ivy-leaved may be grown indoors or bedded out for the summer.
Their flowers are brilliantly hued, orange, pink, white and red. All do well in good light.
Water freely in summer, drying off plants for the winter, unless they are rooted cuttings when they should be kept just moist.
Feed weekly throughout the growing season.
Dig up plants in early autumn when nights grow cool and overwinter them in boxes of soil in a frost-free greenhouse or cold, not freezing, well-lit room.
Take cuttings in August.

Primula obconica
Clusters of rose-pink, red, blue or white flowers in bloom throughout the year. Leaves rounded and slightly hairy. Most reliable house plant. Give it a position in full light at normal room temperature. Water freely in summer, less so in winter. Feed every 7 days in summer.
This primula can cause the skin to develop a rash. Do not grow it if you are allergic to it. Cut back the faded flowers, and pot on in spring if roots are filling the pot. Raise new plants from seed.

Rhododendron indicum
This is the correct name for the plant still probably better known as *Azalea indica*.
Single or double peony-like flowers massed on short stems. Evergreen shrub. Does best in good light or semi-shade. Normal room temperature, humid atmosphere. Spray leaves if the air is hot and dry.

Feed fortnightly while flowers are forming and water freely. After flowering, put plant in unheated but frost-free place, watering less and withholding feed. The soil must not become too dry. Remove dead flowers. Sink pot outdoors in the soil for the summer and continue to feed and water regularly. Bring it back inside in September and repot in peaty soil. Give ample water and feed fortnightly while new growth is forming and flower buds developing.

Saintpaulia (African violet)
Single or double flowers in many shades including pink, carmine, scarlet, cream and azure-blue. Leaves hairy, greyish green.
Thrives in semi-shade or good but not bright sunlight. Flourishes in a humid atmosphere and benefits from an occasional steam bath.
Water whenever the soil is dry in summer, but sparingly in autumn and winter, especially after flowering. Avoid splashing the leaves with water as this can cause brown patches to develop. Summer temperature 18–21°C. (65–70°F.); reduce to 13°C. (55°F.) in autumn and winter.
Feed fortnightly throughout the spring and early summer.
Increase from leaf cuttings.

Saxifraga stolonifera (syn. *S. sarmentosa*) (mother-of-thousands)
Round reddish green, white veined leaves that form an almost flat rosette, from the centre of which slender upright stems of white butterfly-like flower sprays appear.
Ideal for hanging baskets in good but not full sun. Normal room temperature. Keep the soil moist in summer and dryish in winter. Feed fortnightly throughout the spring and summer.
Cut away fading leaves to allow fresh ones to replace them. Young leaves also have brighter markings.
Set out plantlets that form on wiry stems from the centre of the plant.

Sinningia (gloxinia)
Red, blue, white or pink, bell-shaped flowers with plain or frilled petals edged white in some varieties.
Best in light shade away from direct sun, or leaves will flop. Humid atmosphere desirable. Normal room temperature.
Water to keep soil moist in spring and

summer, feeding fortnightly to encourage long flowering and strong healthy growth. In autumn when the flowers fade and leaves wither and die back, cease watering and keep the soil quite dry over winter.

In March, start tubers into growth once more in a tray of moist peat in a warm, moist place. When they are sprouting freely, repot the tubers in peaty potting mix. Pinch out all but the three strongest shoots which are left to form a sturdy plant.

Raise new plants from leaf cuttings or seeds.

Solanum (Christmas cherry)
Popular pot plant for Christmas with orange-red marble-sized berries set on shoot tips amid dark green leaves. Best in bright airy position at normal room temperature. Water freely whenever the soil is dry and spray the flowers to encourage a good set of fruits. Feed every 10 days when flower buds are forming.

Cut back fruited shoots to an inch or two of the main framework, when the berries are over.

Raise from seed or cuttings.

Streptocarpus (Cape primrose)
Striking blue, pink, white or violet trumpet flowers, some attractively veined, on long slender stems. Crinkly primrose-like leaves. Place in semi-shade in humid atmosphere at normal room temperature. Water liberally in summer, hardly at all in winter, or just sufficient to prevent soil getting too dry.

Feed fortnightly when flower buds forming. Rest plant from October to March, in cool, dryish conditions. Raise new plants from seeds or leaf cuttings.

Thunbergia alata (black-eyed Susan)
Open orange-yellow black-centred flowers borne freely on trailing stems. Best in light airy position. Looks well in hanging baskets or cascading from window boxes. Normal room temperature. Give plenty of water throughout the growing season and feed fortnightly to encourage strong growth and many flowers.

Raise from seeds each spring and pot on singly in small pots. Nip out growing tip to make plant branch and form several flowering shoots. Discard after flowering.

Cacti

Epiphyllum
Cactus hybrids with yellow, white, pink and crimson-hued flowers like flamboyant waterlilies. Fleshy jointed stems, flattened and waved at the edges. Best in diffused light; will tolerate light shade. Normal room temperature. Water freely throughout the growing season, and keep the soil fairly moist in winter. Feed weekly from April to September.

Repot annually when flowers fade. Raise new plants from seeds or cuttings.

Mammillaria
This cactus forms its flowers in a ring on top of the plant. They are bell-like with flared petals and mostly purplish, red or creamy white. Full sun and normal room temperature. Water freely in summer but hardly at all in winter.

No feeding necessary unless growth is slow. Raise new plants from cuttings.

Rebutia
Brilliant coloured trumpet flowers in all shades of pink, orange, red and yellow. Blooms last about a week and are freely produced. Cactus body globe-shaped, set with minute spines and hairs. Thrives in full sun, at normal room temperature. Ideal for hot dry conditions.

Water freely from April to September,

keeping the soil fairly dry for the rest of the year. Feed fortnightly if growth slow.

Raise new plants from cuttings.

Rhipsalidopsis (Easter cactus)
Scarlet trumpet flowers borne at the tips of thick, fleshy jointed leaves. Grows best in full sun but will tolerate light shade. Normal room temperature. Water freely throughout the spring and summer but less so during autumn and winter, particularly from December to January when shoots are ripening and flower buds forming.

Feed every ten days from late spring to autumn.

Propagate new plants from leaf cuttings snapped off at a joint.

Schlumbergera (*Zygocactus*, Christmas cactus, crab cactus)
Magenta-rose fuchsia-like flowers borne at the tips of pendent fleshy jointed stems.

Good but not direct sunlight, normal room temperature.

Water freely in spring, sparingly from June to August. Keep soil fairly dry in winter but water freely when flower buds appear. Spray foliage with clear water to keep plants fresh in hot dry air of centrally heated room.

Feed only if growth is slow and then during the late spring and summer. Increase plants from stem cuttings broken off at a joint.

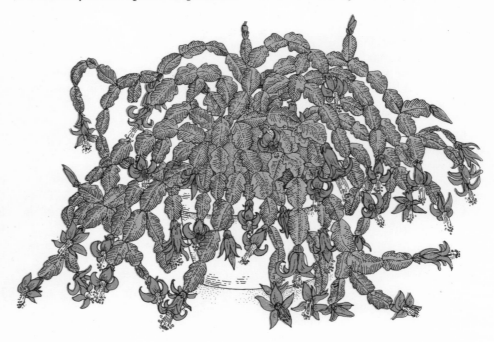

(right) Full advantage has been made here of plants with, in the foreground, the greyish *Ballota pseudodictamnus*

34

Container
Gardening
Outdoors

16

Using Containers

For many people living in the city, the possibilities of growing plants in containers placed wherever space is available outside can be a rewarding compensation for the lack of a garden or patio. Many plants, from small trees and flowering climbers to vegetables, fruit and herbs can be grown on roof gardens or balconies, in window boxes or hanging baskets, or in a tub outside the front door.

Hanging Baskets

These may often be accommodated in a porch or fixed to the wall outside a window.

It is possible to have a show of plants in a hanging basket in the spring if you are prepared to go and buy plants on the point of flowering – primroses, large-flowered daisies, forget-me-nots and, of course, a few bulbs if these have been planted in the basket in the autumn.

Hanging baskets are however usually used for summer-flowering plants. They can be made most attractive with a few upright plants combined with one or two trailers. Good plants which will bloom in a basket all through summer are fuchsias, begonias, particularly the varieties of *Begonia pendula*, ivy-leaved geraniums to hang down and one or two more upright geraniums, lobelias, both the dwarf and the trailing type and both the dwarf and trailing nasturtiums are excellent for hanging baskets.

For easy watering, the baskets may be suspended from the roof of a porch by a rope passed over a pulley which can be used to lower the basket.

Hanging baskets are made of galvanized or plastic-covered wire or of solid plastic material. Some of the latter have a kind of built-in saucer at the base which will catch any surplus water as it drains out of the 'basket' proper. The wire baskets may be lined with sphagnum moss before being filled with potting mix and this gives them a very attractive appearance. Alternatively

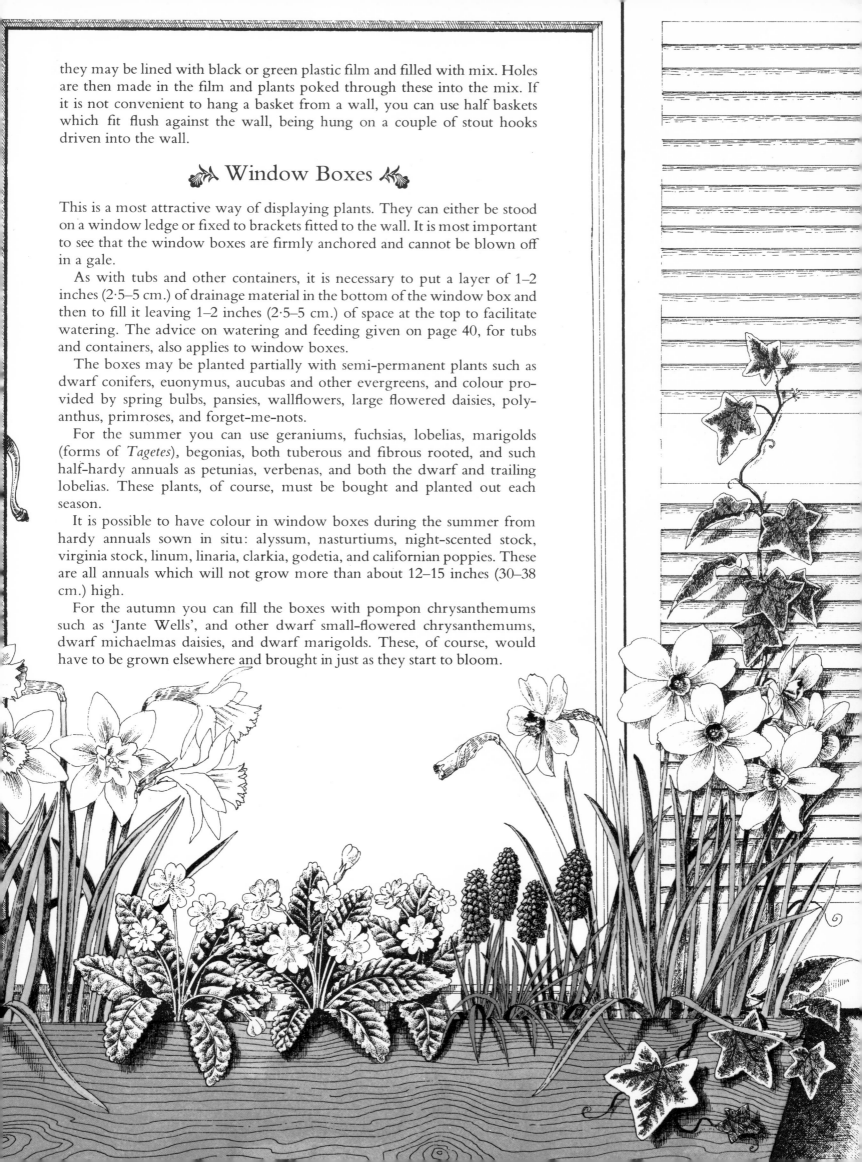

they may be lined with black or green plastic film and filled with mix. Holes are then made in the film and plants poked through these into the mix. If it is not convenient to hang a basket from a wall, you can use half baskets which fit flush against the wall, being hung on a couple of stout hooks driven into the wall.

Window Boxes

This is a most attractive way of displaying plants. They can either be stood on a window ledge or fixed to brackets fitted to the wall. It is most important to see that the window boxes are firmly anchored and cannot be blown off in a gale.

As with tubs and other containers, it is necessary to put a layer of 1–2 inches (2·5–5 cm.) of drainage material in the bottom of the window box and then to fill it leaving 1–2 inches (2·5–5 cm.) of space at the top to facilitate watering. The advice on watering and feeding given on page 40, for tubs and containers, also applies to window boxes.

The boxes may be planted partially with semi-permanent plants such as dwarf conifers, euonymus, aucubas and other evergreens, and colour provided by spring bulbs, pansies, wallflowers, large flowered daisies, polyanthus, primroses, and forget-me-nots.

For the summer you can use geraniums, fuchsias, lobelias, marigolds (forms of *Tagetes*), begonias, both tuberous and fibrous rooted, and such half-hardy annuals as petunias, verbenas, and both the dwarf and trailing lobelias. These plants, of course, must be bought and planted out each season.

It is possible to have colour in window boxes during the summer from hardy annuals sown in situ: alyssum, nasturtiums, night-scented stock, virginia stock, linum, linaria, clarkia, godetia, and californian poppies. These are all annuals which will not grow more than about 12–15 inches (30–38 cm.) high.

For the autumn you can fill the boxes with pompon chrysanthemums such as 'Jante Wells', and other dwarf small-flowered chrysanthemums, dwarf michaelmas daisies, and dwarf marigolds. These, of course, would have to be grown elsewhere and brought in just as they start to bloom.

(above) Fuchsias and begonias form the prominent colour feature of this container planting

(right) This wheel-barrow is planted with lobelia, petunia, fuchsia and ivy-leaved geraniums

(far right) Ivy has been trained up the outside wall of this house and petunias and geraniums planted in the tubs

❧ Tubs and Containers ☙

The various types available are perhaps the mainstay of the city gardener. Available in different sizes, shapes and materials, they are useful both where space is limited, as on the balcony, roof garden or in front of the house and also in a larger area, such as a back yard or patio where the garden soil may be very poor.

Naturally the types of plants to be grown depends largely on the size of the tub. A tub, say, up to 2½ feet (75 cm.) across and about 2 feet (60 cm.) deep can accommodate a wide range of shrubs, climbers or even a small tree. Smaller tubs will of course contain smaller shrubs as well as bulbs and bedding plants.

Tubs, like window boxes and other containers, are made from a wide variety of materials. Wood is popular but there are also troughs made of concrete and various plastic materials including glass-fibre moulded from antique lead containers. All containers should be checked for adequate drainage holes.

The self-watering plastic troughs are a splendid invention: you can fill the reservoir with water and it will supply the plants' needs for 2–3 weeks.

It is worth shopping around wine merchants, large hotels or restaurants as empty wine or beer casks may often be bought quite reasonably. These are then easily cut in half to make plant containers. Tie a piece of string round the middle of the barrel and draw a chalk line along it as a guide when sawing. Drainage holes, 1 inch (2·5 cm.) in diameter, should be bored in the bottom of the tubs, about 6 inches (15 cm.) apart. Treat the woodwork inside and out with a wood preservative – not creosote. Either leave the tubs their natural colour or paint the outside whatever colour you like. Treat the metal bands with a rust-proofing fluid before giving them a coat of paint. Place some pieces of broken flower pot or stones over the holes and then put in a layer of broken bricks, stones or similar material about 4–6 inches (10–15 cm.) deep. This is to ensure adequate drainage since otherwise the tub can become waterlogged after heavy rains.

On top of the drainage layer fill the tub to within about 2 inches (5 cm.) of the top with a proprietary potting mix. The peat-based composts are lighter than the loam-based mixes. If loam-based mixes are used it is wise to fill the tub rather less full, say to 3–4 inches (7·5–10 cm.) from the top and then place a layer of 1–2 inches (2·5–5 cm.) of peat on top of the mix. This

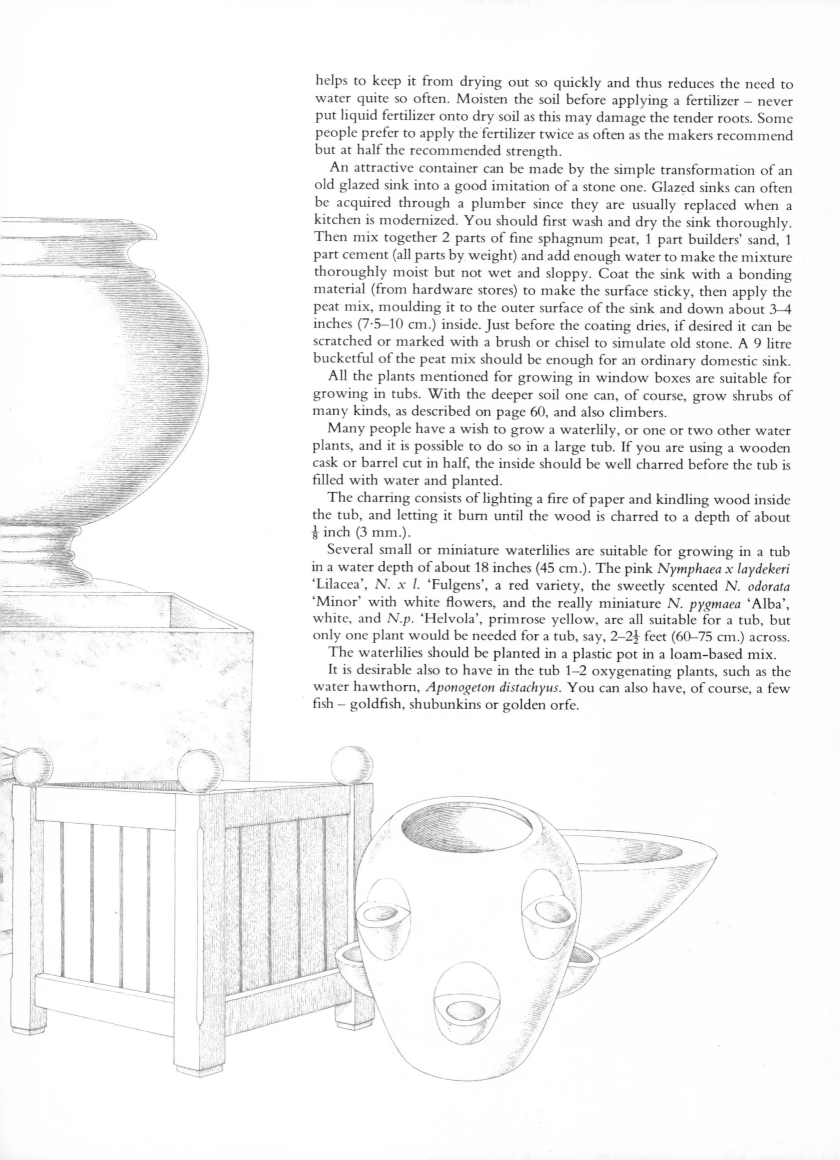

helps to keep it from drying out so quickly and thus reduces the need to water quite so often. Moisten the soil before applying a fertilizer – never put liquid fertilizer onto dry soil as this may damage the tender roots. Some people prefer to apply the fertilizer twice as often as the makers recommend but at half the recommended strength.

An attractive container can be made by the simple transformation of an old glazed sink into a good imitation of a stone one. Glazed sinks can often be acquired through a plumber since they are usually replaced when a kitchen is modernized. You should first wash and dry the sink thoroughly. Then mix together 2 parts of fine sphagnum peat, 1 part builders' sand, 1 part cement (all parts by weight) and add enough water to make the mixture thoroughly moist but not wet and sloppy. Coat the sink with a bonding material (from hardware stores) to make the surface sticky, then apply the peat mix, moulding it to the outer surface of the sink and down about 3–4 inches (7·5–10 cm.) inside. Just before the coating dries, if desired it can be scratched or marked with a brush or chisel to simulate old stone. A 9 litre bucketful of the peat mix should be enough for an ordinary domestic sink.

All the plants mentioned for growing in window boxes are suitable for growing in tubs. With the deeper soil one can, of course, grow shrubs of many kinds, as described on page 60, and also climbers.

Many people have a wish to grow a waterlily, or one or two other water plants, and it is possible to do so in a large tub. If you are using a wooden cask or barrel cut in half, the inside should be well charred before the tub is filled with water and planted.

The charring consists of lighting a fire of paper and kindling wood inside the tub, and letting it burn until the wood is charred to a depth of about $\frac{1}{8}$ inch (3 mm.).

Several small or miniature waterlilies are suitable for growing in a tub in a water depth of about 18 inches (45 cm.). The pink *Nymphaea x laydekeri* 'Lilacea', *N. x l.* 'Fulgens', a red variety, the sweetly scented *N. odorata* 'Minor' with white flowers, and the really miniature *N. pygmaea* 'Alba', white, and *N.p.* 'Helvola', primrose yellow, are all suitable for a tub, but only one plant would be needed for a tub, say, 2–2½ feet (60–75 cm.) across.

The waterlilies should be planted in a plastic pot in a loam-based mix.

It is desirable also to have in the tub 1–2 oxygenating plants, such as the water hawthorn, *Aponogeton distachyus*. You can also have, of course, a few fish – goldfish, shubunkins or golden orfe.

(left) This tiny area has been made an oasis of colour and luxurious foliage with clever and varied planting. All kinds of plants have been used – from a standard rose to a dwarf conifer – and every advantage has been made of the available space

(below) *Cistus*

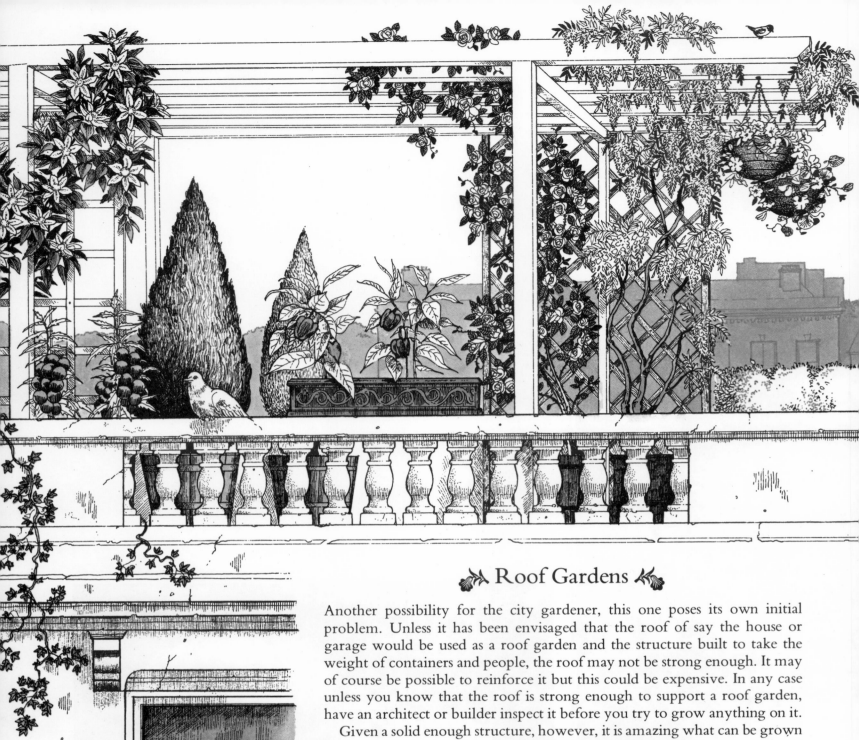

🌺 Roof Gardens 🌺

Another possibility for the city gardener, this one poses its own initial problem. Unless it has been envisaged that the roof of say the house or garage would be used as a roof garden and the structure built to take the weight of containers and people, the roof may not be strong enough. It may of course be possible to reinforce it but this could be expensive. In any case unless you know that the roof is strong enough to support a roof garden, have an architect or builder inspect it before you try to grow anything on it.

Given a solid enough structure, however, it is amazing what can be grown on a roof garden in tubs and other containers. Where there is room you can even have grass, a small pool with fish, a fountain and flood lighting. Trees may be grown with success, up to 10 feet (3 m.) or so in height and a wide range of flowers, vegetables and even some fruits may be grown.

🌺 Balconies 🌺

These may be used and decorated in a number of ways by the city gardener. Plant pot-holders are available which may be attached to the railings or walls of the balcony. It is also possible to attach a square mesh panel of plastic-covered wire to the wall, fixing it to hooks so that it is an inch (about 2·5 cm.) or so away from the wall. Rings of plastic-covered wire may then be clipped on to the mesh and pot plants placed in the rings which are pliable and thus able to hold pots of various diameters. Quite a large number of pots can, in this way, be suspended in a small area.

If the balcony is capable of sustaining the weight of a number of pots, tubs and window boxes, it is possible to make a brave show by growing plants to flower in summer, and also having evergreens to look out upon

44

during the winter. You may, for example, in a large pot or tub, have a climbing plant such as an ivy or a virginia creeper to grow up the wall on either side of the balcony.

All the plants mentioned for growing in tubs and window boxes may be grown on a balcony, or indeed in a roof garden.

Miniature Rock Gardens

When made in a stone sink container these can give much pleasure. It should be filled with a good potting mixture, small pieces of rock placed here and there and the surface of the soil 'landscaped' to make shallow valleys and slight promontories.

There are rock plants that grow well in a stone sink, such as *Aethionema* 'Warley Rose', *Androsace lanuginosa*, *Campanula arvatica* and *C. pulla*, *Erinus alpinus*, *Silene acaulis*.

If you wish to include a miniature tree, the dwarf willow, *Salix x boydii* is suitable. The dwarf conifers are also excellent for sink gardens – *Chamaecyparis obtusa* and its varieties, *C. pisifera* 'Nana', *C. p.* 'Plumosa Compressa', *Juniperus communis*, 'Compressa'.

You can also grow many of the small bulbs, such as *Narcissus minimus*, crocuses, snowdrops, *Iris reticulata* and *I. histrioides*. Miniature roses will also do very well and the various saxifrages, armerias and the dwarf geraniums, such as *G. napuligerum*, will grow very happily in a miniature rock garden.

If the sink is filled with an acid soil you can grow the acid-loving plants which cannot be grown in an ordinary potting mix. A number of plants will happily tolerate an acid soil but most of the gentians, some of the dwarf rhododendrons, the acid-loving heathers, forms of *Erica*, *Calluna* and *Daboecia* must have an acid soil.

Plants for Containers

⚜ Permanent Plants ⚜

A surprisingly large number of permanent plants may be grown in containers, provided these are large and deep enough. Suggestions about the size of tubs and their treatment are given on pages 40–41.

The advantage of growing plants in containers in city gardens – or in gardens anywhere for that matter – is that you can grow plants that require a certain type of soil in separate containers. For example, rhododendrons, azaleas, camellias, gentians and heathers, all of which grow well in tubs in the city, provided the air is not too polluted, need an acid soil. This is provided by mixing plenty of peat moss with ordinary garden soil. When feeding is necessary an application of an acid fertilizer such as sulphate of ammonia should be given.

Practically no plants which the amateur is likely to wish to grow in the city insist on a purely alkaline soil. While there are many that will tolerate an alkaline soil, they will also grow quite well in the ordinary fertile soil of the garden. It is unusual to find soils in cities so alkaline as to prove unacceptable to all but plants that insist on a truly acid soil. As a rule, years of atmospheric pollution have resulted in the precipitation by means of the rainfall of the sulphuric acid which is polluting the atmosphere, and has made the city soil very often unacceptably acid for many garden plants. Usually, for this and other reasons, it is desirable for tubs and other containers to import good soil – one of the potting mixtures is ideal.

Another point in favour of using permanent shrubs in containers is that it is possible, if there is room to spare, to have some evergreen shrubs growing in an inconspicuous corner and have them brought into a more prominent position for the winter months when the last of the summer flowers are over and the spring flowers have not yet begun.

It is not, of course, necessary to have a number of pots for this purpose. It is quite possible to plant the shrubs such as dwarf conifers in any old container – a tin box with holes in the bottom for instance, or cheap plastic containers – which may be slipped inside the more ornamental tub or trough.

Many consumer goods, such as radios and other pieces of household equipment, now come packed in moulded polystyrene containers within a cardboard outer pack. These polystyrene packs are excellent for growing plants in, provided of course that they are deep enough and that holes can be bored through the bottom for drainage. It is important to note however that these containers burn very easily, so they should not be used indoors.

It is both easy and very effective to grow a few permanent plants in a tub or other container, provided there is room, and then plant flowers for spring, to be replaced by flowers for summer and autumn, around the permanent occupants. The dwarf conifers, variegated *Euonymus*, the golden *Lonicera* are excellent for this purpose.

Other charming permanent occupants of containers are the trailing plants which are evergreen and add another dimension to the display. The ivies are the most popular for this purpose, and it·is better to use the smaller leaved varieties, unless of course the container is very large or unless the ivies are required to grow up a wall or other vertical support. The variegated

Snowdrops and winter aconite in container

ivies are most attractive and can be mixed judiciously with the green form. The variety 'Gold Heart' ('Jubilee') is particularly attractive and contrasts well with the small silvery-grey white-edged variety 'Glacier'. Other trailing plants that may be grown in tubs include the Creeping Jenny, *Lysimachia nummularia*, which has attractive yellow flowers in summer. There is also a golden variegated form.

Provided the containers are of a reasonable size and filled with a suitable potting mix, and the plants are fed regularly, it is possible to grow quite a range of wall shrubs and climbers for covering walls or trellises. These include of course the ivies already mentioned, as well as, here, the variety 'Gloire de Marengo' also known as *Hedera canariensis* 'Variegata', and there are also the Virginia creepers and the climbing hydrangea, *Hydrangea petiolaris*. All these climbers attach themselves to the walls or other supports

47

by means of aerial roots. They are not particularly good at clinging to shiny surfaces such as plastic covered wire or similar materials.

Where for example square-meshed plastic covered panels are used for supporting climbers, it is better to use the twining plants such as honeysuckle or clematis which attach themselves to their supports by twisting themselves or their leaf stem around the wire or whatever support is available.

Plants for Spring Flowering

It is the plants for spring flowering, which have to pass the winter in their containers, that are most harshly treated by the weather and which suffer most from impurities in the atmosphere. In cities with a heavily polluted atmosphere the old golden rule of growing plants which go underground in the winter is still very sound. Here of course the bulbs come into their own. Much depends upon the size of the containers whether one can grow permanent herbaceous plants which can be cut down every autumn and which pass the winter safely underground. The majority of these plants flower in summer or early autumn, and it is usually better to stick to bulbs and biennials for the spring display. There are, however, some perennial plants such as aubrieta, bergenia, arabis, and the yellow *Alyssum saxatile*, which are charming in the spring.

If the atmosphere is fairly clean one can plant wallflowers, forget-me-nots, sweet williams, pansies and the large-flowered daisies in the autumn as well as many bulbs. If the atmosphere, however, is very dirty, it is probably best to order some of these plants for collection in the spring, and plant them say in March, or early April when they will soon be in flower.

It is particularly with the spring flowers that it is a good plan to have several 'liners', that is containers which can be placed inside the tub, window box, or other container. The spring flowers do not last very long. Snowdrops probably last the longest as they start to flower at the turn of the year and go on for 2 months. Crocuses, winter aconites (*Eranthis*), and *Anemone blanda* are also flowers of the early spring and succeed well in containers. But as the weather warms up, the daffodils and tulips do not last so long, especially if one runs into a sunny period. For this reason it is a good idea to have a number of spare boxes which can be filled with a succession of daffodils and tulips.

Plants for Summer Flowering

For our purpose let us define summer as beginning at the end of May or early June, and ending when the frosts come, maybe any time from the end of September until early November, depending upon the season and where you live.

The spring flowers, the tulips, wallflowers and the forget-me-nots will have been past their best by the end of May or in colder districts some time in the first week of June. When they are removed you can take the opportunity of adding an organic fertilizer of some kind to the soil, as it is better to do this in the spring in readiness for filling the boxes again in the autumn. The reason is that the plant food will get the summer flowers away to a good start, and there should be enough left in the soil for the spring flowers which are planted in the autumn. It is not wise to plant flowers for spring in too rich a soil as this would encourage them to make soft growth that would be liable to damage in the winter from drying cold winds and frost.

As with all containers it is desirable to have some plants growing up and some hanging down. The most popular plants for bedding in tubs or boxes, or indeed in hanging baskets, are geraniums, fuchsias, lobelias – the tufted

48

and the trailing type, ageratums, petunias, and begonias. All the summer flowers thrive in the sun, although some of them will give quite a good account of themselves in shade or in semi-shade, in positions where the sun reaches them during some part of the day.

There are several ways of going about planting containers with summer flowers.

You can buy geraniums, petunias, begonias, fuchsias and the like and plant these after the spring flowers are over when dangers of frost are past. Some of these flowers, notably geraniums, fuchsias and begonias may be lifted and kept throughout the winter indoors, to be planted out again the following year. If plants are to be bought each year then there is much to be said for a combination of permanent occupants – say dwarf conifers in small window boxes or troughs, larger shrubs such as hydrangeas, or a box bush in the larger containers. Then fewer flowering plants are required to fill the container and while the result may not be so colourful and bright, the foliage plants do set off the brilliant colours of the flowers to advantage.

The cheapest way of filling a window box for summer effect is to use hardy annuals sown in situ. Here again the advantage of having a 'liner' is obvious. Most of the hardy annuals would be sown in March, and some of the half-hardy ones in April or, in cold districts, in May. Obviously if the containers are filled with spring flowers it is not possible to do this unless you have interchangeable 'liners'. But if the expense is a problem and you do not wish to buy considerable numbers of bedding plants, much pleasure can be obtained from hardy and half-hardy annuals sown in troughs or tubs.

Even if only 1 or 2 containers are available, it is worthwhile sowing the seeds of the scented annuals – alyssum, white or purple; mignonette, delightfully scented although a drab looking plant, and night-scented stock. One of the drawbacks about the flowers from seed is that many of them although very attractive do not last very long in bloom. Some, however, do carry on for many weeks, and some like alyssum, linaria and calendulas may be clipped over with a pair of scissors when the first flush of flowers is over, and more flowers will appear. Indeed it is possible to have 3 crops of bloom this way.

Some flowers like nasturtiums, both the dwarf bushy little plants and the trailing type, flower over a long period, as do the sweet peas – the Jet Set varieties – provided the dead flowers are assiduously picked off. The hardy annual chrysanthemums also flower over a long period, and godetias, clarkias, californian poppies and the morning glories or convolvulus last well, but again it is necessary to keep picking off the faded flowers.

For fairly large containers the miniature and Butterfly types of gladiolus are suitable. Unless the containers are in a very windy spot, if the corms are planted about 5 inches (12·5 cm.) deep they will need no support. These gladioli are of course a good investment as they may be lifted and kept through the winter for planting again the following year.

The dwarf bedding dahlias of the Coltness Gem type – there are both single and double dwarf forms – are excellent for providing colour from August until the coming of the frosts. They may be raised from seed if you have the facilities – see page 22 – or boxes of seedlings may be purchased. The plants may be lifted at the end of the season and the tubers stored in a frostproof place for planting out again the following year. They may be increased of course by cuttings taken in the spring.

To give colour well into the autumn, the dwarf marigolds or *Tagetes*, and the dwarf michaelmas daisies are excellent. The tagetes, being half-hardy annuals, will probably be planted out of boxes at the end of May or early June, but the michaelmas daisies, being hardy perennials, may form part of the permanent feature of the containers.

(far left) High up above the city this balcony, with a variety of containers and plants, affords privacy

(left) A gaily coloured window box includes fuchsia, lobelia and ivy-leaved geraniums

(below) This balcony, attractively filled with plants of varying heights, gives pleasure from outside and within the room

Fruits, Vegetables and Herbs

It is possible to grow some kind of fruits, vegetables and herbs quite satisfactorily in containers. There are others which people yearn to grow and which can, in fact, be grown but with mediocre results. However, working on the theory that half a lettuce is better than no lettuce many people are no doubt satisfied with some small result.

Fruit

Perhaps the first fruit a city dweller thinks of growing in a container is the strawberry. In days gone by people used to cut holes 1–2 inches (2·5–5 cm.) across in the side of a large barrel, fill it with soil and plant strawberry plants in the holes. Very pretty and productive they were too. But nowadays wooden casks are becoming scarcer and so are handymen who could cut the holes although it is possible to buy wooden strawberry barrels with holes. Various substitutes have appeared too, notably plastic containers which can be stacked one on top of the other making a tower of strawberry plants. Then from time to time containers of earthenware, concrete or reconstituted stone, with holes for the plants, have appeared on the market. Growing strawberries in containers really only makes sense if the container is of a vertical nature, so that a dozen or more plants can be grown on a very small area such as a balcony or roof.

Then a fig, 'Brown Turkey', will grow quite well, in milder areas, in a large tub. It may be cut down in a severe winter but would probably grow again, from the base.

A grape vine may also be grown in a tub, either trained against a wall or over an umbrella-shaped wire frame as you might grow weeping standard roses.

In all cases these fruits should be grown in full sun.

Apples, pears, peaches, apricots and plums may be grown in large pots or tubs. Naturally this calls for careful pruning and general care and a reliable nurseryman should be consulted about varieties to choose. He should be told that the trees are intended for pot culture and in the case of apples, should supply trees on dwarfing stocks, preferably 'Malling IX' for apples. Melons too may be grown in a tub, trough or similar sized container and for this the variety 'Ogen' or 'Charentais' would be the best to try.

Vegetables

Given containers of reasonable size – not less than a normal sized window box or a 9–10 inch (23–25 cm.) pot – and a reasonably sunny situation, many vegetables may be grown in a small area. Runner beans, however, may be grown in shade.

Probably the most rewarding are the salad vegetables. Tomatoes do very well in containers, usually ripening 4 trusses of fruit in warm areas. There are dwarf varieties, such as 'Pixie' which grows only to about 2 feet (60 cm.) in height or 'Tiny Tim' which grows to about 15 inches (38 cm.) and these are suitable for growing in a window box. The normal sized outdoor tomatoes are really only suitable for growing in troughs or tubs on a balcony or roof.

Lettuce grow well in containers and any of the smaller cabbage varieties are suitable. They need plenty of water and should not be allowed to dry out.

Capsicums, or sweet peppers, are excellent for growing in a large pot 8–9 inches (20–23 cm.) in diameter – or a reasonably deep container – in warm districts. The variety 'World Beater' is a good one.

Radishes, any of the small leaved types like 'Saxa' are easy to grow in containers and so are the white onions for pulling young and green. Even more fun are the cocktail onions which make bulbs of about 1 inch (2·5 cm.)

diameter in 12 weeks. They may of course be pulled smaller and are excellent for boiling with peas and runner beans. The really small bulbs may be used for cocktails.

In warm areas cucumbers may be grown in containers and the white skinned 'White Wonder' or 'Sigmadew', or the green Burpless hybrid are excellent. Many people feel that a cucumber must be green, but 'Sigmadew' is very thin skinned and of excellent flavour. The small apple-shaped cucumber is also worth trying in containers.

A short carrot may be sown in containers and lettuce seedlings planted among the carrots 8 inches (20 cm.) apart. The lettuce will mature first followed by the carrots.

Where there is a fair amount of container space French beans, dwarf broad beans such as 'The Sutton' and even dwarf peas such as 'Little Marvel' may be grown. As indicated above runner beans will also succeed in tubs or large pots. The runner beans, of course, will need strings, a net or some other support up which to climb.

Herbs

All the herbs described on pages 14–15 as being suitable for growing indoors may be grown in containers outdoors and bay trees may be grown to quite large specimens in a tub. Bay trees may, of course, be grown for ornamental purposes, trained as pyramids or as a ball on a stem several feet high. Bay is liable to be damaged in severe winters but may be taken indoors or into a shed or garage during the severest cold spells. The 2 enormous conical bay trees in the garden of the American Embassy in Paris are covered every winter with a fairly close fitting canvas overcoat.

It is probably best, as with herbs in troughs or large containers indoors, to grow the plants in individual pots sunk in peat to prevent rampant plants crowding out the others.

The
Small
Garden

Conditions

We now move on to terra firma as it were because in the past chapters we have been looking at the problems and possibilities of growing plants in window boxes, on balconies, roof gardens and other areas for 'container' planting. Now we have to consider the small back yard or front garden, the terrace or the patio. There may be some soil, or the area may be entirely paved over. Even if an area is paved it is possible that, if desired, some of the paving may be lifted here and there to make a small bed into which a climbing shrub, or even a small tree, could be planted.

Let us first consider the major problems of soil and light, or, more likely, lack of it. The soil in the city, especially if it is many years old, is likely to be thin, dusty, impoverished, devoid of any kind of humus-forming material that will retain moisture, and probably devoid of organic life as well. Soil bacteria are essential as they form a part in the transformation of plant foods into an organic state in which they can be assimilated by the plants. It is usually fairly safe to assume that city soils are acid due to the deposit over many years of acids from the atmosphere.

There are three ways of tackling the problem of city soil. One is to decide to do without it and cover the area if it is small with paving of some kind and then grow plants in containers. There is much to be said for this aspect of city gardening which we will look at in more detail later.

If it is feasible it may be worth while going to the expense of digging up the old soil, or at least part of it in strategic beds or borders, and replacing with fresh good soil from an outside source. This can be, of course, a very expensive operation. However, if the area to be dealt with is not too frightening, this is a good way of dealing with the soil problem.

The third approach would be to set about improving the existing soil, and here it would be necessary either to dig in manure, fresh if possible, if this could be obtained or, failing this, any kind of organic matter, and to give the soil plenty of chemical fertilizers, especially superphosphate, which may be applied up to $1\frac{1}{2}$ ounces (42·5 g.) to the square yard or metre. All this will help to stimulate bacterial activity again.

City soils, too, are liable to be thin and unable to hold moisture well. To assist in moisture retention peat should be dug in as generously as possible, 2–3 pounds (0·9–1·4 kg.) to the square yard, and from about mid-April onwards in the milder climates it would be wise to keep the soil covered with some kind of mulch, peat or spent hops – any organic material that may be available. This will help to conserve moisture in the soil and, important in hot exposed sunny gardens, it will help to keep the roots cool.

Now let us consider the problem of light, or, as is more usual in the city, lack of it. Of course, there will be many gardens, either in front or behind a house, facing due south or west, which will get plenty of sun and if, as often happens, they are surrounded by walls there may be not very much movement of air on hot days and the gardens themselves can become extremely warm. On the other hand there will be gardens with an easterly or northern aspect, or surrounded by other buildings or high walls, into which the sun penetrates possibly only for a short time each day.

There is not much you can do about altering the light factor in a garden except, of course, to paint walls a light colour to help reflect such light as there is and to grow plants that will put up with low light conditions. There are plenty of these, although they may not be the most attractive or desirable plants. The heavily shaded garden is probably at its best in the spring because if part of the shade is cast by trees the early bulbous flowers such as the cro-

cuses, snowdrops, daffodils, and early tulips, muscari, scillas and chionodoxas, will give their display before the foliage becomes too dense.

It is necessary to differentiate between full sun, partial shade and total
shade. With very few exceptions, most of the plants that the amateur wishes
to grow in a city garden flourish in full sun. Ferns and hostas are, of course,
happier in shade and should not be planted in sunny positions. The great
majority of plants that enjoy a fully open position will also give a reasonable
account of themselves in partial shade – that is, in a garden or part of a
garden which receives some sun for part of each day. Others, which are
mentioned elsewhere will do well in a totally shaded position.

Here again, however, we must draw a distinction between shade cast
by buildings or distant trees, and that cast by overhanging trees. Many
plants do not like to grow in the shade cast by a tree immediately above
them, nor do they like the drip of rain from branches of over-hanging trees.
These points have to be borne in mind when planning the planting.

Atmospheric pollution is another major problem for the city gardener.
In many cities the problem has been controlled and it is now possible to
grow almost anything. Where this is not so the golden rule is to grow
herbaceous perennials – those that spend the winter underground, bulbs that
do the same, deciduous trees and shrubs – those that lose their leaves in the
winter – and those often with shiny leaves have demonstrated their ability
to survive even in a polluted atmosphere.

There are other hazards inseparable from life in the city. These are the
depredations of small children, animals, and birds. All one can do with a
front garden is to try to deter children and animals from getting in, using a
low fence or hedge possibly of spiny shrubs, such as low growing *Berberis*.

To deter cats getting into back gardens surrounded by a wall or a fence
it is sometimes effective if 3–4 strands of loose wire are fixed to the top of
the wall or fence. There are also dog and cat repellents to spray in the garden.

Birds, particularly pigeons and sparrows, are a serious problem in the city
garden. You can give young seedlings temporary protection by putting
hoops of wire netting over them, or covering them with close mesh nylon
netting, or even criss-crossing black thread over the plants on sticks 6–8
inches (15–20 cm.) above the ground. This method of stretching black
cotton above plants is often used to keep the birds from destroying crocuses,
primroses, polyanthus, and other spring flowers.

There are also bird repellent sprays which are often effective in protecting
the buds of flowering shrubs and trees, and also fruit bushes, from birds in
the winter. It is not claimed that these bird repellents work 100 per cent all
the time, but if they are applied, say in mid-November and then again
maybe 6–8 weeks later, in areas with a high bird population, you do deter
the birds in very many cases.

Having at length listed the hazards of gardening in the city, there is
something to be said on the credit side. It is usually warmer than in small
towns or villages in the country. The city dweller can confidently hope that
his plants will not be struck down by a frost quite so early in the autumn
and he may hope to escape those sneaky and damaging late spring frosts.

Furthermore, the chemicals that pollute the atmosphere in the city do
at least have an inhibiting effect upon plant disease such as black spot of
roses and other troubles. In towns that suffered from serious air pollution
it was never necessary to spray plants for such diseases. When the pollution
was controlled by, for example, smokeless zones, gardeners had to resort
to protecting their plants by spraying against diseases. This, however, is a
small price to pay for the blessing of clean air.

In spite of the difficulties, with patience, determination, and a wise choice
of plants great pleasure, and some profit, may be had from the city garden.

The Paved Garden

(above) Effective use has been made here of gaps left between the paving stones

(right) An attractively planted terrace

The lawn has become a kind of fixation with many people who will try to achieve a small patch of green in the most unpropitious situations. The city dweller, if he is determined to have his patch of grass, at least starts off with the advantage that the soil in the city is usually acid enough to grow good grass, as one can see in so many city squares and parks. The city dweller has the problem of cutting his little lawn because he possibly has no room for a lawn mower, but if he is prepared to get down on his hands and knees with a pair of shears, good luck to him.

There are, of course, lawn substitutes and vast areas of the lawns in Buckingham Palace gardens, for example, are composed of chamomile. It forms a very close-growing neat sward which does not dry out and turn brown as does grass in hot dry weather. The ordinary chamomile that is raised from seed is a flowering plant and needs to be mown, particularly to keep the plant from shooting up flowering stems. Also, whether you raise chamomile from seed or buy plants, the lawns have to be planted laboriously putting a young piece of chamomile about every 4–5 inches (10–12·5 cm.) apart. Weeds have to be kept under control until the chamomile has covered the area and can do its own job of weed suppression.

There is a non-flowering form of chamomile, 'Treneague', which spreads very rapidly, and with patience you can soon have a small green area which can be walked upon and which needs no cutting, or very little.

In North America chamomile is worth experimenting with, but is not always adapted to the colder or drier areas.

The town dweller would, however, do well to forget the lawn and concentrate on paving over most of the area, leaving perhaps only a few small beds or pockets of soil in which permanent plants may be planted. It will not be too arduous or expensive a job to excavate the soil from these small areas and replace it with good fertile soil.

The holes should be big enough, 6 inches (15 cm.) or more across, to contain a fair amount of soil and, of course, the ground must be excavated to the depth of about a foot (30 cm.), and the hole filled with fertile soil. There are many plants which can be grown in these pockets – thymes, saxifrages, aubrieta, iberis, herbs, or even a few colourful dwarf annuals sown each spring.

No matter what kind of paving is used, old stone paving slabs which can very often be obtained from the local council or building suppliers, or concrete paving which today is made in a wondrous assortment of finishes, it is well worth considering leaving small pockets here and there between the stones into which low growing plants can be inserted to break up the flat expanse of paving.

While some plants will stand a certain amount of traffic, it is not wise to put plants in a position where they will be trodden upon very often.

If you wish to grow rock garden plants, gaps in paving or walls make very useful niches for them, and they often succeed better in such situations than they would in the soil on a rock garden. The reason is that the rain water does not lie around the crown of the plant as it would around plants growing in soil in a rock garden or border, and there is less danger of the crown of the plant rotting.

If a garden is shaded, if it is on a slope or on different levels connected by steps; if it is to be used frequently by elderly people who possibly walk with a stick, it is best to avoid stone paving slabs. These may very soon become covered with green slippery algae and can be very dangerous. So, too, can smooth concrete as this may also be covered in autumn and winter with slippery algal growth. In choosing paving slabs keep an eye open for those with a slightly rough surface as these are less likely to become slippery.

Having once paved the garden, patio, terrace or whatever, the annual labour and expense of trying to keep the area of garden soil fertile has been eliminated. You can then concentrate the expenditure upon a variety of attractive containers – genuine stone sinks which may still be found in certain districts although they are fast disappearing, concrete imitation sinks, tubs, fibreglass imitation lead cisterns, troughs, vases, and indeed a whole range of attractive containers in which to grow plants.

Containers are economical both of soil and plants. A few plants hanging down, and a few standing up are often all that is required to create a charming feature.

As mentioned on page 46, containers such as tubs and sinks, whether genuine stone sinks or imitation stone sinks made from concrete, offer the opportunity of growing a wide variety of plants in a small area. Those that require, say, an acid soil can be grown in one container, and those that prefer soil that is rather more limy can be planted in another container. Plants that need a certain amount of shade can be grown together and placed in a shady part of the garden.

The plants mentioned earlier as suitable for growing in tubs and containers are also, of course, all quite suitable for growing in a back yard or patio. Whether in patio or back yard, there is usually more room for plants to grow than on a balcony or on a roof, and a list is appended of shrubs which will succeed well in containers provided these are large enough.

Shrubs for Containers

The following shrubs, or varieties of them, may be grown successfully in large containers:

Aucuba, Berberis, Camellia, Caryopteris, Chamaecyparis, Choisya, Cistus, Clematis, Cotoneaster, Deutzia, Escallonia, Euonymus, Forsythia, Hebe, Hedera, Hydrangea, Hypericum, Jasminum, Kerria, Laurus, Lavendula, Lonicera, Mahonia, Parthenocissus, Passiflora, Pernettya, Prunus, Pyracantha, Ribes, Rosa, Rosmarinus, Spiraea, Syringa, Tamarix Vitis, Weigela, Wistaria.

Naturally shrubs and climbers grown in containers need more care and attention and feeding than their counterparts growing in the ground. Generally speaking shrubs in containers should grow to 4–5 feet (1·2–1·5 m.) high and 3–4 feet (0·9–1·2 m.) across, depending of course on the variety. Climbers should, with proper care and feeding, reach the roof of a 2-storey building.

Plant in a good potting soil – a loam or peat-based mix, with the addition of a general fertilizer according to the maker's instructions. No further feeding should be required in the first year, after which liquid fertilizer should be given regularly to keep growth active and healthy.

Some pruning is obviously necessary to keep shrubs shapely and to restrict growth of the more vigorous types. Root pruning as well as pruning of branches may be necessary after, say 4–5 years. This will entail taking the shrub from its container, and removing the outer layer of soil and roots – say 4–5 inches (10–13 cm.) from the outside of the root ball. Then scrub out the container and replace the shrub, filling it with fresh potting mixture.

Plants for Sun and Shade

As mentioned on page 57, most plants will grow in sun or partial shade – that is with sun during some part of the day. There are others that tolerate complete shade, others, like hostas and ferns, that prefer it.

Trees

It is sad that over many years the city dwellers have thoughtlessly planted trees that inevitably grew too large for the space available. The result is a good living for the tree surgeons who have to be called in every few years to cut back these trees – brutally perhaps, but necessarily. Yet it is splendid to plant more trees in towns. There are plenty small enough for many situations, or trees which can be kept small by careful pruning which will not disfigure them.

The smaller cherries, species and varieties of *Prunus*, especially upright varieties like the pink 'Amanogawa', hawthorns, laburnums, catalpas, some magnolias such as *M. soulangeana*, are superb town trees. The robinias, or false acacias, also make excellent town trees as do the crab apples, varieties of *Malus*.

Let us not think that only the small and comparatively short lived trees should be planted in cities. Where there is space for large trees such as limes, or lindens, poplars, oaks, and the plane tree, probably the finest city tree of them all, they should be planted. Many of the more unusual trees flourish in the city – the tulip tree, *Liriodendron tulipifera*, *Paulownia imperialis*, *Cercis siliquastrum*, the Judas tree, varieties of *Gleditschia*, *Cotoneaster frigida*, *Liquidambar styraciflua*, *Koelreuteria paniculata* – all these and many more flourish in the cities largely because they are deciduous. The pines and the spruces – indeed, many evergreen conifers take rather unkindly to smoky cities. Yews, hemlocks and hollies, though, are exceptions among the evergreens.

Shrubs

To learn which shrubs will thrive in your particular city, study your local parks and the mature gardens visible to the passerby.

Again, broadly, except in cities with clean air, concentrate on the deciduous shrubs, taking the risk with evergreens only when you know that local conditions offer a good chance of success.

All the shrubs suggested on the opposite page as suitable for growing in containers may obviously also be grown in beds or borders in the garden. In addition there are some which would not succeed so well in a tub, but are excellent growing in the ground. The butterfly bush, *Buddleia davidii*, in its lilac, reddish purple, purple or white forms, and the exciting *B. alternifolia* are excellent city plants. The latter grown as a standard on a 6–8 foot (1·8–2·4 m.) stem has long 'ropes' of lavender flowers festooning the branches which hang down to the ground.

The *Chaenomeles*, varieties of the Japanese quince, which used to be called *Pyrus japonica*, enjoy the city life; so do varieties of *Philadelphus*, the mock orange, *Viburnum*, *Dipelta* and *Diervilla*.

61

(right) Japanese quince

(far right) *Clematis* 'Nelly Moser'

(below) *Cordyline australis* is the dominant feature of this attractive patio with pelargoniums and fuchsias in the pots in front

In mild areas, most brooms, forms of *Cytisus* and *Genista*, and the yellow Spanish broom, *Spartium junceum*, the hollies, green, golden or silver-variegated, *Skimmia*, and the varieties of *Ulex* or gorse, are worth trying.

Shrubs for Heavy Shade

There are many shrubs that can be grown in heavy shade although they do not necessarily demand it and will grow well in other situations. These, however, are worth a trial in shade – *Aucuba, Buxus* (box), *Camellia, Elaeagnus, Euonymus, Fatsia japonica, Hypericum, Mahonia, Prunus lusitanicus, Skimmia* and *Viburnum davidii*.

We seize enthusiastically upon south and west facing or protected walls against which we can grow the rather more tender wall shrubs and climbers – also figs, pears, peaches and other fruits. But there are many climbers and wall shrubs that will do well on a north or east facing wall. Good climbers for these cold walls are *Celastrus orbiculatus*, ivies, *Hydrangea petiolaris, Parthenocissus* (Virginia creeper) and *Schizophragma hydrangeoides*. Of climbing roses for these less protected walls there is a very wide variety, both the so-called hardy climbers and the more tender climbing hybrid teas if there is enough sun. Some of the best to try are 'Danse du Feu', 'Félicité et Perpétue', 'Gloire de Dijon', 'Hamburger Phoenix', 'Mme Alfred Carrière', 'Mme Caroline Testout', 'Maigold', and 'Paul's Lemon Pillar'.

Shrubs that will grow against north or east walls include *Berberis stenophylla, Camellia, Chaenomeles, Choisya ternata, Euonymus fortunei, Jasminum nudiflorum, Kerria japonica* 'Pleniflora', *Pyracantha* and *Viburnum grandiflorum*.

Ground Cover

The city dweller with limited space to grow plants may feel that he is not making the best use of his ground if he just fills it with permanent ground covering plants. In the larger suburban or country gardens where any help is difficult to find, very expensive, and probably not very knowledgeable when you find it, weed-smothering, labour-saving ground cover plants are almost essential if the garden is not to become a burden.

Even in small town gardens it may be that not much time or labour can be given to the garden, and parts of it, probably under trees or shrubs, can usefully be planted with ground cover.

The ground cover plant par excellence is the ivy in all its forms – green, gold or silver variegated, large or small leaved. It grows under trees or in partial shade; if tree leaves fall on it they may be swished off with a besom or broom, to fall underneath the ivy foliage there to rot and form a nice organic top dressing for the ivy plants.

The periwinkles (*Vinca*), green or variegated, blue or white, are excellent in shade, and so is *Pachysandra terminalis*, but it does not like alkaline or limy soils. The low growing *Hypericum calycinum* does well in sun or shade.

Then there are the various dead nettles, forms of *Lamium*, for sun or shade, but where space is limited *Lamium* 'Chequers', green and white, is a more restrained variety. Other good ground coverers for reasonably sunny areas are *Sedum spectabile* and its varieties, *Veronica gentianoides*, with blue flowers, London pride, and most of the true geraniums, not to be confused with the tender plants generally referred to as geraniums, but more correctly known as varieties of *Pelargonium*, we use for bedding out. Then the epimediums, *Alchemilla mollis* and *Euphorbia robbiae*, are all good ground cover plants.

Most people like to grow a few roses in the garden, but they are not at all attractive for 8 months of the year. So some of the ground cover plants mentioned above, violas or pansies, dwarf bulbs for the spring as well as aubrietas, forget-me-nots and other dwarf flowers that bloom before the roses are very welcome, used to provide interim colour.

If, however, you grow other plants among your roses you must feed the beds or borders rather more generously than you would for roses alone. Give the roses their recommended feeds of a rose vegetable garden fertilizer and supplement this with a granular general fertilizer in the spring, watered in to prevent any danger of scorching the foliage of the ground cover.

Herbaceous Plants

Turning now to herbaceous plants, once again the types that go below ground in winter – that is, whose top growth dies down and is cut off in the autumn – are the most reliable, but others are worth trying in all but the most polluted towns. For early spring we have, besides pansies and English daisies, aubrietas, perennial *Alyssum saxatile*, bergenias, *Helleborus corsicus*, primroses and polyanthus.

A little later come campanulas, aquilegias, oriental poppies, irises, peonies and then the whole galaxy of summer flowers. The phloxes are fine town plants, and should be planted deep, 6–8 inches (15–20 cm.). The campanulas, rudbeckias and heleniums, lilies, *Hemerocallis*, sedums – these and many more do well, including most of those listed below for shade.

When considering plants suitable for growing in shade we have to make a difference between dry shade and moist shade. In a wood there is probably a good depth of moisture-holding organic material, the result of many years of leaves falling and decomposing to form a rich layer of nature's compost. Shady areas in a town are more than likely to be arid areas with thin, dead soil woefully deficient in moisture-holding organic material. Such sites need not be dry as there are plenty of small watering devices as well as permanent and even automatic watering systems that can be installed to keep the areas moist. Naturally it pays handsomely to dig in peat or some other bulky organic material before planting to help conserve the moisture in the soil. Even newspapers soaked and shredded, if dug into the soil, help to hold the moisture.

Some reliable herbaceous perennials for dry shade are *Anaphalis*, *Epimedium*, *Euphorbia*, *Geranium* and *Polygonum*.

For reasonably moist shade there is a much wider choice of herbaceous plants. These include those already mentioned for ground cover, and also *Astilbe*, *Anemone hybrida* (*A. japonica*), *Filipendula*, *Hemerocallis*, *Hosta*, *Lysimachia*, *Polygonum*, *Rodgersia*, *Thalictrum*, and *Centranthus* (valerian).

Annuals

All the hardy and half-hardy annuals find their place in the town garden, but most need a fair amount of sun. The following, however, will give a good account of themselves in partial shade: annual *Anchusa*, *Antirrhinum*, begonias, annual *Delphinium*, *Impatiens* (busy lizzie), *Linaria*, *Matricaria*, *Mimulus*, *Nemophila*, *Papaver* (poppies), *Salvia*, and *Viola*.

When buying boxes of annual flowers, look suspiciously on those that are already in full flower. This probably means they have been sown and pushed along too early and are already starved in the boxes, which is why they are flowering prematurely; such plants may not be the best buy.

Vegetables

In addition to the vegetables mentioned on page 52 for growing in containers, there are several worth while growing in a bed or border, not only for their crop but for decorative effect. I have mentioned training runner

(following page)
Camellia japonica 'Kimberley'

A collection of ivies – climbing and trailing – add interest to the dimensions of this garden

beans against a wall. Another way to grow them, which is very economical of space, is to place a 7–8 foot (2–2.5 m.) pole each side of a garden path so that 6 feet (1.8 m.) of it is above ground. Then bend over a whippy cane or a piece of stout wire into a half circle, and tie each end to the top of a stake.

If pairs of poles are placed about 3 feet (90 cm.) apart, a charming tunnel of greenery, flowers and eventually pods is formed. Grown like this it is not necessary to trample on the ground to pick the beans.

Yet another method is to push in 1–2 stout poles about 6 feet (1.8 m.) apart, and sow or plant a ring of say 10 runner beans around the pole – say about 2 feet (60 cm.) away from the pole. Then tie strings or thin wires to the top of the pole and anchor them firmly, each string alongside a bean plant, tying them to a loop of stout wire or a peg pushed firmly into the ground.

Jerusalem artichokes grow well in towns, and their roots are rather like potatoes. The stems will grow to about 6–7 feet (1.8–2 m.) high and effectively hide an ugly shed or other eyesore.

Globe artichokes are a very different matter. Their leaves are large, deeply cut and very ornamental in a bed or border. Each shoot on a plant will produce three flower heads, which of course are the part of the plant that is eaten. Each year after the first year, in March or April, scrape away the soil and reduce the number of side shoots to three per plant. If more are left the heads will be small. Plant a new row or clump with some of the offsets. After a plant has cropped for a third year, discard it.

Sweet corn too may be grown in small groups of 2–3 plants in a border of flowers. They are always best grown in a group rather than in a straight line as this ensures pollination no matter which way the wind is blowing.

If you like spinach, the New Zealand spinach makes a large spreading low growing plant which gives masses of fleshy leaves all summer. Seeds may be sown in peat pots indoors in April, or outdoors in early May for planting in late May or early June. This plant is excellent for covering bare ground among other plants provided the site is not too shady.

Rhubarb too will grow well in towns and while not particularly ornamental it is certainly not an eyesore.

Marrows or squashes of the long or trailing variety may be used to cover a rubbish heap. It is best, however, to plant them or sow the seeds at the base of the heap and to allow the plants to ramble up over it. Planted on top of the heap they may not receive enough water.

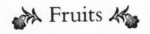

Fruits

All the fruits that can be grown in containers may be grown in the ground, and there are also a few more that are impracticable to grow in containers.

Obviously fruit trees may be grown more successfully in the ground.

An apple, pear or mulberry makes a good shade tree if there is room for it, and a fig, peach, apricot or Morello cherry may be grown against a wall. All, except the Morello cherry, which thrives on an east or north facing wall, need to be grown on a south or west facing wall.

Soft fruits, such as gooseberries, red, white and black currants, thrive in a town. The gooseberries, red and white currants, but not the black currants, may be grown as single, double or triple cordons against a wall or fence, or against canes tied to wires stretched across the garden. This way of growing them is very economical of space and the cordons can be grown to 6 feet (1·8 m.) or more high and carry a very useful crop. However, neither currants nor gooseberries, which serve as alternate hosts, are permitted to be grown in white pine country because of the white pine blister rust.

A few loganberries or cultivated blackberries can be grown against a wall or fence. Alternatively they may be grown against wires stretched between posts and they will form an excellent screen to hide any eyesore. There are thornless loganberries and thornless blackberries and these are the most convenient to grow as they are so easy to prune and tie to their wires.

Raspberries will grow well enough in the city, but they do need full sun and this is not always easy to provide.

Black currants too need an open site, but 3–4 bushes, well grown, will produce a worthwhile crop.

Herbs

All the herbs described as being suitable to grow, indoors or outside, in tubs or other containers may, of course, be grown in beds or borders in a front or back garden. Many of them such as sage, rosemary and bay, may be allowed to grow to their full stature, and do not have to be kept artificially dwarfed by pruning or pinching back.

There are several plants which we can classify as herbs because they have some domestic use but which are also handsome ornamental plants. These include lavender, which may be grown as an individual bush or as a low hedge, and there are over a dozen good varieties. Probably the best all round lavender is 'Munstead' variety, dwarf, dark coloured, growing to about 12 inches (30 cm.) high. Taller, and very free flowering is 'Hidcote' variety. At the other end of the scale are the real dwarfs, excellent for a rock garden or for a pocket in paving.

The bergamots, or varieties of *Monarda*, although invasive, are attractive flowering plants; their leaves when dried are useful mixed with tea.

Fennel makes a handsome tall plant with its finely cut foliage.

Garlic is very easy to grow. Split up a garlic bulb into its segments and plant each one 2 inches (5 cm.) deep and about 6 inches (15 cm.) apart.

The Third Dimension

As city gardens are usually small it is important to make the best use of the third dimension – height. Many attractive plants may be grown against walls or fences, over arches and pergolas, and indeed against screens made of wooden trellis, plastic-covered wire mesh or meshed plastic panels.

There are really only 4 plants which cling to walls or other supports by means of aerial roots – 4, at least, that are commonly found in gardens. These are the ivies in their various colours and forms, virginia creeper, *Hydrangea petiolaris*, the climbing hydrangea, and *Schizophragma hydrangeoides* which is not unlike the climbing hydrangea.

If necessary all of these may be grown in a large tub, but it is best to plant them in the ground even if this means taking up paving to create sufficient space to accommodate the plants, and give them a fair chance of success. It is often thought that plants would object to having their roots covered with concrete or paving, but in fact roots will ramify and flourish.

While these self-clinging climbers are not necessarily the most attractive they are the most trouble free. True, the climbing hydrangea will need a certain amount of clipping back from time to time in order to encourage flowering. Also, if it is allowed to grow out too much from the wall it may

(below) A small pond makes an attractive feature in the corner of this garden

(right) Good use has been made of the third dimension in this garden, ivy is climbing up the rustic pole with the rose 'Iceberg' beneath; runner beans are trained up the wall in the foreground with clematis behind

be blown away from the wall in a fierce gale or by the weight of snow.

Among the other climbers, the most colourful wall plants are, of course, wistaria, climbing roses, clematis and honeysuckles. Colourful too are runner beans – their red flowers contrasting gaily with white or cream walls.

There are various methods of training wall shrubs. The time-honoured method is to drive vine eyes or hooks into the wall – vine eyes are large nails with a hole at the top – and then to thread galvanized, copper or plastic-covered wire horizontally along the wall between the vine eyes. Wires spaced about 2 feet (60 cm.) apart up to a height of about 8 feet (2·5 m.), are usually sufficient to make the training of wall shrubs and climbers easy. A simple method of keeping the wires taut is to thread the wire through the lowest row of vine eyes up to and along the next row and so on until the topmost vine eye is reached. The wire is then made tight to this vine eye and at the bottom a bolt strainer or turnbuckle is fixed between the wire and the lowest vine eye. By tightening up the bolt strainer all the wires are tightened.

Other more expensive but very effective and labour-saving ways are wire panels, preferably plastic-covered panels, which may be fixed to the walls and kept just 1–2 inches (2·5–5 cm.) away from the surface by wiring them to vine eyes or large nails driven into the gaps between the bricks. Where the concrete pointing is very hard it may be necessary to drill holes and plug these before driving in or screwing in the fasteners.

With many types of wall shrubs it is not necessary to tie the shoots to plastic-covered mesh panels as such climbers as honeysuckles will twist themselves in and out of the meshes, clematis will cling to the wires by means of their leaf stalks, and the young growths of climbing roses for example, can be woven in and out of the meshes by hand as they grow.

There are, of course, many shrubs that will grow to a reasonable height, 6 feet (1·8 m.) or more, against walls and which may need no support. The firethorn, or pyracantha, is one and there are others such as forsythias, the flowering currants and *Kerria japonica*; for north walls there are camellias.

Considerable use may be made of arches and pergolas that will give height to a garden and add welcome colour. The arches may be constructed of virtually any material – rustic poles, squared and planed timber, or even of plastic covered wire. The arch itself is not necessarily a thing of great beauty, but it is usually almost obscured when it is covered by a climbing rose, clematis, honeysuckle or other flowering plant.

The introduction of plastic mesh netting and plastic covered wire panels has made the construction of pergolas to provide a shady sitting place in a town garden, very easy. A framework of uprights and 1–2 rafters for the roof is constructed, then the wire mesh panels may be attached to one or more sides and to the roof, thus giving a shelter as well as privacy.

The Russian vine, *Polygonum baldschuanicum* is a great plant for the city, and it grows prodigiously in almost any conditions – indeed, its common name, the mile-a-minute plant, indicates how rapidly it will grow. It is, of course, deciduous, but it makes a fairly thick mass of branches which, even without their leaves, form a useful screen. It may be clipped back as hard as desired with shears each spring. From midsummer until the coming of the frosts it covers itself with billowy white blossoms.

A grape vine does well, or one of the ornamental vines such as *Vitis coignetiae*, with enormous leaves that turn to crimson scarlet in the autumn.

All the plants mentioned can, of course, be grown in tubs, and climbing nasturtiums may also be grown in tubs or containers to climb up a support.

There is often some kind of an eyesore to be screened or camouflaged in a garden. Here again, simple panels of wire mesh fixed between wooden posts or metal uprights form a convenient support for such climbers as sweet peas, honeysuckles, or the Russian vine.

Pools and Flood-Lighting

Separately, or, even better, in combination, these two features can be used to great effect in the tiniest area. A pool opens up the possibilities of growing water plants and also provides a wonderfully cool relaxing atmosphere. Flood-lighting will enhance this, or any other feature of the garden.

☙ Pools ❧

Even the smallest courtyard, patio, or back garden can be greatly enhanced by a small ornamental pool in which 1–2 waterlilies and other aquatic plants may be grown (see p. 41).

If a small fountain is installed, the movement of water and the gentle sound it produces make a pleasant feature of the patio, and if some discreet floodlighting is also installed, the effect is charming.

Small submersible electric pumps may be placed in the pool, and there are models which will automatically give a changing pattern of jets.

Waterproof lighting equipment is available so that you can have an electric light, plain or coloured, submerged in the pool.

As regards the pool itself, we do not today consider digging a hole and building a pool with concrete walls and base. Prefabricated plastic pools may be had in various shapes and sizes, and these are just dropped into a hole of suitable shape and size.

For town gardens, square or rectangular shaped pools are usually the most appropriate. Irregularly shaped pools are more suitable for the more informal settings that you would have in a country garden.

It is often not possible to dig a hole to accommodate a prefabricated pool. In such situations the pool can be set on a brick and concrete base and a low wall of brick or flat stone built around it. If the wall is thick enough, say, a double wall with a cavity of about 15 inches (28 cm.) left between the 2 walls, a flat coping stone may be placed on top of the walls all round the pool, and this makes a useful seat.

When laying an electric cable to the pool – a job for a competent electrician – it is wise to lay a piece of plastic pipe from a mains supply to the pool also, so that the water level can be raised by turning a tap or faucet.

☙ Floodlighting ❧

A garden should be used as an extra room to the house whenever possible, and in a city on a hot evening it is very pleasant to dine or sit outside. Some discreet floodlighting is therefore an asset. This may take the form of a few fixed lights, or a small set of, say, half a dozen lights, plain or coloured, or a mixture of both.

It is possible to buy a kit of half a dozen portable lamps powered by a 12 volt transformer. These may be moved about as required – a lamp which has been illuminating a clump of early tulips can be moved to light up a lilac or some other feature.

Whatever type of lighting is installed, it is essential to specify waterproof equipment suitable for use outdoors, and any mains wiring should be done by a competent electrician.

73

A-Z of Plants

Climatic differences throughout the world affect the range of plants available. Many varieties are available on both sides of the Atlantic; where a variety is particular to a certain country, this is indicated in the text.

Bulbs

Chionodoxa (glory of the snow)
Small starry flowers borne singly or in sprays on slender stems a few inches high, from February to March. Varieties: *C. luciliae* 'Rosea', rose-coloured, 'Pink Giant', 'Gigantea', violet-blue. Height 6–8 inches (15–20 cm.).
Ordinary soil, including limy; light shade for most intense colours.
Plant in autumn, 2–3 inches (5–7.5 cm.) deep and 4 inches (10 cm.) apart in groups.

Crocus and Colchicum

Chalice-shaped blooms in many colours; certain kinds, particularly autumn-flowering, appear before the leaves. Flowers from early autumn to late spring. Ordinary soil, best in sun or the blooms fail to open fully. Varieties: *Crocus speciosus* in blue or white, autumn-flowering; *C. chrysanthus* varieties: 'Snow Bunting', white, 'Zwanenburg Bronze', bronze with yellow inside petals; 'E. A. Bowles', rich yellow; spring-flowering.
Plant corms in early autumn, 3 inches (7.5 cm.) deep, 6 inches (15 cm.) apart.

Eranthis hyemalis (aconite)

Buttercup-like flowers surmounting a ruff of narrow leaves, February to March. Height 4 inches (10 cm.). One of the first spring bulbs to appear, often in the hardest weather. Any soil, including limy. Shady site best, often naturalizes beneath trees. Plant tubers in late summer, 1 inch (2.5 cm.) deep, 4 inches (10 cm.) apart.

Fritillaria

Pendent bell flowers borne singly on slender arching stems or clustered thickly on upright fleshy stems. Flowers from April to May. Any fertile soil, sun or light shade. Species and varieties: *F. imperialis* (crown imperial), reddish yellow flowers formed in a circular cluster beneath a rosette of glossy green leaves on top of the stem, 2–3 feet (60–90 cm.); *F. meleagris* (snakeshead), solitary or paired flowers on thin stems; petals chequered many shades: 'Aphrodite', white, 'Saturnis', violet-red, 'Poseidon', purple-spotted.
Plant bulbs in autumn, 4–6 inches (10–15 cm.) deep. The crown imperial should be an inch (about 2.5 cm.) or so deeper. Leave plants undisturbed or they may not flower well.

Galanthus (snowdrop)

Bright little winter-flowering bulbs. Flowers are made up of 2 sets of petals: 3 long ones and 3 inner short ones; blooms nodding on short slender stems among narrow leaves. Species and varieties: *G. elwesii*, bluish leaves, inner petals deep green; *G. nivalis*, common snowdrop; *G. nivalis* 'Flore-plena' has double flowers; 'S. Arnott' is much taller with large single blooms.

Fritillaria meleagris

74

Good in shade or sun, ordinary soil, thrive on limy.

Increase plants by dividing clumps after flowering, before the leaves disappear, and replanting pieces 6 inches (15 cm.) apart.

Hyacinthus

Sturdy spikes of flared and starry tubular flowers, in shades of blue, red, pink, white and yellow. Height 6–8 inches (15–20 cm.). Best in fertile soil; sun or light shade. Blooms appear from December to May.
Varieties: 'City of Haarlem', yellow; 'Delft Blue', light blue; 'Jan Bos', red. Roman hyacinths have looser spikes of bloom with fewer flowers in white, pink or blue.
Plant 5–6 inches (13–15 cm.) deep in early autumn for flowering in spring.

Iris

The flowers comprise 3 upright petals – the standards – and 3 broad lip-shaped petals – the falls. Narrow leaves arise from the base of the plant. Ordinary soil, sun or light shade. Plants do well in limy areas.
Species and varieties: *I. reticulata*, small rock-garden kind in deep blue with an orange blotch; plant 2–3 inches (5–7.5 cm.) deep.
Hybrids: Dutch, Spanish and English. Dutch kinds in white, yellow, blue or purple, flower from early to mid June. 2 feet (60 cm.).
Spanish: flower 2 weeks later and come in many attractive shades. 18 inches (45 cm.).
English: late flowering – in July – white, pink, blue or purple. Only yellow is missing from the colour range.
Plant bulbs 4 inches (10 cm.) deep and 6 inches (15 cm.) apart in early autumn.

Lilium (lily)

Flared trumpet- or chalice-shaped blooms in many colours. Flowers borne on slender stems clothed with narrow glossy green leaves. Most lilies prefer light shade and a cool root run, ideally among other shrubs which can support them as they grow up and between them. Heights from 2–6 feet (60 cm.–1.8 m.).
Species and varieties: *L. auratum rubrum*, white red-striped petals; *L. candidum*, pure white trumpet blooms; *L. tigrinum*, turk's cap bloom in orange red with black spots; Bellingham Hybrids, orange, red, yellow and

bicolours, all marked with brown spots.
Planting depth depends on the habit of the plant. For example, *L. candidum* is set 2 inches (5 cm.) deep, *L. tigrinum*, 6 inches (15 cm.), *L. auratum*, 6–12 inches (15–30 cm.). Those set deeply are stem rooting and others set shallowly are basal rooting.

Muscari (grape hyacinth)

Clusters of narrow green leaves and tightly packed cones of bloom, except for *Muscari comosum* 'Plumosum' which has feathery tassel flowers. Any soil, sun or quite deep shade. Perfect edging plant, completely hardy, multiplies freely.
Varieties: *M. armeniacum*, pale blue, 'Heavenly Blue', bright blue. Height 8 inches (20 cm.). *M. comosum* (as above in clear sky blue); *M. tubergenianum*, light and dark blue flowers clustered on the same spike. Height 8 inches (20 cm.).
Plant bulbs in late summer and autumn, 3 inches (7.5 cm.) deep, 6 inches (15 cm.) apart.

Narcissus (daffodil)

Broad or narrow, trumpet or tubular flared blooms in yellows and whites. For borders, woodland, or rock gardens. Best in well-worked soil in sun or light shade. Good for brightening gloomy spots. From 2 inches to 2 feet (5–60 cm.).
Species and varieties: *N. bulbocodium* (the hoop coat daffodil), circular, flared yellow trumpets; 'Golden Harvest', deep yellow trumpet; 'Mount Hood', white trumpet; 'Ice Follies', yellow cup with white petals; 'Mary Copeland', double pinkish white ruffled petals, orange centre; 'Actaea', the pheasant's eye, pure white petals with bright orange cupped centre.
Plant in autumn for flowering in spring. Set bulbs to 3 times their depth in the soil.

Raise new plants from old clumps by splitting up bulb clusters after flowering.

Tulipa (tulip)

Single, double or flared chalice-shaped blooms for many weeks in late winter and spring. Ordinary soil in sun or light shade.
Varieties: among the botanical tulips, reddish starry bloomed *T. kaufmanniana* 'Shakespeare', yellow, flushed-red *T. clusiana*, *T. chrysantha*, and scarlet *T. praestans* 'Fusilier', are outstanding. Heights around 12 inches (30 cm.). The single early tulips such as orange-red 'Couleur Cardinal', white 'Diana' and 'Pink Perfection' have narrow chalice blooms. Heights from 6–15 inches (15–38 cm.). Completely different are the double late tulips. Resembling full double peony blooms, red 'Brilliant Fire', deep yellow 'Gold Medal' and white 'Mount Tacoma' are magnificent. Heights about 18 inches (45 cm.).
Raise plants from bulbs set 3 times their depth in the soil in autumn and early winter.

Biennials

Bellis (double daisy)

Bright little pompon flowers are borne on 6 inch (15 cm.) stems from May to June. Sun or semi-shade, ordinary soil.
Varieties: 'Colour Carpet', shades of red, pink and white; F$_1$ hybrid 'Fairy Carpet', rose or white double flowers; 'Pomponette Pink Buttons', quilled petals forming dainty ball heads in shades of rose or pink.
Raise plants from seed sown in a nursery bed in May. Plant out seedlings when they are large enough to handle and set 6 inches (15 cm.) apart where they are to flower.

Campanula medium (Canterbury bells)

Large single or double bell-shaped blooms set in huge clusters on sturdy stems. Ordinary soil, sun or light shade.
Varieties: the single types such as 'Bells of Holland', blue-mauve, rose or white blooms on 15 inch (38 cm.) stems; Cup and Saucer varieties with semi-double blooms: often offered as Pure White, Deep Rose-Pink, Blue and Special Mixture.
Either sow in gentle heat in late winter to flower in summer, or raise plants in June, in light shade to have them flowering the following spring.

Cheiranthus cheiri (wallflower)
Dense spikes of gaily coloured blooms in spring and early summer. Ordinary soil, including limy in which they are less liable to contract club root disease which can cripple growth. Sun or light shade.
Varieties: 'Giant Blood Red', 'Giant Yellow', 'Giant Fire King', scarlet, all 18 inches (45 cm.) high; 'Persian Carpet', cream, apricot, rose, purple and many other shades of flowers on 15 inch (38 cm.) stems, perfect for bedding and spreading.
Raise plants from seed sown in May in a nursery bed. Plant out seedlings 4 inches (10 cm.) apart to grow on for finally transplanting to their flowering positions in early autumn, to bloom in spring.

Dianthus barbatus (sweet william)
Massed auricula-type blooms in huge clusters on short stems. Sun or light shade, ordinary soil, including limy.
Varieties: both Single and Double Mixed as well as single colours in many shades of salmon, scarlet and purple, each flower having distinctive white eye. Heights from 6–18 inches (15–45 cm.).
Grow as an annual, raising plants early in spring to flower the same year, or as a biennial, sowing seed in June to get plants flowering the following early summer.

Myosotis (forget-me-not)
Intense, mostly blue, flowers in sprays or clusters on short stems. Perfect for interplanting with tulips.
Sun or light shade. Ordinary soil, including limy in which they thrive.
Varieties: 'Royal Blue', 12 inches (30 cm.); 'Bouquet', 'Indigo Blue', 10 inches (25 cm.); 'Carmine King', 8 inches (20 cm.); 'Miniature Blue', ball-shaped flower clusters, 5 inches (13 cm.), ideal for edging.
Raise plants in June for flowering the following May to July.

Primula vulgaris (polyanthus)
Vivid-hued primrose-like flowers borne in huge semi-circular clusters on short thick stems. Ordinary soil best enriched with plenty of old manure to encourage sturdy growth and fine flowers; will tolerate limy soil. Light shady position to prevent flowers being burnt up by the sun; this also prolongs the display.
Varieties: 'Triumph' Strain, huge

blooms, around 2 inches (5 cm.) across in white, yellow, pink, red and blue shades; 'Pacific Dwarf Jewel' Strain, plants only 7 inches (18 cm.) high, wide range of colours; 'Suttons' Giant' Strain, many brilliant hues, plants tough and weather resistant. Heights of all varieties range from 6–9 inches (15–23 cm.).
Raise plants from seed sown in gentle heat in late winter or early spring. Prick out seedlings in trays of good soil and harden them off before setting them outdoors in early autumn where they are to flower. Birds peck at yellow-petalled varieties, so you may find that black netting or thread may have to be strung over the plants.

Viola tricolor or **V. x wittrockiana** (pansy)
Low growing spreading plants massed with open almost circular, plain or 'faced' blooms in many colours. Ordinary soil in full sun for finest flowers. Varieties: 'Roggli Giant' strains – 'Alpengluhn', red, 'Jungfrau', creamy white, 'Eiger', yellow with black blotch, 'Thunersee', blue.
Raise plants in summer for planting out in autumn to bloom the following spring. Alternatively, sow seed in February or March to bloom the same year.

V. hybrida (viola)
Smaller blooms than pansies, freer flowering, compact plants.
Many and varied varieties.
Raise plants as for pansies, above.

Hardy Annuals

Calendula (marigold)
Orange, yellow or creamy, single or double large daisy-like flowers, 2½–4 inches (6–10 cm.) across. Ordinary soil. Full sun. Thrive without special care.
Varieties: 'Orange Coronet', 1 foot

(30 cm.), golden orange; 'Dwarf Golden Gem', 10 inches (25 cm.), golden yellow; 'Happy Talk' mixed, 2 feet (60 cm.), lemon, yellow-gold and orange; 'Double Art Shades', 2 feet (60 cm.), soft cream to deep yellow.
Raise new plants from seed sown indoors or outdoors in situ; thin plants to 6–8 inches (15–20 cm.) apart.

Centaurea cyanus (cornflower)
Narrow upright plant with tapering leaves and stems topped by double pompon-like flowers, blue, pinkish or white.
No special soil, best in full sun, though will tolerate light shade. Support plants with small twigs in windy districts. Discard after flowering.
Raise new plants from seed sown outdoors in spring when frosts over or indoors earlier.

Clarkia
Erect stems clustered with rounded blooms in many colours. Best in full sun, happy in ordinary soil which, if slightly poor, induces better flowering.
Varieties: *C. pulchella* mixed, 1 foot (30 cm.), semi-double flowers in white, violet, carmine rose and other shades. Good cut flower.
Raise new plants from seed sown in situ outdoors in spring when soil workable. Also makes a good pot plant for conservatory or greenhouse. In sheltered areas, sow in autumn, cover plants in severe weather and look forward to earlier flowering plants in summer.

Godetia
Flamboyant, flared, cup-shaped blooms in vivid colours, borne in masses on short stems. Thrives in ordinary soil, best in full sun. May also be grown in pots for flowering indoors.
Varieties: 'Scarlet Emblem', 15 inches (38 cm.), rich crimson-scarlet; 'Monarch Dwarf Bedding', 1 foot (30 cm.), rainbow-hued blooms, single flowered; 'Sybil Sherwood', 1 foot (30 cm.), pinkish orange.
Raise plants from seed sown in situ outdoors in spring; for earlier flowers sow in September but cover with cloches if weather severe.

Lathyrus odoratus (sweet pea)
Flowers in red, pink, maroon, blue,

cream, lavender and many other shades, including picotees in rich cream with deep rose frilly edged petals. Heights vary from 12–18 inches (30–45 cm.), to 6–8 feet (1·8–2·4 m.). Best in deep fertile soil in full sun.

Varieties: among the free flowering, vigorous Spencer varieties are white 'Swan Lake', cerise 'Percy Izzard', scarlet 'Air Marshal' and mid-blue 'Noel Sutton'.

Jet Set varieties are about 3 feet (90 cm.) high but are as prolific as the taller kinds. 'Blue Naples', salmon, cream-pink 'Killarney' and scarlet 'Madrid' are superb. Knee-Hi varieties carry sturdy stems of 5–10 blooms in a mixture of colours and are splendid for window boxes. Where scent is important, this is provided by a group called 'Old-fashioned Scented' mixed. Flowers are fairly small in comparison to the others mentioned, but more than compensate by their richness of scent. Raise plants in autumn and over-winter in a cold frame, planting out in spring, or sow in situ in spring. Insert twiggy sticks to support plants or grow them up canes and pinch out their side shoots and tendrils. Huge flowering stems develop on these specially trained cordon plants.

Linaria (toad flax)
Snapdragon-like flowers in dainty spikes around 9 inches (23 cm.) high. Blooms in many colours including violet, blue, crimson, pink and yellow. Ordinary soil in sun or light shade.

Variety: 'Fairy Bouquet', a colourful mixture. Shear off faded flowers to encourage more to grow in late summer and early autumn.

Raise plants from seed sown in situ in spring. Thin to 3–4 inches (7·5–10 cm.) apart.

Malcolmia (Virginia stock)
Slender stemmed plants carrying heads of cruciform flowers around ½ inch (1·3 cm.) across. They are sweetly scented and bloom for several weeks.

Will grow almost anywhere but thrive in full sun.

Varieties: *M. maritima* mixed, in various colours – red, lilac, rose or white; 'Nana Compacta', a dwarf form, again in several shades. Height around 8 inches (20 cm.).

Raise plants from seed sown in March and successively at monthly intervals to give flowers over a long period. September sowing gives plants for overwintering and flowering early the following spring.

Phacelia campanularia
Gorgeous upturned gentian blue-bell flowers borne on 9 inch (23 cm.) stems. One of the really true blue annuals. Flowers for most of the summer and these attract bees. Best in full sun; ordinary soil.

Raise plants from seed sown in situ in spring. Space plants to 6 inches (15 cm.) apart.

Fuchsia 'Snowcap'

Reseda (mignonette)
Tall thin spikes of sweetly scented flowers. Beloved by bees, this fragrant annual is best planted close to the house where its scent can waft through open windows. Thrives in full sun in ordinary soil and limy areas.
Varieties: 'Suttons' Giant', 12 inches (30 cm.), ideal for pots, very fragrant; 'Sweet-Scented', a 15 inch (38 cm.) high variety of great merit. Flowers of all varieties greenish yellow, except 'Machet', golden yellow and 'Red Monarch', red and green.
Raise plants from seed sown in situ in March. Thin to 6 inches (15 cm.) apart.

Tropaeolum (nasturtium)
Carpeting or trailing plants with distinctive rounded leaves and showy flared trumpet flowers, often with short spurs. Thrive in ordinary soil, the less fertile the better, or too many leaves appear and swamp the few flowers that form. Fine plant for tubs, window boxes or for climbing over trellis-work.
Varieties: 'Golden Gleam', 'Scarlet Gleam', 'Cherry Rose' (dwarf double). The canary flower, *Tropaeolum canariense* (*T. peregrinum*), is a vigorous climber whose leafy stems are massed with exotic looking clear yellow

flowers with shaped and frilled petals. Raise plants from seed where they are to flower. Provide netting or trellis for the climbing forms, which also trail.

Viscaria (syns *Lychnis*, *Silene*)
Slender stems topped by single pink-like flowers in pink, red, blue or white. Ordinary soil in full sun, though will grow well in limy areas.
Varieties: 'Sutton's Brilliant' mixture; 'Nana Compacta' mixed, delightful colour range: flowers borne on low growing plants 6–9 inches (15–23 cm.) high. Grow as a massed display for effect.
Raise plants from seed sown outdoors in spring; thin to 6 inches (15 cm.) apart.

Summer Bedding

Ageratum
Fine edging or carpeting plant massed with thickly clustered bobble flowers on 5–9 inch (13–23 cm.) stems. Good for sun or light shade in ordinary soil.
Varieties: F_1 hybrid 'Blue Blazer', F_1 hybrid 'Summer Snow', 'Little Blue Star' and reddish-blue 'Blue Mink'. Raise plants in gentle heat in late winter or early spring. Prick out seedlings into seed boxes, harden them off and plant outdoors in late spring or when frosts are over.

Phacelia campanularia

Alyssum (now *Lobularia maritima*)
Effective edging plant with spreading clusters of tiny flowers. Also grows on walls or between crazy paving. Ordinary soil, sun or light shade.
Varieties: white 'Little Dorrit', 'Carpet of Snow'; rose-pink, 'Rosie O'Day', 'Lilac Queen'.
Sow in spring where plants are to flower and thin seedlings to 4 inches (10 cm.) apart, or start indoors and transplant for early bloom.

Antirrhinum (snapdragon)
Showy spikes of tubular lipped flowers. Full sun, ordinary soil.
Types: Carpet (6–8 inches, 15–20 cm.); Bedding (16 inches, 40 cm.); Giant Tetraploid (28 inches, 70 cm.); Butterfly or Penstemon-flowered (30 inches, 75 cm.); Double (36 inches, 90 cm.); Rocket (36 inches, 90 cm.) all with wide varieties of colour. Raise plants from seed sown indoors with gentle heat in late winter or early spring. Prick out seedlings in seed trays of potting mix and harden them off ready for planting outdoors in late May or early June or plant outdoors directly when soil is workable.

Shear off first flush of blooms when they fade, to encourage flowering side shoots.

Begonia semperflorens (bedding begonia)
Glossy rounded bright green, coppery or purplish leaves and thick clusters of red, pink or white flowers from late spring to early autumn. Sun or semi-shade. Ordinary soil. Water freely and feed well for strong flowering shoots.
Varieties: F_1 hybrid 'Bella', carmine-rose; 'Fireball', carmine-scarlet with puckered leaves; 'Snowball', white, green leaves; 'Pink Comet', salmon-pink; (North America only, 'Red Planet', 'Northern Lights').
Plant out for summer display when frosts are over. Dig up some plants in autumn, overwinter in a frost-free place and take cuttings of the young shoots in early spring. Alternatively, raise plants from seeds.

Callistephus (China aster)
Floppy chrysanthemum-like blooms all summer. Best in full sun in ordinary soil.
Types: Carpet (8 inches, 20 cm.); Cactus; Powderpuff; Full Double; Super Giant semi-formal; all with wide varieties of colour.
Raise plants from seeds sown with gentle heat indoors in spring. Prick out seedlings in shallow trays and harden them off before setting outdoors in late May to flower from June onwards or sow outdoors as soon as soil conditions permit.

Dahlia
Flowers in many shades of colour. They highlight late summer with their brilliant hues, continuing until cut down by frost in autumn. There are several classic shapes; blooms can

range from 4–10 inches (10–25 cm.) across.
Single-flowered – consisting of an outer ring of petals and a large yellow boss in the centre.
Anemone flowered – blooms like anemones.
Collerette – ring of tubed petals overlapping outer ring of flat spoon-shaped petals.
Peony flowered – flowers consist of 2 or more circles of flattened petals.
Decorative: magnificent double flowers subdivided into Giants, with 10 inch (25 cm.) blooms, large, medium, small, miniature.
Ball – ball-shaped blooms.
Pompon – similar to ball-flowered dahlias but with smaller and more globular flowers.
Cactus – sharply quilled petals.
There are hundreds of varieties in almost every shade imaginable. Best in full sun though will tolerate light shade. Ordinary soil enriched with old manure to prolong the display.
Raise plants from seeds, tubers, or cuttings.

Dianthus chinensis (Indian pink)
Vivid-hued blooms, single or double in self or mixed colours. Full sun. Thrive in most soils, particularly those rich in lime.
Varieties: 'Baby Doll', single flowers, many brilliant shades, petals attractively patterned, 6 inches (15 cm.); *D. heddewigii* 'Fireball', glorious scarlet, 9 inches (23 cm.); (North America: 'Snowflake', single, white).
Pinch out growing points to encourage bushiness and plenty of flowers.
Raise plants with gentle heat indoors in late winter or early spring. Prick off seedlings in shallow trays of gritty compost, harden off and plant outdoors in late May or early June or sow directly outside when soil permits.

Fuchsia
Tubular ballet-skirted flowers borne along slender arching shoots. Plants hardy or tender. Blooms brighten late summer and early autumn. Heights from 2 inches (5 cm.) with the carpeting form of *F. procumbens*, to 8 feet (2·4 m.) or more and as much across with *F. magellanica*. Best in deep fertile soil in light shade, though will tolerate full sun. Coloured leaved varieties best in good light.

Some hardy varieties. Most, however, make excellent bedding subjects but must be overwintered in a frost-free greenhouse: 'Texas Longhorn', large double red and white flowers; 'White Spider', gorgeous slender petalled flowers.
Prune back flowered shoots to within a few inches of the main framework in spring, to encourage sturdy new flowering shoots.
Raise new plants from seed or cuttings.

Heliotrope (cherry pie)
Clusters of small deeply coloured flowers top stems set with broadly spear-shaped, deeply veined leaves, 12–18 inches (30–45 cm.) high. Ordinary soil in good light, but will tolerate light shade. Stake plants in windy districts.
Varieties: deep blue 'Marina'; violet-blue 'Lemoine's Giant'. All have a strong sweet scent. Can be grown as standards. Best sown in gentle heat in February or March, pricked out to grow on strongly and set outdoors in late May or early June to flower throughout the summer.
Increase plants from seed, or cuttings taken in September and kept growing steadily in a frost-free greenhouse throughout the winter.

Impatiens (busy lizzie)
Bright flattish or cup-shaped flowers borne singly or in small clusters on fleshy stems. Height, 6 inches (15 cm.) to 2 feet (60 cm.). Ordinary soil, in sun or light shade.
Come in a wide variety of colours including light pink, rose, plum, scarlet, salmon, tangerine and white; some with variegated leaves. New are Elfin Series and fancy-leaved sorts.
Raise new plants from seed or cuttings. Frost-tender.

Lobelia
Tiny broad-lipped tubular flowers borne in immense numbers on spreading or trailing stems. Excellent edging plant for borders or window boxes. Any good soil, sun or light shade.
Varieties: *L. erinus* 'Blue Gown', sky-blue; 'Mrs Clibran Improved', deep blue with a white eye; 'White Lady'; 'Rosamund', carmine-red; 'Sapphire', azure-blue, with distinctive white eye, good trailing variety.
Raise plants in gentle heat and bed them out for the summer when frosts

are over or sow outdoors directly for later blooming.

Lobularia maritima, see **Alyssum**

Nicotiana (tobacco plant)
Tubular blooms, richly fragrant, borne in large numbers atop slender stems. Ideal for sun or light shade in any soil.
Varieties: 'Evening Fragrance', petunia-like flowers in many shades emit superb fragrance, especially at dusk, 3 feet (90 cm.); 'Affinis', pure white, very fragrant, 32 inches (80 cm.); 'Dwarf Idol', bright crimson; 'Lime Green' or 'Lime Sherbet', flowers of that colour; 'Sensation' mixed, many colours, and blooms remain wide open in daylight.
Raise new plants from seeds sown in gentle heat in late winter and planted outdoors in June or when frosts are over.

Pelargonium (geranium)
Mostly round-headed clusters of single or double flowers, with plain or frilled petals. Foliage particularly attractive in the zonal and ivy-leaved varieties. Good rich soil, full sun or light shade. All groups include a wide selection of colours.
Types: Best known are the zonals, so called because their leaves are zoned or patterned: come in a wide selection of varieties and colours, also miniatures.
Regal or 'Martha Washington' pelargoniums: less hardy and floriferous than the zonals; waved or crinkled leaves.
Scented geraniums with leaves of varied fragrances.
Ivy geraniums: perfect for cascading from tubs or window boxes. Care-free strain, a group more readily grown from seed for use the same year.
Overwinter bedded-out geraniums from October onwards in a frost-free greenhouse, a cold room or store in their soil in a cellar. Take cuttings in August. Again keep them growing through the winter in a cool, but frost-proof place.

Petunia
Very showy, single or double saucer-shaped flowers borne on short stems that spread freely in sun or shade. Ordinary soil, best enriched with old manure to prolong flowering.
All colours, singles and doubles, plain-petalled and frilled, dwarf or tall.
Raise plants in gentle heat in winter and, after hardening them off, plant them out for blooming throughout the summer. Propagate doubles by cuttings taken before frost.

Tagetes (French and African marigold)
Single, daisy-like blooms or double, carnation-like blooms are borne freely on short stems from June to late autumn, or as soon as nights grow cold. Ordinary soil in sun or semi-shade.
Types: single, double and anemone-flowered; yellow, orange, brown and two-toned; 4–18 or 20 inches (10–45 or 50 cm.).
Raise plants from seeds sown in gentle heat in late winter or spring and, after pricking off seedlings and hardening them off, plant them where they are to flower, in late May or early June.

Herbaceous plants

Acanthus (bear's breeches)
Handsome with large, deep green leaves and upright flower spikes of hooded blooms from July to August. Ordinary soil, sun or semi-shade.
Species: *A. mollis*, 4 feet (1·2 m.) high, leaves roughly heart-shaped with wavy edges, flowers white and purple; *A. spinosus*, 3–4 feet (90 cm.–1·2 m.) high, long narrow finely cut leaves, white and purple flowers offset by green bracts. Both species bear their flowers on 18 inch (45 cm.) spikes. Shorten stems back to near ground level after flowering.
Raise new plants by dividing the clump in autumn or spring. Take root cuttings or sow seeds.

Aubrieta (rock cress)
Carpeting plant with small silver greyish green leaves and tiny flowers that completely cover the shoots in spring and early summer. Ideal for growing in full sun in poorest soil, between crazy paving, cascading from walls or on a rock garden. Grows well in limy soil. Height 4 inches (10 cm.), spread several feet.
Colours: purple, lavender, white, reddish. Cut back flowered stems when blooms fade to keep plant compact. Top dress crowns with rich gritty soil to boost strong growth.
Raise new plants from cuttings or seeds.

Campanula (bellflower)
Striking open, starry or tubular bell-flowered plants which bloom from spring to late autumn. Sun, semi-shade. Ordinary soil, best if lime added where it is light and sandy.
Herbaceous kinds: *C. lactiflora*, 5 feet (1·5 m.), immense spikes of blue cup-shaped flowers; *C. glomerata* 'Superba', the clustered bellflower, violet bells, does well in shade.
Bedding kinds: *C. medium*, Canterbury bells – 'Bells of Holland', large bell-shaped blooms in pink, blue, white or mauve shades, 15 inches (38 cm.).
Alpine kinds: *C. garganica*, deep blue, mats, 3 inches (7·5 cm.); *C. portenschlagiana* 'Major', violet mauve, 6 inches (15 cm.), excellent for dry walls.
Raise new plants from seeds or rooted offsets of parent clump.
Raise biennial kinds every year, in late spring and plant out in autumn for flowering the following year.

Cineraria maritima (syn. *Senecio cineraria*)
Excellent foliage plant with silvery white, finely cut leaves. Height 2 feet (60 cm.). Small yellow flowers borne in late summer. Sun or light shade, ordinary soil. Fine plant for growing in tubs. Pinch out growing tip to make plant bush out.
Take cuttings in August and over-winter them in a cold frame for planting out the following late spring and early summer.
Prune away faded flower stems and trim to shape. Remove straggly stems when necessary.

Convallaria (lily-of-the-valley)
Spreading, ground-covering plant about 9–12 inches (23–30 cm.) high. Sprays of small white bell-shaped flowers, richly scented, broadly spear-shaped leaves. Blooms in April and May. Ordinary soil, including limy. Sun or quite deep shade.
Flowers white or faintly pink-tinted.
Varieties: *C. majalis*, the common lily-of-the-valley.
Raise new plants from rhizomes dug up in autumn and planted 4 inches (10 cm.) apart, just below the soil surface.

Erigeron (fleabane)
Imposing daisy-like flowers for sun or light shade, mid to late summer. Ordinary soil.
Varieties: 'Foerster's Liebling', 2 feet (60 cm.), semi-double pink; also lavender-blue and violet-blue varieties. Trim off dead flowers occasionally to encourage new blooms.
Raise new plants from rooted offsets of established clumps.

Euphorbia (spurge)
Easy growing perennial for sun or deep shade in ordinary soil, including limy areas. Flowers, actually bracts, are usually well coloured in shades of yellow or green. Leaves handsome, especially in *Euphorbia wulfenii*.
Species and varieties: *E. epithymoides*, saffron-yellow flower heads, spring, early summer. 1 foot (30 cm.); *E. wulfenii*, bold clusters of bloom held like clubs on long fleshy stems above stems massed with narrow blue-green leaves; *E. griffithii* 'Fireglow' has flame-coloured bracts; *E. myrsinites*, sun lover for hot spots in dry soil; trailing stems clustered with blue-grey leaves.
Increase plants by splitting up the

Campanula persicifolia

rootstock and setting out rooted portions in autumn or spring.

Grasses (annual and perennial kinds)
Easy, trouble-free plants for admiring in the border or for drying and arranging in the home. Ordinary soil, best in sun.
Annuals: *Briza maxima*, nodding heads, $1\frac{1}{2}$ feet (45 cm.); *Coix lachryma-jobi*, $2\frac{1}{2}$ feet (75 cm.); *Lagurus ovatus* (hare's tail), 1 foot (30 cm.).
Perennials: *Cortaderia selloana* (pampas grass), 5 feet (1·5 m.), towering plumes; *Acorus gramineus variegatus*, 8–10 inches (20–25 cm.), narrow leaves striped silver; *Helictotrichon sempervirens*, upright blue tufts, 2 feet (60 cm.); *Miscanthus sinensis gracillimus*, 5 feet (1·5 m.), blue-green leaves turning yellowish in autumn.
Raise new plants from seed or divisions of older plants.

Helleborus
Generally open cup-shaped flowers on

short stems with sometimes quite striking sculptured leaves. Sun or deep shade. Ordinary soil, grows well in limy. Evergreen leaves.
Species: *H. niger* (Christmas rose), 1 foot (30 cm.) high, bright white flowers in winter; *H. orientalis* (Lenten rose), white, pink or purplish flowers, 1–2 feet (30–60 cm.) high, several to a stem; *H. corsicus*, 3 feet (90 cm.) architectural leaves, light green flowers in clusters.
Raise new plants from seeds or pieces from established clumps.

Heuchera (coral flower)
Massed panicles of tiny bell flowers borne on slender stems among deep green heart-shaped leaves, from June to September. Good in full sun or light shade; leaves make a weed suppressing carpet. Ordinary soil. Colours: red, rose and pinks. *Heucherella* is a bi-generic hybrid between *Tiarella* and *Heuchera* and is vigorous with plentiful sprays of light pink flowers from May to October; flowers longest in light shade. Raise new plants by dividing clumps into rooted pieces.

Hosta (plantain lily)
Superb foliage plant for sun or deep shade. Leaves mostly spear-shaped, bright green, bluish, margined with silver or yellow striped. Best in moist soil. Bold flower spikes of lily-like flowers appear in summer.
Species and varieties: *H. albo-marginata*, lilac flowers, white-edged leaves; *H. fortunei*, fresh green leaves, heliotrope flowers; *H. sieboldiana*, blue-green leaves, effectively crimped, whitish flowers. All grow around 2 feet (60 cm.) high.
Protect succulent shoot tips in spring by baiting against slugs.
Raise new plants by splitting up clumps.

Iberis (candytuft)
Cushions of bloom amid lustrous deep green leaves – a spectacle in spring. Ordinary soil, sun or light shade.
Annuals: *I. umbellata*, white, some rose or lavender-tinted.
Perennials: *I. gibraltarica*, flowers opening pink and turning to white; *I. sempervirens*, bright white flowers, evergreen leaves.
Increase plants from seeds or softwood cuttings.

Nepeta (catmint)
Silver-grey leaves attractive all summer and autumn, flowers lavender-blue, in spikes 1–3 feet (30–90 cm.) high. Full sun, ordinary soil.
Species and varieties: *N. mussinii*, 1½ feet (45 cm.), 'Six Hills', 3 feet (90 cm.) darker coloured flowers, vigorous. Perfect edging plant. Leave foliage all winter for its silvery effect. Raise new plants from rooted offsets taken in autumn or spring.

Penstemon
Sprays of snapdragon-like flowers borne in sprays in late spring and early summer. Ordinary soil, sun or light shade.
Varieties: 'Firebird', scarlet, 3 feet (90 cm.); also many species of varied heights and colours, reds, roses, pinks, lavenders, whites. Cover plants with cloches in winter if severe frosts likely. Raise new plants from cuttings in late summer and overwinter in a cold frame.

Euphorbia, crown of thorns.

Polygonatum multiflorum
(Solomon's seal)
Arching stems set with oblong
pointed leaves. Flowers small, white
and narrowly tubular, borne singly, in
pairs or trebles along the entire length
of the underside of the stem. Spreads
by means of underground stems.
Any soil, thrives in limy. Best in
light shade where the leaves develop
well.
Raise new plants by dividing the
rootstock in autumn and planting out
rooted pieces 9–12 inches (23–30 cm.)
apart.

Tolmiea menziesii (pig-a-back plant)
Curious maple-shaped green leaves
produce baby plants from their centres.
Slender sprays of greenish flowers
appear in summer.
Ordinary soil, excellent for carpeting
in light shade beneath trees, or growing
as a pot plant in unheated conservatory.
Increase by removing sturdy plantlets
from leaf centres and potting them on
in small pots of rich gritty soil.

Shrubs

Aucuba (spotted laurel)
Rounded bush of evergreen leaves and
striking marble-sized berries in
autumn and winter. Species and forms:
A. japonica (male or female) glossy
spear-shaped leaves, scarlet fruits;
grow both sexes for fruiting.
'Crotonoides', mottled gold leaves;
'Fructu-albo', handsome leaves,
yellowish berries. Thrives in shade or
semi-shade, ordinary soil. Does well in
smoky atmosphere. Water freely in
summer, less in winter. Feed
fortnightly to encourage sturdy
growth in summer.
Raise plants from seed or cuttings.

Berberis (barberry)
Upright or spreading, deciduous or
evergreen bushes grown for their
spring flowers, autumn fruits and
autumn-tinted leaves. Stems and
leaves are spiny. Evergreen varieties:
B. linearifolia, orange flowers;
B. verruculosa, dark green leaves, pale
yellow flowers. Deciduous varieties:
B. thunbergii, red fruits; *B.t.* 'Aurea',
striking golden leaves; *B. wilsonae*,
golden yellow flowers, bright red
fruits, autumn-tinted foliage.
Ordinary soil, sun or shade. Water
freely in summer, hardly at all in
winter, but make sure soil stays damp.
Feed fortnightly if growth poor,
otherwise, not necessary.
Raise plants from seeds or cuttings.

Camellia
Glossy-leaved evergreen shrubs
(tender in coldest parts of North
America) with single, semi-double or
fully double flowers in many colours
including pink, white, scarlet and
blotched pink and white. Winter and
spring-flowering, acid soil essential or
leaves turn yellow and growth is poor.
Varieties of *C. japonica*: 'Adolphe
Audusson', crimson-scarlet; 'Gloire de
Nantes', rose-pink; 'Mathotiana Alba',
large white.
Feed with sequestered iron at regular
intervals through spring and summer
to induce strong healthy foliage.
Water freely, semi-shade.
Raise new plants from leaf bud
cuttings.

Caryopteris (blue spiraea)
Low spreading edging shrub with
spires of blue flowers in late summer.
Leaves silvery grey, aromatic. Sun or
semi-shade. Ordinary soil. Deciduous.
Varieties: 'Heavenly Blue', rich blue,
free flowering.
Water freely in summer, feed
fortnightly and water sparingly in
winter.
Pruning: cut back flowered shoots in
March to encourage strong new
growth from the base.
Raise new plants from cuttings.

Chamaecyparis (false cypress)
Evergreen conifer with upright or
rounded habit, with blue-green,
silvery, golden or grass-green foliage.
Grows best in acid soil though
tolerates ordinary soil.
Sun or shade. Golden variegated kinds
do best in sun.

Varieties: very numerous, especially of
C. obtusa and *C. pisifera*. Vary greatly
in size, shape, type of foliage and
colour. All grow slowly in tubs or
pots and need watering frequently in
summer, less in winter. Ideally feed
fortnightly throughout the summer.
Clip to shape in spring if shoots get
straggly.
Raise new plants from cuttings.

Choisya ternata (Mexican orange)
Glossy-leaved evergreen with bunches
of small cup-shaped, white, richly-
scented flowers in spring and
intermittently throughout the summer
and autumn. Ordinary soil in sun or
semi-shade, even dense shade.
Water freely in dry spells. Feed
fortnightly throughout the summer if
growth needs spurring along.
Raise new plants from cuttings.

Cistus (rock rose)
Large open flowers in white, red or
pink, often maroon blotched at the
base of petals: May to October. Ideal
for hot dry situations. Full sun,
ordinary soil with added peat.
Evergreen shrub with rounded or
spreading habit. Water freely in dry
spells, feed fortnightly if growth poor.
Varieties: *C. x corbariensis*, white;
C. x cyprius, white, blotched maroon;
'Silver Pink', silvery pink;
C. x purpureus, rosy crimson.
Raise new plants from seeds or
cuttings.

Clematis
Twining climber with mostly open
flat-petalled (sepalled) blooms in a
range of colours from white through
pink, red, blue, violet and purple.
There are even some yellow-flowered
kinds. Grow best with their roots in
the shade and shoots in the sun.
Deciduous and a few evergreen sorts.
Thrive in limy soil, though grow well
in most soils that drain freely and
have adequate plant foods.
Varieties: essentially there are the
large flowered hybrids such as purple
'Jackmanii', red and magenta 'Ernest
Markham', and bluish 'Mrs
Cholmondeley', and the species such
as *C. alpina*, blue with white stamens,
white *C. montana*, pink *C. montana*
'Tetrarose' and yellow *C. orientalis*.
Water freely throughout the summer,
less in winter. Feed fortnightly when
strong growth is made in spring and
early summer.

Raise new plants from layers, cuttings or seed. Prune by either cutting back previous year's growth to 2 feet (60 cm.) off the ground each February or early March, or simply shorten flowered shoots to within a few inches of the main upright branching system. Pruning given depends on variety.

Cotoneaster

Deciduous and evergreen kinds. Upright, rounded, spreading or ground covering shrubs with attractive leaves and berries. Sun or shade.
Varieties: accommodating evergreen kinds include ground-hugging, red-berried, glossy-leaved *C. dammeri*, sulphur-yellow-berried *C. rothschildianus* and handsome white-flowered, red-berried *C. lacteus*. Deciduous kinds are the herringbone cotoneaster, *C. horizontalis*, with masses of orange red berries on wiry flattened branches, perfect for growing close to a wall, and *C.* 'Hybridus Pendulus', a weeping variety usually grown as a standard.
Keep the soil moist in summer, less so in winter. Feed fortnightly if growth slow.
Raise new plants from cuttings or seeds.

Escallonia

Evergreen shrub with upright or spreading habit. Clusters of pink, red or white flowers borne along shoot tips in summer.
Varieties: 'Pride of Donard', rich red flowers in May; 'Iveyi', white flowers; 'Donard Seedling', apple-blossom pink.
Ordinary soil in full sun or light shade. Water freely in summer, less in winter. Feed to encourage sturdy growth.
Raise new plants from cuttings or layers.

Euonymus (spindle berry)

Attractive for its brilliant red autumn tinted leaves, coral-pink fruits and green variegated leaves. Sun or deep shade. Evergreen or deciduous.
Varieties: *E. alatus* is small roundish shrub with winged stems and bright autumn-tinted foliage; *E. europaeus* 'Red Cascade' is grown for its masses of large fruits; *E. fortunei* 'Emerald Gold' makes good ground cover with leaves margined with gold. Water freely in dry spells. No feeding necessary unless growth poor. All

forms of *E. fortunei* also excellent for training over walls provided suitable supports are erected.
Increase from layers, seeds, or cuttings.

Forsythia (golden bellflower)

Golden tubular starry flowers in spring. Bushes rounded and vigorous; cascading shoots in *F. suspensa*, which also makes a fine wall shrub. Varieties include: 'Lynwood', most free flowering; 'Beatrix Farrand', largest blooming variety; 'Arnold Dwarf', ideal for small tubs or window boxes. Ordinary soil. No feeding necessary, water freely in dry spells. Sun or semi-shade.
Raise new plants from layers or cuttings.

Hebe

Hardy, semi-hardy and tender, upright or spreading, evergreen, with mostly glossy leaves and cone-shaped flowers throughout the summer and autumn.
Varieties: *H. x andersonii* 'Variegata', with waxy, creamy leaves and lavender flowers; 'La Séduisante', plum purple flowers with reddish green leaves; 'Carl Teschner' dwarf, ideal for rock gardens, violet-blue flower sprays; *H. pagei*, grey-blue silvery leaves, white flowers, excellent for ground cover.
Sun or shade, normal soil. Water to keep roots moist in dry spells, hardly at all in winter.
Raise new plants from cuttings or layers.
No pruning needed apart from removing straggly shoots in early spring to keep bush shapely.

Hedera (English ivy)

Self-clinging evergreen climber. Ideal for sun, shade or deep shade. Leaves palmate or arrow-shaped, green or variegated.
Types: very numerous, large, small, all shapes, green and variegated.
Normal soil, water freely in dry spells. Feed only if growth poor. No pruning necessary apart from cutting back unwanted shoots in early spring.
Increase from layers or cuttings.

Hydrangea

Deciduous bushes or self-clinging climber. Mostly hardy. The lace caps have flattened blooms of fertile florets surrounded by sterile florets; the mopheads (hortensias) have roughly globe-shaped blooms of sterile florets.

Flowers lilac or reddish in neutral or limy soils, violet or blue in acid soils. Add hydrangea blueing powder to the root area to change red or lilac flowered varieties into blue-flowered specimens. Blooms in summer.
Varieties: 'Altona', red; 'Mariesii', pale rose or blue; 'Grayswood', violet purple and white, flushed red.
The one climbing hydrangea, *H. petiolaris*, has white flower discs in early summer and sticks to rough surfaces by means of stem roots, like an ivy.
Water whenever the soil is dry as hydrangeas need ample moisture to produce luxuriant leaves and fine flowers. Feed fortnightly throughout the summer. Plant in light shade. Prune in late spring, thinning out dead or weak shoots from centre of bush and cutting back faded flowers to healthy buds just below the blooms.
Raise new plants from layers or cuttings.

Hypericum (St John's Wort)

Starry or cup-shaped yellow flowers on upright or spreading shoots. Deciduous and evergreen.
Species and varieties: *H. calycinum*, large blooms with pronounced boss of yellow stamens; 'Hidcote', massed yellow flowers on rounded bush; *H. elatum* 'Elstead', grown for its salmon-red berry clusters and yellow flowers. Ordinary soil. No feeding necessary, but water freely in dry spells.
Prune *H. calycinum* back hard in March to induce strong new growth from the base. 'Hidcote' and *H. elatum* should have their side shoots shortened to within a few inches of the older shoots in spring.
Raise new plants from seed or cuttings. Grow plants in good light or light shade. Blooms in summer and early autumn.

(above) *Mahonia aquifolium*

(left) *Prunus subhirtella* 'Pendula'

(right) *Clematis* 'King George'

Jasminum (jasmine)
Deciduous wall shrubs with scented
tubular flowers, for mild climates.
Species: *J. nudiflorum*, with bright
golden yellow flowers in winter; *J.
officinale*, with pure white flowers on
twining shoots, in summer.
Ordinary soil. No feeding necessary
unless growth is slow. Water freely
when soil dry in summer. *J. officinale*
grows best in full light, but *J.
nudiflorum* does not mind light shade.
Raise new plants from cuttings.
Pruning: shorten flowered shoots of
J. nudiflorum to within 2–3 inches
(5–7·5 cm.) of the main framework;
simply thin out stems of *J. officinale*;
no cutting back of flowered shoots
necessary.

Kerria (Jew's mallow)
Rounded bush with single or double
orange-yellow flowers on shoots set

86

with green or silvery variegated foliage. Blooms in April and May.
Varieties: *K. japonica* 'Picta', silvery green leaves; *K. j.* 'Pleniflora', double flowers. Ordinary soil. This is a very hardy shrub and tolerates cold winds, shade and drought with little sign of discomfort. Looks well against a wall, too. Water freely through the summer, less so in winter. Feed only if growth is slow.
Prune flowered shoots back to strong new growth.
Raise new plants from cuttings or division of the rootstock.

Laurus nobilis (sweet bay, bay laurel)
Dark green spear-shaped leaves, small white flowers in spring. Leaves used in flavouring many dishes.
Makes a rounded bush if grown naturally, but often clipped to form a pyramid or standard with a ball head. Sheltered position in good light, not fully hardy. Ordinary soil. Water freely in summer, less in winter. No feeding required unless growth slow.
Trim to shape in summer. No other pruning necessary.
Raise plants from cuttings.

Lavandula (lavender)
Evergreen rounded shrub with greyish silvery leaves and sweetly scented. Low growing. Flowers in summer.
Varieties: *L.* 'Hidcote', deep violet-blue.
Best in well-drained soil in full sun. Does not mind long periods of drought. Water freely in summer or whenever the soil is dry. Feed fortnightly if growth poor.
Raise new plants from cuttings. Trim off flowered shoots in late summer; cut back old growth if straggly, in late spring.

Lonicera (shrubby and climbing honeysuckle)
Shrubby: *L. tatarica* most common, large, red-berried.
Climbing forms: semi-evergreen or evergreen – *L. japonica halliana*, creamy yellow flowers all summer. Deciduous: *L. periclymenum* 'Belgica', flowers with peaches and cream tints in early summer; *L. periclymenum* 'Serotina', creamy white, suffused purple flowers in summer and late summer; *L. heckrotii*, red and yellow flowers. The climbers twine their shoots round a supporting framework. Water and feed

regularly as climbing forms have extensive root system and can quickly deplete a tub of soil of its plant foods.
Pruning: cut out old or weakly shoots on both climbing and shrubby sorts after flowering.
Raise new plants from layers or cuttings.

Mahonia
Evergreen sculptured shrub with statuesque leaves and yellow flowers in winter.
Varieties: *M. aquifolium*, creeping habit with bunches of bright yellow flowers followed by blue-black berries – late winter; *M. bealei*, larger, coarser, with larger leaves; 'Charity', probably the finest upright form with large stiff pinnate leaves and stems topped by pendulous flower sprays. Ordinary soil, sun or deep shade. No feeding necessary unless growth slow. Water well in summer, hardly at all in winter. Leaves suffer from wind burn in exposed places.
No pruning required, apart from cutting back *M. aquifolium* fairly hard if shoots become straggly.
Increase plants from seeds or cuttings.

Parthenocissus (Virginia creeper)
Self-clinging climber grown for its magnificent autumn-tinted leaves.
Species: *P. henryana*, variegated white and pink palmate leaves; *P. quinquefolia* (true Virginia creeper), palmate leaves that take on brilliant scarlet hues in autumn.
Sun or shade. Ordinary soil. No feeding required.
No pruning necessary but cut back unwanted shoots in summer.
Raise new plants from cuttings.

Passiflora (passion flower)
Semi-evergreen climber with striking creamy white and blue flowers in summer.
Varieties: *P. caerulea*, flowers as above, and 'Constance Elliott', white. Thrives in sheltered, sunny position away from cold winds.
Ordinary soil. Water well in summer, less in winter. Feed fortnightly while flowers forming.
Prune side shoots back to 6 inches (15 cm.) of the main framework in early spring.
Raise new plants from layers or cuttings.

Pernettya
Ground hugging shrub with small

pointed leaves, tiny white flowers and highly attractive marble-sized berries in white, pink, mauve or scarlet. Winter decoration.
To get berries have one male plant together with several females.
Varieties: *P. mucronata* 'Bell's Seedling', red berries; *P. mucronata* 'Alba', white berries.
Grow plants in peaty soil free from lime. Water freely in summer, less in winter, sun or shade, mild climate. No pruning necessary.
Raise plants from cuttings or layers.

Philadelphus (mock orange)
Upright or rounded shrub from 3 to 12 feet (0·9–3·7 m.) high, depending upon variety. Pure white, single or double, often maroon-blotched flowers borne freely along arching stems in mid-summer. Sun or light shade. Ordinary soil.
Varieties: 'Beauclerk', large white, cerise throated blooms; *P. coronarius* 'Aureus', white flowers, golden leaves; *P. microphyllus*, white flowers. *P. grandiflorus*, tallest sort with scentless flowers, often used for flower arranging as the sweet peppery scent of other varieties can cause irritation of eyes and nose.
Pruning: remove some of the older stems when the flowers fade. Retain young growth for flowering the following year.

Prunus (flowering cherries, plums, almonds, peaches)
Large family of deciduous trees and shrubs which flower mostly in spring. Some have brilliant autumn-tinted leaves. Branches are hung with blossom. Best in full sun; ordinary soil, with or without lime.

Varieties: (ornamental almond), *P. tenella* 'Firehill', dwarf habit, bright red flowers on every branch.
Ornamental cherries: *P.* 'Amanogawa', pillar of pink flowers, narrow upright growth, ideal for confined spaces; *P. subhirtella* 'Autumnalis', white winter flowering; *P.* 'Okame', small tree with rosy pink flowers.
No pruning necessary, but should a branch need taking out, do this in late summer to reduce risk of attack by silver leaf disease.
Keep the soil moist in dry spells, feed if growth poor, otherwise not necessary.
Raise new plants by grafting varieties on to vigorous stocks; also by cuttings.

Pyracantha (firethorn)
Evergreen shrub. Grow as a specimen in the open, or against a wall or fence. Masses of foamy white flowers in early summer followed by clusters of berries in autumn and winter. Branches spiny.
Species and varieties: *P. angustifolia*, orange-red berries; *P. atalantioides*, red berries; *P. rogersiana* (syn. *P. crenulata rogersiana*) 'Flava', yellow berries.
Water freely throughout dry spells in summer. Feed fortnightly if growth slow.
Clip wall-trained shrubs with shears in early summer.
Raise new plants from cuttings.

Ribes (flowering currant)
Deciduous shrub draped with clusters of flowers in early spring. Makes a roundish bush. Ideal for deep shade or full sun. Ordinary soil.
Varieties: *R. sanguineum* 'King Edward VII', intense crimson; 'Pulborough Scarlet', deep red; 'Praecox', pink.
No feeding necessary. Water freely in dry spells. Shorten back old non-flowering shoots to near ground level in spring.
Raise new plants from cuttings.

Rosa (rose)
Single or double flowers borne on miniature, low growing, medium or large bushes. Deciduous, ordinary soil, sun or light shade. Climbing kinds also have single or double flowers.
Species: *Rosa rugosa* 'Frau Dagmar Hastrup', single pink flowers followed by rounded bright red tomato-sized hips.
Climbing species: *Rosa filipes*, vigorous, greyish green leaves, huge clusters of white flowers.
Old-fashioned roses: 'La Reine Victoria', double pink cup-like blooms; 'Mme Hardy', flattish pure white flowers.
Hybrid tea roses: 'Colour Wonder', orange salmon; 'Grandpa Dickson', creamy yellow pink-edged flowers; (North America: 'Mirandy', velvety wine-red; 'Eclipse', chrome-yellow).
Floribundas: 'Blessings', coral pink; 'Allgold', yellow; 'Fashion', coral peach; (North America: 'Fire King').
Climbers: 'Golden Showers', yellow.
Ramblers: 'Dorothy Perkins', bluish pink flowers.
Miniatures: 'Baby Masquerade', flame and gold; 'Coralin', orange and pink; 'Cinderella', white; (North America: 'Crimson Gem').
Pruning: aim at keeping in as much young wood as possible. Cut away bare lengths of non-flowering wood and keep the centres of bush roses well thinned. Remove faded flowers and stems of rambler roses completely, tying in new growths to flowers the following year. Leave the species roses and most of the old-fashioned kinds well alone, apart from keeping them shapely. Carry out all pruning in mid-February, early March or before growth begins in spring.
Raise new plants from cuttings or budding varieties on to appropriate stocks.

Rosmarinus (rosemary)
Aromatic evergreen with narrow leaves and upright spikes of flower. Ideal for dry, windy spots and hot sunny areas. Useful culinary herb.
Varieties: *R. officinalis*, light blue; *R. o.* 'Albus', white flowers.
Ordinary soil in sun or shade. Keep the soil moist in dry spells, though plant can tolerate long periods without water.
Pruning not required. No feeding necessary unless growth poor.

Spiraea
Deciduous shrubs with low rounded habit or arching stems. Starry flowers borne in flattened heads or tapering plumes. Mostly spring flowering.
Species and varieties: *S. thunbergii*, white clusters of bloom; *S. menziesii*, bright rosy pink flower cones in summer; *S. bullata*, low growing, ideal for rock gardens, crimson flowers in umbrella heads; *S. x bumalda* 'Anthony Waterer', crimson flowers.
Sun or deep shade, normal soil. Water freely in summer. Feed only if growth is weak.
Prune back flowered shoots of *S. x bumalda* in February or March. Prune *S. menziesii* after flowering – simply cut back flowered stems to strong buds below.
Raise new plants from cuttings and layers.

Syringa (lilac)
Upright deciduous shrubs with imposing spires of bloom in late spring and early summer. Single or double flowers. *Syringa palibiniana*, dwarf kind, ideal for containers.
Large varieties: 'Esther Staley', clear pink; 'Primrose', creamy yellow; 'Charles Joly', dark red; 'Edith Cavell', white.
Sun or semi-shade, ordinary soil. Water freely in summer, feed only if shoot growth weakly.
Prune off faded flowers in summer. Raise new plants from cuttings or grafting varieties on to stock plants.

Tamarix (tamarisk)
Feathery rose-pink flowers borne in mid-summer among bright green ferny leaves. Height: 9–12 feet (2·7–3·7 m.). Full sun. Deciduous. Ordinary soil but hates lime.
Varieties: *T. parviflora*, deep pink flowers; *T. pentandra* 'rubra', rose-red

flowers; *T. tetrandra*, pink flower plumes borne on shoots produced the previous year.
Pruning: keep bush shapely by cutting back around half of the previous season's shoots. Deal with *T. pentandra* from early autumn to late winter and *T. tetrandra* when the flowers fade.
Raise new plants from cuttings in October.

Vitis (ornamental vine)
Vigorous climber ascending by means of clinging tendrils. Can grow to 60 feet (18 m.) or more in favoured situations. Deciduous, ordinary soil, sun or light shade. Perfect for covering walls, fences, arbours, trees or pergolas.
Species and varieties: *V. coignetiae*, the Japanese crimson glory vine. Large heart-shaped leaves of striking appearance which turn scarlet and

orange in autumn; *V. vinifera* 'Purpurea', handsome claret-coloured vine-shaped leaves, deeply lobed, colouring well in autumn.
Prune out congested shoots in summer. Encourage new growth to fill allotted area.
Raise new plants from stem cuttings in November, but increase *V. coignetiae* by layering stems.

Weigela (syn. *Diervilla*)
Rounded shrub with arching branches bearing sprays of foxglove-shaped flowers in spring and early summer. Leaves green or variegated. Height: 6-8 feet (1·8-2·4 m.).
Ordinary soil in sun or light shade.
Varieties: *W. florida* 'Foliis Purpureis', purple-hued leaves, rosy purple blooms; *W. florida* 'Variegata', leaves margined white, pink flowers; *W. middendorffiana*, large sulphur-yellow flowers.

Pruning: shorten flowered stems and some older shoots back to ground level when the flowers fade. Aim at keeping young free-flowering growth.

Wistaria
Vigorous twining climber with handsome pinnate leaves and long racemes of bloom in spring.
Deciduous, ordinary soil, full sun.
Varieties: *W. floribunda* 'Alba', long white flower clusters; *W. sinensis*, lavender-blue flowers.
Pruning: shorten all side shoots back to 2-3 buds from the base of the previous year's growth in late winter, early spring.
Raise new plants from seeds, layers or cuttings.

Berberis

Care
of Plants

❧ Watering ❧

One of the disadvantages of gardening in the city is that only too often the gardens or patios are very hot in summer and plants tend to dry out quickly.

If suitable materials can be obtained – spent hops, peat, or even sawdust – a layer 1–2 inches (2·5–5 cm.) deep over the soil, whether in borders, tubs or window boxes, helps to retain moisture and reduce the frequency of watering. It also helps to suppress weeds which in themselves rob the plants of moisture.

It is well worth while going to the expense of installing an outside water tap or faucet. Some water authorities object to the installation of permanent sprinklers or watering devices, such as punctured hose spray lines, if these are in contact with the soil. These objections can often be overcome if a non-return valve is fitted into the system.

There are now many different types of sprinkler for watering large or small areas, and there are even water- and electric-operated timing devices which can be set to apply water for given periods.

You can tailor-fit a garden for water by laying a plastic main or pipe down one side if it is a rectangular garden, or round several sides if it is of irregular shape. Then fittings, rather like electric light sockets, are fitted at intervals in the main. A similar but 'male' plug is then fitted to a short length of hose pipe, at the other end of which is a sprinkler or a length of spray line.

When you wish to water a given part of the garden you just 'plug into the main'. With several outlets, it is only necessary to have a short, easily carried length of hose connecting the main or supply pipe to the sprinkler, and it is just moved round the garden as required.

If a series of irregular beds or containers of various sizes have to be watered, it is possible to connect them all to the water main by means of a length of semi-rigid plastic pipe. Then above the bed or container, holes are punctured or drilled in the pipe in sufficient number to water the bed in a reasonable time. If water is required more quickly you just make some more holes. Again, if a hole should become bunged up for any reason, it is simple enough to puncture another one. A simple tool for making the holes is a bradawl filed down to about the thickness of a gramophone needle.

There are, of sourse, the sub-irrigation kits originally designed for use on greenhouse benches, which can be used to water plants in pots outdoors. Basically these consist of shallow trays connected, if more than one tray is used, by a plastic tube. The trays are filled with sand and then connected by another tube to a small tank or cistern which is filled with water. This keeps the sand in the trays wet and pot plants are stood on the sand. The roots draw up moisture as they require it. The cistern may be filled as required by means of a hose pipe, but it may be connected to the mains supply and fitted with a ball valve. The sand trays will thus be always kept moist.

Such equipment, of course, may be used to keep house plants watered while the owner is away, provided there is room to set it up although those with an octopus-like arrangement of tiny tubes are better for such a purpose. These self-watering trays may even be used on a balcony or on the floor of a kitchen, to keep the plants watered when the owner is on holiday.

91

❧ Overwintering Plants ❧

In days gone by, when plants and bulbs were relatively cheap, the city gardener was happy enough to buy new bedding plants every year. Now it is important to preserve certain of our bedding plants from year to year.

Ideally, bulbs such as daffodils, tulips and hyacinths grown in containers should be allowed to die down naturally; then the top growth is removed, the bulbs cleaned up, dried off and kept in a cool dry place for replanting in the autumn. This means that you need spare boxes, or inner containers, which can be put in some out-of-the-way corner and watered until the foliage begins to wither naturally. Or better still, if you have an odd corner in the garden or in a friend's garden, the bulbs can be laid in a trench, covered up to half the length of their stems with soil and dried off gradually.

The summer flowers that we should try to lift and preserve through the winter are geraniums, fuchsias, dahlias, gladioli and begonias.

Before frosts arrive in the autumn, lift the geranium plants, trim back the roots, cut the stems down to about 8 inches (20 cm.) long and pack the plants fairly close together in a large pot or box. Pack them in sandy soil, or peat and keep this just slightly moist all winter. In spring pot the plants separately, or plant out when frost danger is over. Treat fuchsias similarly.

With dahlias wait until the foliage has been blackened by frost. Cut the plants down to 12 inches (30 cm.) above ground. Lift the roots carefully. Stand them upside down in a frost free place for 10–12 days. Then put them in boxes and cover the tubers with peat but do not cover the 'crown' of the plant – the point on the stem to which the tubers are attached. It is from this point that new shoots will appear next year and it is important that no rotting takes place here. Keep the peat just moist all winter, and store the plants in a frost free place. Divide into separate pieces each with a tuber and a live growing shoot and replant the tubers in late April; see that there is 6 inches (15 cm.) of soil over the crown of the plant.

Lift gladiolus plants as soon as they have finished flowering. Cut the stems to about 3–4 inches (7·5–10 cm.) above the corms. Store the corms in a single layer in trays in a frost free place.

Lift tuberous begonias before the onset of frost. Put them in a tray or box and allow the stems to wither naturally. Then break them away from the tubers and store these, covered with peat, in trays in a frost free place. In early spring start them into growth by moistening the peat, and plant them in pots or out again when danger of frost is passed.

❧ Frames and Cloches ❧

If there is no space for a greenhouse or a home extension, there may be room for a frame and this can be a great asset. It can be used to raise seedlings and root cuttings and in summer to grow 1 or 2 cucumber plants.

If it is fitted with an electric soil warming cable buried in sand, it is even more useful as seeds may be sown several weeks earlier, and it may be used to grow lettuces and early carrots in the winter, and early spring.

Even more valuable is a frame fitted with both soil and air warming cables. The air warming cables are fitted by special clips to the inside of the frame. With thermostatic control the frame may be kept free of frost, and running costs are not high. It may be powered from a power socket in the house.

Such a frame may be set up on a patio or small terrace at the back of the house, say in late September, and used for overwintering geraniums and other tender plants if the climate is not too severe. In the spring it could be used to raise seedlings of tender annuals, tomatoes and sweet corn plants for planting out. Then, say at the end of May, it may be disconnected and the

frame stood on end, covered with a sheet of plastic, to make more room.

If there is no space for a frame, or you do not want to go to that expense, a few glass or plastic cloches are an excellent investment. Not only will they permit the sowing of tender plants like sweet corn, French and runner beans, and marrows in late April, ahead of season, but also planting of these in early May if they have been bought in or raised indoors or in a heated greenhouse.

Cloches also hasten the growth of peas, broad beans, lettuces and carrots sown under them in late February or March. With lettuces, the cloches give protection against damage by birds.

❧ The Greenhouse and Frames ❧

For anyone who enjoys growing plants, a conservatory, a home extension with glass walls, however small, or a small greenhouse can be a great joy. Such a structure enables you to work with the plants at any time – after dark if need be, and in the winter when there is little to do in a small garden.

Even more rewarding, however, are the benefits such glass protection can provide in the way of better plants and the saving of money.

There are many pot plants which can do a turn in the home for a few weeks, but then need to be given a period of convalescence in a greenhouse with more congenial conditions of light and humidity.

Many plants may be propagated by cuttings, or raised from seed in a greenhouse or conservatory, saving a considerable outlay at the florists. Plants for tubs, window boxes, beds or borders can be propagated, and the tender plants such as geraniums and fuchsias overwintered without difficulty.

By a careful choice of plants you can have flowers in the greenhouse all the year round and, of course, plenty of foliage plants. You can also grow a grape vine, or tomatoes, cucumbers and salad plants in a greenhouse.

While some people prefer wooden greenhouses, the modern trend is towards aluminium, either as a lean-to or as a free-standing house. They used to be much more expensive than wooden houses, but now, as wood is so expensive, they are as cheap as a really good quality wooden house. They need no maintenance and of course last for many years.

While a cold greenhouse or conservatory is better than no greenhouse, one that is equipped to keep the minimum night temperature at 7–10°C. (45–50°F.) is infinitely more valuable. A cold house may be used to push bulbs and other hardy flowers to bloom a little earlier than they would outdoors. But a heated house permits a vast variety of plants to be grown. The heat may be provided by paraffin, kerosene or gas or bottle-gas heaters, by electric heaters, or as an extension of a central heating system.

Apart from enhancing the pleasure of gardening, a greenhouse can effect savings if you usually buy pot plants, cut flowers or bedding plants.

A greenhouse should be sited to obtain most of the available sunlight and is best if its long side faces south, south west or west.

❧ Useful Equipment ❧

If there are beds and borders to be dug over, a spade and a fork are necessary. For small areas a small spade or fork is all that is required.

A rake, a long handled hoe, a short handled or onion hoe, a trowel, and a small hand fork are also necessary. Secateurs or pruning shears will be required for pruning and cutting down woody or herbaceous plants.

Also very handy are a trug, plastic bucket or basket for gathering rubbish and some kind of incinerator for burning woody garden rubbish if outdoor burning is permitted in your area. Soft rubbish – leaves and stems of plants that are finished should be rotted down in a compost heap.

String and plastic covered wire which can be cut into short lengths for tying plants to stakes are essential; so is a small sprayer for applying insecticidal and fungicidal sprays. A watering can fitted with a fine rose is also a necessity, and if there is any paving to be kept clear of weeds, an old table fork bent over at right angles is useful.

❧ Pests and Diseases ❧

Let us dispose of diseases first because these are not so serious in most towns as in country districts. This is because the impurities in the atmosphere help to prevent the spread of diseases. However, these are the most common:

Black spot Affects roses, showing as black or purple spots; afterwards leaves yellow and fall prematurely. Spray with captan or maneb every two weeks after pruning. Burn or otherwise remove and destroy all prunings and fallen leaves and petals.

Mildew White powdery patches, affects roses, tomatoes, chrysanthemums and many other garden plants. Spray with a fungicide recommended for use on the affected plants immediately the disease is noticed. Another year apply preventive sprays *before* disease appears.

Peach leaf curl May affect almonds, apricots and peaches and nectarines. Leaves become swollen, puckered, red and distorted. Spray with lime sulphur or Bordeaux mixture in January or February, again a fortnight later. Spray also at leaf fall in the autumn.

Rust Many plants are affected by rust diseases, brown or black spots on the foliage. Roses, hollyhocks and many other flowers, and some vegetables are affected. Rusts are not easy to control. Burn all diseased foliage at the end of the season. Spray with a copper fungicide as soon as the disease is noticed, and repeat every 14 days.

Tomato blight This disease is similar to the blight that affects potatoes, and may affect outdoor tomatoes. Spray with a copper fungicide in early July, and repeat twice at 14-day intervals.

Apart from birds, cats and dogs which have been mentioned on p. 57, the following are the pests most commonly found in city gardens:

Aphis This group consists of green and black fly. Greenfly are found on roses, lilies, chrysanthemums and many other plants. Black fly are common on beans and dahlias. Spray with a suitable insecticide as soon as pests appear. Check plants once or twice a week, especially the underside of the leaves.

Caterpillars Many caterpillars – the larvae of butterflies and moths – attack ornamental plants, fruits and vegetables. Inspect plants once or twice a week, and spray with derris or any recommended insecticide immediately the pests are noticed, repeating the spray as advised by the manufacturers.

Earwigs These pests damage the blooms of dahlias, chrysanthemums, clematis and other plants. Keep the gound clear of fallen leaves and other rubbish under which they may hide, and dust on and around the plants with BHC or trichlorphon.

Leaf miners These caterpillars tunnel into the leaves of chrysanthemums and cause white 'mines' in the leaves. They seldom cause much damage, but in severe infestations spray with BHC or other recommended insecticide.

Slugs and snails Every garden suffers from these pests which can do untold damage to your seedlings and tender young shoots of delphiniums and other perennials. Keep the ground clear of fallen leaves and weeds under which slugs and snails can hide in the day time. Immediately their slimy trails are noticed put down metaldehyde slug bait, or water the ground and plants with liquid slug killer. Remove and destroy dead or moribund slugs each morning. Some may only be drugged and may recover.

Index

Acknowledgments

The author is grateful to Mr. John Negus for his assistance with the A-Z plant descriptions.
The publishers are grateful to the following people for their permission to reproduce the photographs in this book.
A-Z Botanical Collections Ltd: 26–27, 77, 90 Elli Beintema: 66–67 British Tourist Authority: 38 below Camera Press: 10, 22–23, 70 W. F. Davidson: 66 inset, 87 House Beautiful: 42–43 G. E. Hyde: 30, 43 right, 47, 63, 79, 82, 83, 86 above, 86 below W. McLaughlin: 62 below Picturepoint Ltd: 38 above, 39 H. Smith: 58, 59, 75 Spectrum Colour Library: 11, 31, 62 above Violet Stevenson: 14–15, 51 above, 71 Syndication International Ltd: 18–19 Linda Yang (The Terrace Gardener's Handbook): 50, 51 below
Illustrations by:
Barrington Barber: 16–17, 36–37, 44–45, 68–69; Andrew Farmer: 20, 21, 24, 25, 92–93; Vana Haggerty: 1, 29, 32, 33, 34, 48–49, 53, 76, 77, 80, 81, 84, 85, 88, 89; Rodney Shackell: 4–5, 8, 9, 28, 40–41, 74.

SO-BZN-827

TEACH BEYOND YOUR REACH

SECOND EDITION

An Instructor's Guide to Developing and Running
Successful DISTANCE LEARNING Classes,
Workshops, Training Sessions, and More

Robin Neidorf

Information Today, Inc.
Medford, New Jersey

First Printing, 2012

Teach Beyond Your Reach: An Instructor's Guide to Developing and Running Successful Distance Learning Classes, Workshops, Training Sessions, and More, **Second Edition**

Library of Congress Cataloging-in-Publication Data

Neidorf, Robin.
  Teach beyond your reach : an instructor's guide to developing and running successful distance learning classes, workshops, training sessions, and more / By Robin Neidorf. -- Second edition.
       pages cm
  Includes index.
  ISBN 978-1-937290-01-6 (pbk.)
  1. Distance education. 2. Teacher-student relationships. I. Title.
  LC5800.N45 2012
  371.35--dc23

2012030851

Printed and bound in the United States of America

President and CEO: Thomas H. Hogan, Sr.
Editor-in-Chief and Publisher: John B. Bryans
VP Graphics and Production: M. Heide Dengler
Managing Editor: Amy M. Reeve
Editorial Assistant: Brandi Scardilli
Cover Designer: Lisa Conroy
Copyeditor: Barbara Brynko
Proofreader: Beverly Michaels
Indexer: Beth Palmer

www.infotoday.com

Contents

Chapter 6: Individual Learners 141

Chapter 7: Creating a Community of Learners 163

Acknowledgments

The usual cast of thousands has contributed to the ideas in this book. I'm grateful to many individuals and organizations for their trust in me and their willingness to co-create learning experiences with me.

The following people generously gave their time and shared their expertise by granting interviews, sharing resources, pointing me in the right direction, and providing assistance and support of many kinds: Michael Allen, Scott Brown, Monique Cuvelier, Kim Dority, Beth Edwards, Christine Hamilton-Pennell, William Hann, Rabbi Hayim Herring, Stephanie Hoffman, Jan Knight, William Males, Jan Zanetis, my terrific colleagues at FreePint, and my writing ebuddies in the Bennington Collective.

The following organizations and people have helped me become a better instructor, writer, thinker, and *mensch* by giving me opportunities to test ideas and stumble, as well as succeed: The Bennington Writing Seminars, Compleat Scholar at the University of Minnesota, JSkyway, FreePint, STAR (Synagogues: Transformation and Renewal), the University of Phoenix, the University of Gävle, and my writing instructors and mentors, particularly Sven Birkerts, Susan Cheever, and Morgan Grayce Willow.

I could not have completed this book—or really much of anything in my life—without the support of my husband, Andrew Sullivan, and our daughter, Talia Sullivan Neidorf.

To the countless students who have allowed me to work with them, changing their thinking and sometimes their lives—my gratitude.

To my colleagues in the field of instruction—my best wishes.

About the Website

Distance learning is a rapidly changing field, like any other environment deeply involved with and affected by technology.

You can find case studies of organizations adding distance learning components to their strategy, commentary on and links to distance learning resources, downloadable versions of the worksheets in this book, and announcements of "train the trainer" opportunities at the website associated with this book.

The site is part of FreePint, a publisher dedicated to supporting the value of information in the enterprise. Excellence in learning principles, using all the tools at our disposal and those still being developed, is critical to creating agile organizations.

Visit web.freepint.com/go/research/learning
Or start at www.freepint.com and click on "Learning"

Disclaimer

Neither the publisher nor the author make any claim as to the results that may be obtained through the use of this webpage or of any of the internet resources it references or links to. Neither publisher nor author will be held liable for any results, or lack thereof, obtained by the use of this page or any of its links; for any third-party charges; or for any hardware, software, or other problems that may occur as the result of using it. This webpage is subject to change or discontinuation without notice at the discretion of the publisher and author.

Those Who Can, Teach

Becoming a Teacher

My first teaching opportunity came when I was still in high school. I served as a math tutor, working with junior high students struggling with algebra. In a one-on-one setting, often lounging with my students on their bedroom floors, I explained polynomial functions and abstract numbers. I also answered questions about life beyond eighth grade graduation. From the lofty distance of 3 years, I could reflect on how I had risen to the challenge of high school. My willingness to talk and to respond to their questions helped several of them express and then ease their fears about moving into the next stage of their education.

From my first experience in that intimate setting, I've expanded my teaching to classrooms both virtual and traditional. I've taught several hundred students of varying skills and interests, covering topics including research skills, communication and marketing, professional leadership, college composition, business strategy, nonprofit branding, creative writing, and more.

I never see most of my students and only rarely speak to any of them on the phone. We communicate primarily through web conferencing, voice-over-internet protocol (VoIP) systems, asynchronous discussion, email, and social media; they send assignments via web depository or email, and I respond digitally with detailed feedback. Yet I find that in many ways the relationships we have are not altogether different from those I had as a math tutor. I am doing much more than serving as a conduit to the mastery of a specific subject or skill. Rather, I am changing the way they think about themselves and interact with their entire world. I am helping them build confidence, be willing to take risks, and believe in themselves and their ability to perform in a quickly changing world.

When I am teaching, whether face to face or on the other side of the world, I am engaged in one of the most rewarding, challenging, and connected roles I take on in my busy life.

1

Why Write This Book?

I first came to distance learning with some skepticism. Despite the fact that I had earned my own master's degree in creative writing through a low-residency program (a hybrid form of distance education involving brief on-campus periods followed by 6-month stretches of work through the mail with a mentor), I wasn't convinced that distance methods could adequately serve the needs of a dynamic classroom. From my comic book reading days, I remembered the "Draw me!" ads, offering to train me to be an artist although I could barely draw a 3D cube with any degree of accuracy. Was it really possible to deliver high-quality learning experiences if I couldn't see and immediately respond to my students?

When I first explored the possibilities of distance learning early in 2002, my experience included teaching in a live classroom, as well as years of experience (naturally) on the other side of the gradebook. I was comfortable with traditional classrooms, and so I took them as the norm against which distance learning would have to be measured. In front of a class, I knew (more or less) what to expect and how to prepare. I knew how to read expressions, think on my feet, adapt, take a little more time with a challenging topic, or allow an unexpectedly profound discussion to run long. How could an online classroom ever compare?

What a different world we live in, only one short decade later! Since then, I've taught countless courses through a variety of distance learning formats, as well as organized and run many informal learning opportunities via web conference, discussion board, and one-on-one mentoring through the likes of Skype and Google Chat. I've learned how to adapt both what I teach and how I teach so that I maximize the features and benefits of different learning environments. I've learned more about learning styles, as well as my own strengths and weaknesses as an instructor. Most importantly, I've become more conscious of what I need to do and prepare to deliver an engaging, educational course—a development that has had a deep and positive impact on all my teaching, no matter the venue.

What's more, this reorientation is hardly limited to my instructor relationships: My entire professional life has migrated into a distance format, and even a good number of my personal relationships are deeply enriched by digital, distance interactions. At the turn of the 21st century, the online world was still specialized and largely populated by early adopters. Today, it's a fundamental part of how many of us conduct our lives.

My Experiences With Distance Learning

In 1996, I graduated with a master's degree in creative writing with the inaugural class of the Bennington Writing Seminars (BWS) at Bennington College in Vermont. BWS is based on a low-residency format: four semesters of one-on-one work through the mail with writing mentors, interspersed with "residencies" in January and June, when we participated in workshops, lectures, and graduation for the outgoing class. At the time, there were half a dozen low-residency master's programs in writing in the country; today there are more than 30, with new ones being established each year.

After graduation, I began teaching occasionally in traditional classrooms, primarily through the adult enrichment program at the University of Minnesota in Minneapolis. Around the same time, I started my research and communications business, which enabled me to start developing and conducting customized trainings for clients in business research, public relations basics, audience-focused communication, and more. When I couldn't travel to a client site, we would naturally move to a teleconference format. I started to become more interested in finding other ways to reach geographically remote audiences.

In 1999, I joined an online writer's group for BWS alumni. Although I've never met the majority of the writers in the group, our exchanges on both writing and the woes of the artistic struggle have allowed us to develop very close relationships. One of my dear colleagues in this group is William Males, a lecturer at the University of Gävle in Sweden, where he lives. Before we had ever met face to face, William invited me to become a co-teacher in his Creative Writing in English course, which was taught online under the auspices of his university.

In late 2001 and early 2002, my business (and many others) was in a slow mode. Seeking additional income sources, I responded to an online faculty recruitment advertisement from the University of Phoenix Online. I was accepted into the intensive 1-month training program, and I successfully taught my first class—Essentials of College Writing—at the University of Phoenix in August 2002.

By mid-2003, I was eagerly looking for more ways to incorporate distance learning principles into my consulting practice. I found the perfect opportunity in my relationship with a national nonprofit, Synagogues: Transformation and Renewal (STAR), which provides training, education, and capacity building for synagogues and their leaders through its programs. As STAR's communications consultant, I was charged with the exciting and challenging task of creating and consulting on distance learning opportunities for rabbis, synagogue professionals, and volunteers in a variety of key areas including synagogue marketing, which I taught as well as developed.

In 2006, I accepted a full-time job with my current employer, FreePint Ltd. (www.freepint.com), a U.K.-based publisher of resources that support information professionals—researchers, analysts, corporate librarians, and other professionals with information at the heart of their work. We work closely with many trade associations, such as the Special Libraries Association (SLA; www.sla.org) and the Software and Information Industry Association (SIIA; www.siia.net). A big part of FreePint's mandate is to deliver meaningful professional development opportunities to our audience, even in an economic environment in which budgets have been cut and conference attendance is declining. The creation of FreePint webinars as a distance learning opportunity that meets the needs of today's busy and practical-minded professionals is only one way we serve the learning needs of our many audiences.

Teaching through distance learning is just as rewarding as teaching in a traditional classroom setting, and often more so. I teach through distance learning in part because flexible formats enable me to work with students I wouldn't otherwise be able to reach and to add classes to an already busy schedule. The students I encounter through distance learning have diverse backgrounds, abilities, and needs, bringing a new richness to my own experiences as an instructor.

Still, these benefits weren't achieved simply through migrating to a distance learning platform. Making distance learning such a positive experience for myself and my students has taken focus, attention, training, and a willingness to experiment. It also requires an attitude of continuous improvement: Distance communication and instruction are changing too rapidly in response to technology and culture for anyone to get complacent. Taking advantage of distance learning always makes me take a critical look at every element of my formal and informal teaching and think differently about exactly what I'm offering to students.

When I was first invited to teach a seminar in a traditional classroom setting, I had only one decision to make: What was I going to present, based on the requested topic and the knowledge level of the students? Now that I'm developing distance learning offerings, I have a whole host of additional decisions to make, including which platform to use, how to format materials, which ways to integrate technology to enhance the learning experience, and how to manage and guide a student's "classroom" experience.

The biggest surprise for me in the shift from classroom to distance learning has been the relationships I have with my distance students. From the moment I conceive an idea for a possible distance learning program, the students are present. As I craft objectives, activities, lesson plans, the arc of a learning experience, the integration of technology, and even the content of assignments, I am in a silent dialogue with the students who live in my head—asking questions, pointing out inconsistencies in the classroom experience, and giving me a deer-in-the-headlights stare because I've failed to provide the requisite background information to complete an assignment.

In distance learning, ironically, the students are *always* present.

I love that connection with students and the potential for creating meaningful change (in them) and exchange (between us). So many talented instructors and potential instructors dismiss the idea of distance learning because the traditional classroom is their norm, as it was for me before I started teaching at a distance. They may assume, as I did, that it's too difficult or even impossible to craft those connections without being in a face-to-face environment. My hope is that this book helps you expand your ideas about the creative possibilities in distance learning and gives you the practical knowledge you need to make it happen at the same time.

But What Exactly *Is* Distance Learning?

Does distance learning mean web-based education? Correspondence courses? Self-paced activities? Virtual teams? Webinars? Satellite courses? Interactive video? Here's a short, easy answer: any and all of the above. Distance learning is more visible today than ever before because of the way the internet is now embedded in corporate, academic, and consumer life. But it has existed longer than the web, and if, as some doom-and-gloomers predict, the web collapses one day under the monstrous weight of its unsupportable growth, distance learning will continue to be a viable option for education of all kinds.

It's true that web-based education dominates the current development in the field, given its many advantages for instructors, developers, and students. But even within the category of "web-based classrooms," we can find a lot of variation in learning platforms and instructional approaches. A webinar usually refers to a real-time web-based presentation, with or without viewer interaction. Web-based classrooms can be synchronous (e.g., real-time chat rooms) or asynchronous (e.g., threaded discussions in a dedicated space or forum). Instructional models can even be built around downloadable ebooks with interaction provided through email.

In other words, you have options. By uncoupling instruction from the traditional classroom restrictions of time and place, you have an opportunity to focus on the following questions:

- What information and knowledge do you want to share with students?

- What outcomes do you want your students to achieve (e.g., what should they be able to say, think, or do as a result of the learning experience)?

- What is the best combination of instructor resources, student resources, materials, technology, and expense to achieve a successful outcome?

This book will help you answer these questions and develop the materials, resources, tools, and processes you need to act on your answers. It is intended to be platform-agnostic. No matter which tools you choose (or are chosen for you), the guidance provided will help you plan and deliver instruction, and reflect on how to become a more effective instructor.

Who Should Read This Book?

This book is written by an instructor for instructors. It is intended primarily for those who are interested in enhancing their teaching skills, broadening their student pool, challenging their own assumptions about what goes into a functional classroom, and those who are just plain intrigued by the possibilities of distance learning but want a guided approach to make it work for them.

The pressure on institutions and instructors to find ways to develop and deliver effective distance learning is intensifying. Universities now regularly ask instructors to incorporate nonclassroom and online components into all courses, and the number of distance-delivered degree programs in all areas of study has exploded. Consultants, trainers, and topic experts are exploring distance learning as a way to expand their reach (and potential revenue sources) while minimizing airport time. Associations facing increasing competition for their members' time, dues, and loyalty are turning to distance learning as a way to add value to their memberships; they can offer training, professional development, and networking opportunities that members can access at their convenience without the expense and hassle of attending an on-site meeting or conference. Corporate training departments are pushing the boundaries between knowledge management and on-the-job learning with online knowledge repositories that can deliver in-the-moment training. And all of these institutions need instructors who are creative, confident in their choices of distance learning tools, and ready to meet the needs of a wide range of students.

How This Book Is Organized

This book is not designed to be a "soup-to-nuts" compendium of steps in implementing a distance learning program. You will not learn how to develop webpages, install or troubleshoot software, provide student support services, or fulfill other critical needs in developing and delivering an effective distance learning program. There are many other books and resources you can turn to for that kind of assistance (although in my opinion, you have enough to do to teach without needing to learn to create a webpage, too). Resources can be found on the book's companion website at web.freepint.com/go/research/learning. But only go as deeply as you feel compelled to in these other areas. Learn enough to be a good partner to others who have the same passion for software or support services that you have for instruction.

One of the underlying themes of *Teach Beyond Your Reach* is that distance learning is best created in collaboration with others. I do not believe it is even possible to excel at performing all of the roles that go into a successful distance learning program. So, know that this book focuses strictly on the requirements for instruction and points out where you need to partner with others to create the best possible educational environment for you and your students.

Content Overview: It's All About Interaction

The core of learning is interaction.

In traditional classrooms, interaction takes place primarily in a face-to-face setting—a classroom usually, or perhaps team meetings or instructor conferences. It's what most of us are used to and expect at some unconscious level.

In distance learning, interaction is still the beating heart of the educational experience. The interaction, however, occurs at a temporal and spatial disconnect. Learners, instructor, content, and social community are no longer contained within the same four walls at the same time. Yet learning occurs. The job of the instructor is to create the right conditions for interaction with the instructor, content, and learning peers, regardless of the distance between the elements.

Ultimately, the instructor does not create learning (whew!); the instructor can only create the environment, distance or not, in which learning can be *co-created* through the *interaction of content, peers, and instructor* (see Figure 9.1 on page 192).

The tools of distance learning are the media through which these interactions are enabled. Chapter 1 discusses the current tools available for distance learning and suggests how they may be used, individually and in concert with one another.

Best practices in instruction put the focus on the learner rather than the content. Chapter 2 describes what the distance population looks like and how it behaves. Focusing on adult students, this chapter lays out different learning styles, generational differences, and attitudes toward education that can make a difference in how students enter your class, work with you and the material, and communicate their educational goals.

Chapters 3 and 4 focus on creating content for distance learning that encourages interaction while achieving learning objectives. Chapter 3 guides you through the questions and processes to help you create the overall course design, while Chapter 4 offers detailed information on the actual craft and implementation of course content elements, such as lectures, presentations, assignments, and so on.

The role of the instructor in a distance learning environment can be neither "sage on the stage" nor "guide on the side." Depending on the degree of comfort your students have with distance learning, your own pedagogical style, the tools you have on hand, and the objectives of the course, you may find yourself taking on any combination of many different roles: mentor, coach, instructor, facilitator, referee, trainer, and even a shoulder to cry on.

Within a traditional classroom, expectations for the role of an instructor are fairly clear, particularly if all participants have been raised in similar cultures. Everyone agrees on what the words *instructor, student, classroom, performance,* and *you are on the verge of failing* mean. Move into a distance learning environment, though, and expectations become much more amorphous. Often, instructors who are new to distance learning are surprised to find that their interactions with learners are quite a bit more intense and intimate than they might be in a traditional classroom, leading to close and rewarding relationships of mutual development. Though that can be an exhilarating experience for an instructor, this degree of intimacy with students can require skill development in areas not previously considered to be part of your pedagogy—for instance, in motivational skills or boundary setting.

On the other hand, instructors are also surprised at how much effort they have to put in to hear a peep out of some of their students. The primacy of interaction in a successful distance learning environment requires that instructors prepare students to interact. This is harder than it sounds. Years of conditioning through everything from lecture-hall classes to television viewing have not prepared students for active engagement with instructors, materials, or each other. Motivation and creative use of interactive tools will be essential to making students succeed. Satisfied distance learning students are those who have had appropriate expectations raised, are trained in how to get the most out of the experience, and are encouraged, coached, prodded, and urged to be as active as possible in their own educations.

Chapter 5 provides insight and ideas for managing the distance learning "classroom" and helping your students interact effectively with you to maximize their learning. In this chapter, you will find tips and wisdom from the field on what to expect and how to foster the kinds of interaction that make great learning possible. Chapter 6 provides guidance on getting to know your students as individual learners, working with their strengths and weaknesses, and motivating them to their peak performance through mentoring and feedback.

We humans are social creatures. The importance of collaborative work in creating an effective distance learning environment has been documented in many studies. If you foster positive group interaction, your students will reap the benefits, even if they sometimes grumble about the additional challenges that participating in a community may create.

Fostering positive group interaction is also harder than it may seem at first glance. The mandate to create community seems nonsensical when you consider the logistical challenges of learners at a physical distance from one another, with limited means to get to know each other on a personal level. Distance programs tend to attract a diverse range of students, which makes it even more challenging to establish common ground for group bonding. More subtly, the dominant culture of education is one of competition rather than collaboration; distance learning instructors have to shift student expectations from eyeing one another suspiciously to treating every classmate as a valued part of the process.

Of all the kinds of interactions distance instruction presented to me, building a community of learners was one of the hardest to handle. At first, I didn't see the value of collaborative work, in part because, in my experience as a learner, interaction with peers has never been my preference. Throughout my schooling, I dreaded participating in group projects and invariably wanted to go to my corner and work on my own. But I've found that the work I put into helping the students develop teams and mutually supportive relationships brings rich rewards to everyone. Distance learning classrooms are usually diverse in terms of learner experience, background, skills, and perspective. The work we do together, as a collaborative community, adds to everyone's education, including the instructor's.

Of course, chemistry is always a bit uncertain, but an instructor can do plenty to improve the odds of creating a bit of interpersonal magic. Chapter 7 introduces the key ideas in creating effective learning communities at a distance.

While much of this book addresses the needs of formal instruction, many of our educational experiences during our lifetimes are relatively informal. There are many opportunities for ad hoc, informal, and gentle instruction—workshops, peer-to-peer learning sessions, communities of practice, brown-bag lunches, and even book groups and affinity groups.

Informal learning moves easily from in-person to distance environments, and many organizations take advantage of the ease with which people now reach out and connect online by turning those connections into learning. Chapter 8 explores some of the opportunities you may have as an instructor in informal settings and how to adapt the principles of this book to make the most of them.

Distance learning is fundamentally a collaborative enterprise. You can be an outstanding instructor, but without assistance and support from knowledgeable partners, it's difficult to offer high-quality distance education. One of the goals of this book is to help decision makers (e.g., administrators, deans, directors of training, knowledge managers, and executive directors) and supporting experts (e.g., web designers, technical support folks, instructional designers, and even marketing staff) understand what you, the instructor, are trying to create and how they can contribute to the process.

To create a successful team, it is important to first create a shared understanding of the place, purpose, and objectives of a distance learning program. Chapter 9 is designed to serve as a stand-alone "state-of-the-environment" review of the challenges, potential, and collaborative roles involved in distance learning. For individual instructors, this chapter integrates the details of the book into the broader context of the practical world of business education, personal enrichment, and academia. You will also find this chapter to be helpful preliminary reading for the entire team involved in distance learning—including students. Use the worksheet discussion guide following Chapter 9 to establish shared understanding of your particular situation within the cultural, social, academic, professional, and technical context of distance learning.

Those Who Can, Teach ... Beyond Their Reach

Not every expert can teach. We've all been in classes and lectures where the talking head clearly knew her stuff but just as clearly didn't have a clue about how to communicate—let alone teach—competency in said stuff. Teaching is a skill that is too often overlooked or underestimated.

Connection, communication, motivation, and response: These are all required for effective instruction, above and beyond knowledge of the specific subject to be taught. In fact, I've found that, when necessary, I can wing it in the area of subject knowledge more easily than I can fake the core skills needed to connect, communicate, and motivate students to succeed.

Because distance instruction takes us out of a comfortable environment and throws us into an unfamiliar one, it gives us the opportunity to challenge every expectation we may have about how, to whom, and the reasons why we teach. The concepts and processes covered in this book will help you create and deliver effective distance learning programs. They are also likely to make you a more effective instructor in traditional environments. If most of your own education has been in competitive environments that focus on finding errors, teaching to the test, and mastering skills rather than building knowledge, you will discover a new model in these pages. Learner-centric teaching, on which successful distance learning programs are based, puts the learner's needs, skills, and strengths at the heart of the classroom experience. It recognizes the learner's need to receive positive reinforcement even while accepting correction. At its best, it creates a safe place for people to try out new ideas and new skills, make unique human connections, and discover their own potential.

So I encourage you to explore the possibilities of distance education to teach management strategy, technical topics, poetry craft, higher math, computer programming, graphic design, parenting skills, foreign language, web development, literature, music history—even how to create and deliver effective distance learning courses.

Whatever your expertise, and whatever your passion for instruction and connecting with students, open your arms and your creative sense of what's possible. Find the distance venues and methods that work for you, and teach beyond your reach.

New Tools of the Trade

"Each medium, independent of the content it mediates, has its own intrinsic effects which are its unique message."
—Marshall McLuhan,
Understanding Media: The Extensions of Man

In 1964, Marshall McLuhan first articulated what has become a mantra of the Information Age: "The medium is the message." The tools that support the interactions of your distance learning program are more than a collection of functions and features; they create more complex challenges than access or costs. Your choice of tools and how you use them will impact which students come to you, how successful they are, and the subtle messages you project about the value, purpose, and goals of your program.

The role of media in how information is received, absorbed, and processed should not be underestimated. Consider a somewhat extreme example:

Scenario 1: Employee enters the human resources (HR) director's office for a private meeting. The HR director says, "Jane, you've been doing an outstanding job. As you know, though, we're moving toward a complete restructuring of your department, and your particular job is going to be eliminated. I'd like to talk with you about the options, both for accepting severance and utilizing our job search services."

Scenario 2: Employee receives an email from the HR director, which states:

Subject line: We need to meet
Jane, you've been doing an outstanding job. As you know, though, we're moving toward a complete restructuring of your department, and your particular job is going to be eliminated. I'd like to talk with

you about the options, both for accepting severance and utilizing
our job search services.

Sam Smith
Director of Human Resources
Widget Co.: Excellence is our Passion!

It's a bad day in either case, but put yourself in Jane's position: Which
communication makes you more willing to work with the person presenting the information? The same words are used, but the impact is quite different if they're said by a person rather than having the employee read the
news on a screen. The medium is an inextricable component of what is
communicated.

A distance learning instructor needs to have an understanding of the
following factors:

- Tools potentially available

- Impact the tools of choice may have on the delivery of a course
  and on student and instructor satisfaction

- Availability

- Budget

- Applicability of available tools to the needs of a particular
  project

This chapter will discuss the characteristics of the various tools that
a distance instructor may decide to use, including pros, cons, and uses
of each.

However, an essential consideration for any communication tool is the
ease of use for the recipient of the message. Therefore, a fundamental
question is always, "What are the expectations, skills, and norms of my
students?" New methods of communication are constantly introduced
into our networked world, and different audiences adopt these tools at
different rates. When I was researching the first edition of *Teach Beyond
Your Reach* in 2005, I would not have incorporated instant messaging into
a learning toolkit aimed at mid-career professional adults because I
wouldn't have been sure about their comfort level with the tool. However,
by 2012, I don't hesitate: I believe that this audience is now more comfortable with such tools for effective communication.

This variability creates exciting times for instructors, with opportunities to grow and learn new skills. If you embrace that change, it will help your teaching and interactions become that much more creative.

Who Chooses Your Tools?

You may have no control over the tools you are able to use. You may be hired to teach a course and then handed a particular platform or set of tools for delivering the instruction. Or you may be in a situation of creating a learning environment entirely on your own without a budget or any technical support. Any teaching scenario will involve some requirements that are more or less out of your control.

Regardless of the degree of control you have over the tools, however, understanding all the variables involved and the pros and cons of each tool will enable you to make effective instructional choices to achieve your goals with your students.

But at the outset, it's important to keep a basic set of assumptions in mind about the technology, orientation, and comfort of both you and your students:

- *Connected online:* Business, social lives, and education have all irrevocably moved online. Using email or text messaging is as commonplace as using the phone for voice calls (or more so). You and your students have at least one internet-connected communication device (PC, laptop, smartphone, or tablet computer) for personal use.

- *Access level:* At least some of the web is accessible to you and your students, although you may have to address firewall issues and/or content that requires authentication to access (with IDs and passwords, or other form of validation). An additional assumption is that you and your students have high-speed access to these resources.

- *Comfort:* You and your students undergo some degree of online interaction—with colleagues, peers, or friends—through personal choice and because it is an increasingly comfortable medium.

- *Customization:* You and your students increasingly expect to have the option of customizing an online experience to your preferences, such as delivery methods (e.g., access via a website or having summaries emailed), priority topics, or the ability to share online material with selected contacts.

This is a fundamentally different set of assumptions than I used in the first edition of *Teach Beyond Your Reach* (published in 2006) or what I would have presented 2 years ago. The combination of technology advances, deeper penetration and adoption of online tools, and a generation entering the workforce that has been raised in an always-connected world has created this new—and exciting—environment in which we all interact.

Common Distance Learning Platforms

As more organizations are incorporating distance learning into their outreach, training, and support, more adults have become familiar with the most common platforms now being used. In a corporate environment, for example, it's common to have training or education delivered via web conference platforms such as WebEx (www.webex.com) or GoToMeeting (www.gotomeeting.com). In an educational setting, common platforms include complete course management or learning management systems such as Blackboard (www.blackboard.com) or Moodle (www.moodle.com; see Figure 1.1).

These certainly are not the only packages out there, but they are the most commonly used, and it is likely that you—and your students—have encountered them at some point or will soon.

If you don't have access to these options, don't worry: Many of the functions are available on their own through other providers. Following this brief overview of the full-featured platforms, we'll take a closer look at each of the key functions, how you can use them to their best advantage, and where you can find them for your courses.

Web-Based Meeting Package

A web-based meeting package usually includes screen sharing, integrated voice conferencing, integrated recording capabilities, participant polling,

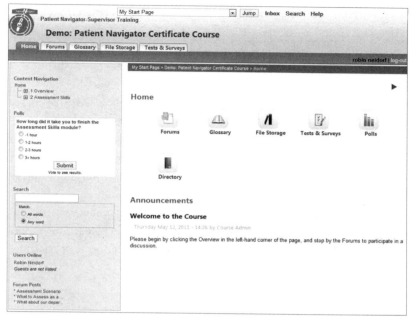

Figure 1.1   The Patient Navigator Online Certificate Program was built and hosted by Talance, Inc. on the Moodle platform.

questions, and text chat functions. Some packages also include additional collaborative capabilities, such as a shared whiteboard. They support multiple presenters, and presenters can pass the control of the environment to each other. Most packages also include the ability to manage registrations and to automatically email reminders prior to an event and follow-up materials after an event, as well as post-event reporting on participation levels and interactions during the session (e.g., questions asked, attentiveness to the screen during live sessions.

Online Education Platform

An online education platform typically includes asynchronous discussion, private journals, electronic attendance and presentation, gradebooks, group functions that enable and enhance teamwork among dispersed students, file sharing, live event capability, whiteboards, lecture postings, links to other resources and readings, and library or online resource connections. Courses often offer in-class email systems and/or a "digest" feature that allows instructors to collect responses to given discussion topics and distribute them automatically via email to class participants, turning a "pull" communication (one that a user has to go out and get) into a "push" communication (one that a user receives directly). Some vendors also make course content available in the form of a course library that instructors or organizations can access and implement "off the shelf" or with some customizations.

And, of course, proprietary web-based classrooms have the benefits offered by any web-based solution: access to other web-based resources with the click of a mouse.

If you are teaching under the aegis of a university, association, corporation, or other entity that offers a significant portfolio of learning opportunities, you will probably use one or both of these platforms or packages to deliver instruction.

Effective Educational Components

Although distance learning platforms and web-based meeting packages have a full suite of tools embedded in them, you may decide that you want to use some elements but not others, and it's always helpful to have a clear idea of when and how each component in the platform will be most useful to you and your students.

Furthermore, you may want to adapt some materials to move from a complete distance learning platform to other environments—for example, to take course materials from one institution or program to another—and laying out your tools and options will help you make that leap.

As virtual teamwork, distance collaboration, and distance learning have become more commonly recognized, a number of tools are now on the "most likely to be used" list. You've probably already thought about these or even used them as a professional, instructor, or student at some point. It's helpful to have them laid out in detail to establish a clear understanding of when and how to use each in a thoughtful manner. They are ordered here based roughly on my preferences for their usefulness to the distance instructor.

And don't forget: The medium is the message. The choices you make regarding delivery of instruction are interwoven with the messages of instruction itself.

Asynchronous Discussion

When any participant can access class discussion at any time, from anywhere he or she has a computer connected to the internet, that's called asynchronous discussion (AD). AD is the heart and soul of many distance learning programs. Proprietary web-based course management systems incorporate AD as part of their standard feature sets.

But AD is neither complex nor expensive. In fact, it is an increasingly common form of communication through LinkedIn, Facebook, and other social networks for professional and personal use. As these tools have become commonplace in usage, students of all kinds take to them quite naturally, but they've existed in other guises for a long time.

Professional associations have fostered AD for years through online bulletin boards and listservs, which can incorporate online discussions, as well as email "digests" of recent posts and/or subject lines, to push the conversation out to participants. Other free tools can be found through such providers as Yahoo! Groups. The basic AD format follows the same flow of interaction: A point for discussion is posted as a new message. A participant can reply to all by posting a response to the message. Another participant can reply to the first response. The entire discussion appears as indented entries, one after another, under the main "thread" established by the first posting. The result is anytime, anywhere access to the interactions and activity of the classroom (Figure 1.2).

AD is a critical component of distance learning in its online forms because of the immense benefits it offers students and instructors—benefits that cannot be matched in the face-to-face classroom. While many traditional classrooms rely on discussion to deepen the learning of participants and share information, the potential for thoughtful contribution from diverse groups of students is far greater in online AD because it

- Benefits students who tend to hang back in face-to-face discussions, preferring to think through their responses before jumping in.

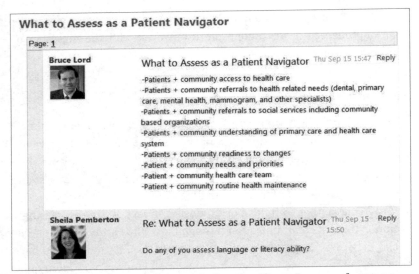

Figure 1.2   The Patient Navigator Online Certificate Program fosters an asynchronous discussion environment.

- Benefits students who tend to learn through reading rather than through listening.

- Offers greater flexibility to students, which contributes to the diversity in the classroom. As an instructor, I find this diversity to be particularly stimulating, bringing my own thinking to places I never expected to go.

- Enables simultaneous discussions on multiple topics, adding to the richness and depth of the dialogue.

- Enables use of linking and bringing nontext content into the discussion.

- Automatically archives all contributions for later review (making it easier to grade on the basis of what actually took place rather than your recollection of what took place) and allows searching and sorting by date, contributor, topic, etc.

If AD represents the excellent potential of online distance learning, it is also the proving ground for many of its weaknesses, including:

- *Lack of immediacy:* Yes, it's a recurring theme in the challenges of distance learning, but I repeat it because it's so often a source of anxiety and dissatisfaction for participants. If you wait 24 hours for a response to a discussion contribution, it can dampen the spark of your intellectual excitement.

- *Poor written communication skills:* Frequent typos, ignorance of grammar rules, flat-footed attempts at humor that turn into gross interpersonal misunderstandings … You'll see it all. And not just with new students.

Despite the challenges of AD, it is an invaluable tool for distance learning. For me and for many distance learning instructors, incorporating AD into a new program isn't a decision; it's a given.

Asynchronous Discussion Quick View

Pros: Widely accepted; if you have any students who have already been involved in distance learning (and even some who haven't), they are likely to have experienced AD. Easy to incorporate into a system with other features or as part of a comprehensive course management system. Appropriate for all levels and all topics of study. Available low-cost options often included with a larger package.

Cons: Some learning curve at first to understand how best to use the tool and how to respond effectively and efficiently. (A busy class can mean a lot of reading and responding. You may find yourself acting as a de facto writing and communication coach, in addition to teaching your actual subject. And if your own typing/writing communication skills need work, there are a number of distance learning courses you can look into to improve your skills …)

Works best for: In-depth discussion among multiple students; group dialogue.

Messages it sends: Convenience and flexibility; words matter and "neatness" counts.

Collaborative Online Workspace

Collaborative online workspaces were a mystery to most people 5 years ago. Today, they are better understood by many adult learners as more and more organizations have introduced them into the workplace. It's easier than ever for teams of people to collaborate online to access documents, spreadsheets, and presentations, and these technological and cultural advances have enabled collaborative online workspaces to adapt to the needs of distance learning.

Within a collaborative online workspace, an instructor can designate core content components, establish team projects, track assignments, and manage deadlines. Participants can chat in real time about documents or projects, or add comments to materials for others to review. Workspaces also maintain a history of changes, so individuals can go back to review who made changes to a document or resource and what those changes were.

Costs for these systems range from free (Google Documents, for example) to more expensive proprietary platforms. Some hosted solutions charge by the seat; others offer licenses for small and mid-sized groups, and there are enterprise editions that handle users in the thousands.

Perhaps the biggest challenge of using a collaborative web space for an instructional program is that the software was not originally designed to solve the particular problems of distance learning. Education-focused solutions such as course management platforms were built from the ground up with the needs and interests of instructors and students in mind; collaborative web space lacks this focus and may need some heavy handling to get it to behave the way you want.

Collaborative Online Workspace Quick View

Pros: Allows many different kinds of interactions and a multiplicity of ways to present and interact with materials. Creates pages and resources "on the fly," in partnership with students.

Cons: Despite broader acceptance, there is still a learning curve involved, particularly for participants who haven't used such a workspace before. Software is not designed with educational applications in mind.

Works best for: Student groups (and instructors) who are comfortable with technology and visually literate.

Messages it sends: Convenient and active classroom; geared toward collaborative learning experiences; students will be an active part of creating the space in which learning will take place.

Video and Multimedia

In the first edition of this book, I counseled against relying too heavily on video or multimedia because of the production costs involved. At the time, an instructor who invested time and resources in video or multimedia needed to be ready to stay with that material for a long time.

But what a difference a few years can make! Video is now incredibly easy to create, manipulate, and make available online. YouTube dedicates an entire section of its site to educational offerings (www.youtube.com/education; Figure 1.3), where you can find everything from university lectures to homemade "how-to" demos.

Video—yes, even *good* video—can be captured with a cell phone or basic digital camera. One of my favorite software publishers is TechSmith (www.techsmith.com), which publishes a variety of tools including Snagit, Camtasia, and Jing, enabling anyone to capture activity as you complete it on a computer screen. Jing is even free and quite simple to use.

High-quality, professional-grade multimedia is still a more expensive and complicated proposition, but you can approximate it better by using the software for recording audio and visual and then adding instructional components such as callouts, highlighted text, and even user-driven actions (e.g., click a button to make the next action happen). Some tools will even create a transcript of your audio.

Video and multimedia have so many potential applications and uses that it would be impossible to list them all here. You can now

- Record segments of an audio or video lecture to post online for students to view and add comments.

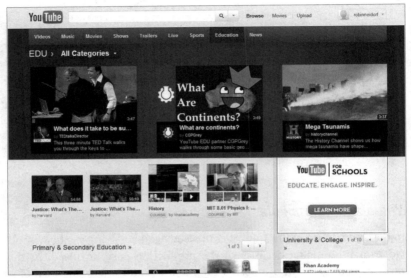

Figure 1.3   In the education section on YouTube, instructors and organizations can create their own channels to share video content.

- Demonstrate tasks, project steps, calculations, and anything that's easier to show rather than to describe.

- Provide alternative formats of instructional materials to meet the needs of different learning styles (more on learning styles in Chapter 2).

- Record live web-based meetings or conference calls to share with others who cannot attend.

And all of this is cost-effective and easier than ever. The once-significant barriers are no longer obstacles.

Video and Multimedia Quick View

Pros: Creates a "see, touch, and do" environment and enables easy capture of material that's better suited or more compelling to convey in a nontext format. Meets the learning needs of students who prefer demonstration instead of text-based learning.

Cons: Depending on the degree of complexity, expensive to create and update (though the costs decrease all the time). Although students can interact with the content itself, they do not interact with an instructor or other students unless other media (e.g., email, links to web-based chat or discussion, opportunity to turn in results, or other form of response mechanism) are incorporated into the program.

Works best for: Instruction that benefits from visual elements, simulation, or demonstration.

Messages it sends: Sophisticated experience.

Synchronous Chat

Synchronous chat is another medium that has gone from unusual to commonplace in a very short time. Voice-over-internet protocol (VoIP) has brought voice communications online, and a variety of platforms have channeled voice, text chat, and file sharing into the environment as well. The best known of these is Skype (www.skype.com), a free tool now owned by Microsoft that enables one-on-one synchronous interaction or group interactions with anyone who has a free account. Synchronous chat is also found integrated into Google (Google Chat and Google Voice), Facebook, and lots of customer service applications.

Synchronous chat was once limited to typing messages into the chat window to share. Skype, Google Chat, and other providers have added reliable video to their chat functions, as well as the ability to share screen views and files. Additionally, chat software keeps records of the chats, making handy references for later viewing.

I often use synchronous chat in my business to discuss project details with partners in Europe and Australia, as well as throughout North America; my students often use synchronous chat to conduct learning team meetings to divide assignments and check in on any problems. I've also used chat to connect with support services, including those associated with distance learning, to troubleshoot and resolve issues that inevitably come up while using complex software and tools.

As with AD, one of my favorite benefits of synchronous chat is the documentation it creates. I can pull up the record of a chat and search it, as I would any document, for words or phrases, and thus return very quickly to the place in the chat where someone shared a key idea or a critical instruction.

Synchronous Chat Quick View

Pros: Many synchronous chat options available at no cost with immediacy and an ability to archive results. Availability of web-based resources during chat for reference and research. Some synchronous chat systems can be accessed with a cell phone or tablet computer, making it an extremely portable tool.

Cons: Learning curve for anyone not used to using it, although the programs get easier all the time and the likelihood that students have used it is always increasing. However, as with any software requiring download or updates, challenges (particularly around incompatibility) can arise. Requires everyone to be online at the same time, with a functional account, access to compatible IM systems, and reliable internet access. Can be hard to follow in-depth discussion among many participants. Participants logging in from business or government locations may not be able to use free chat tools due to security restrictions.

Works best for: Focused team projects; quick one-on-one updates; just-in-time coaching.

Messages it sends: Instant, sometimes at the expense of depth.

Web-Based Conferencing

Web-based conferencing, web-based meetings, and webinars are commonplace tools of training today. WebEx and GoToMeeting are two of the most popular platforms that enable one or more presenters to share screens, video captures, and interactive tools such as surveys or polls with groups of people, all sitting at their own computers anywhere in the world (Figure 1.4).

For instructors, web-based conferencing provides some of the benefits of a live classroom, coupled with features for chat, managing questions, and integrated recording (handy if you want to share the session with others who couldn't attend). However, in practice, instructors should be aware of what corporate trainers and presenters have long known: Those "participating" in a web-based conference may actually be updating their Facebook pages, reading blogs, or checking email. The interactivity you build into the session is essential for maintaining participation.

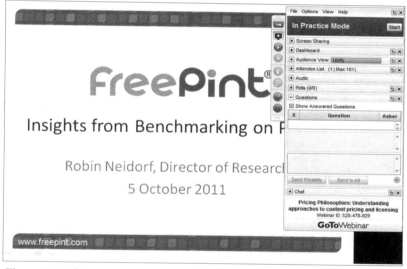

Figure 1.4   This screenshot shows the active presentation plus the webinar management interface for a GoToMeeting instructor. Through the interface, the instructor can see what participants see, monitor attentiveness, review submitted questions, ask and answer questions with the whole group or privately, administer polls, and record the session. [Used with permission from "Pricing Philosophies: Understanding Approaches to Content Pricing and Licensing," created by FreePint Webinars (www.freepint.com)]

Because there are many moving parts to a web-based conference (potentially including video, web access, presentation slides, Q&A, polls, etc.), rehearsal before a session, particularly for new instructors, is a must. In a very complex session, you may want to consider hiring an assistant who can help keep the classroom running, freeing you to teach.

Finally, let's not forget that there are many instructors who could use a bit of coaching on their in-person presentation style. Someone who is merely dull in a live classroom becomes practically coma-inducing in a web-based session.

Web-Based Conferencing Quick View

Pros: Can approximate the visual and audio stimulation of a classroom. Enables far-flung groups to see and hear one another in a synchronous environment. Offers a number of additional features such as chat, questions, polling, and integrated recording to enhance and archive the session.

Cons: Can be complex to run all the pieces; usually requires local software installations, which can be difficult for some students (or impossible, depending on IT requirements). Participants tend to multitask during the session unless it is very well-planned and well-executed.

Works best for: Presentational sessions (though be sure to incorporate interactivity); geographically distributed groups; lectures you want to archive for later viewing.

Messages it sends: High-tech can also be personal; anywhere, anytime instructional experience.

Email Correspondence

Email is such an integrated part of our everyday world today that it's almost hard to remember when using it was novel and unsettling. I remember the first time I emailed an article to an editor rather than faxing it or bringing it to an office. We were both giddy with the thrill and were completely amazed that it worked.

Email is an instructional tool used in just about every educational environment you can think of. However, when considering email as a planned component of a distance learning program, think of it in terms of how it can build relationships among members of a group, as well as between an instructor and an individual student.

It is possible to develop an entire distance learning program based solely on email usage, just as instructors have created distance learning programs based solely on traditional correspondence. The advantage of email over snail mail, in addition to the speed of response, is the relative ease of adding additional people into a dialogue, creating an opportunity for shared communal experiences rather than just one-on-one interactions.

Email Quick View

Pros: Almost universally accessible. Fast response and the ability to create group discussion. An expected component of any professional relationship today. Free, or at least very cheap.

Cons: May encourage "off-the-cuff" responses from both student and instructor. Managing group dialogue can be challenging, especially if responses run long. Many individuals feel overwhelmed with email, especially with spam so rampant, and may tune out email communications.

Works best for: Smaller discussion groups (up to about five) and as an integrated component of other distance media; one-on-one instruction, turning in assignments, informal instruction, or mentoring, etc.

Messages it sends: Quick, easy, and convenient.

Snail-Mail Correspondence

The original distance learning program was the mail correspondence course. It's unlikely to be a model that you choose today, but you shouldn't immediately dismiss the place of physical mail in your bag of tricks.

When I was writing the first edition of this book in 2005, snail mail was still a more commonly used tool than it is today. Real, tangible paper is invaluable for making handwritten notes on an assignment and exchanging materials that do not travel well by digital methods (such as original artwork), and nothing but nothing in the digital world can match "real" mail for posterity. I completed my Master of Fine Arts in creative writing through the Bennington Writing Seminar's low-residency program, organized around monthly packets of writing mailed back and forth between student and writing mentor; though nearly 10 years have passed since I completed that degree, I still have every single letter my instructors sent to me during my tenure in the program. Had I received their comments via digital means, I know I would not have them anymore. The instruction I was not yet ready for 10 years ago is now a valued part of my self-awareness as a developing writer.

Mail continues to have its place and special uses, despite the shift many of us have made to communicating electronically. In fact, I was pleased to learn that as of 2012, the Bennington Writing Seminars still requires the exchange of physical, snail-mail packets between student and mentor as part of the degree program. The rise of electronic communication has actually enhanced the status of "real" mail as the medium to use when posterity matters.

Snail-Mail Quick View

Pros: Universally accessible. An important form of personal touch in a context that can otherwise be impersonal. Relatively cheap for both implementation and usage.

Cons: Snail mail moves like, well, a snail. Not as effective for communication between multiple parties. Long delays in sending, receiving, and responding, which can be an instructional challenge.

Works best for: Mentored relationships that require primarily a one-to-one interaction between a student and instructor; material with an archival component—something that you or your students would want to keep.

Messages it sends: The work is worth taking time over, so don't rush; rather, consider how to create something worth printing, copying, and mailing.

Flexible Combinations: Blended Learning

Any and all of these tools can be part of a distance learning program. In fact, most of them can be part of a nondistance learning program. Many traditional classrooms today incorporate a web component, and even elementary school students may now incorporate online collaboration for group projects or access a remote desktop to submit assignments. As learning and education continue to evolve, the distinctions between teaching techniques are quickly becoming difficult to detect.

For our own work as instructors (and indeed, as students of what it means to be instructors), the keyword is *flexibility*. Evaluate what you want to impart to a group of students, their readiness (and yours) to use different tools, your budget, and your technical resources. Then examine all the potential options to create the right combination of interaction, presentation, teamwork, research, creative thinking, response, and feedback. You may find a combination that feels right and comfortable for many kinds of teaching situations; you also may find that you need to start from scratch with each course you design.

I've presented these tools as if there were bright lines separating one from another. In reality, the boundaries are quite a bit fuzzier. Evolutions and revolutions in telecommunications technology are blurring the borders between teleconference and webinar, between AD and a collaborative web space. My experience with a wide range of students and tools suggests that the readiness factor will dictate the usability of a technology for a given project even more than the functionality of the technology itself.

For example, I once worked regularly with a group of professionals on nonprofit marketing skills and knowledge. This group was very comfortable with a teleconference and very *un*comfortable with a web-based conference. My efforts to push them into moving our teleconferences online met with enormous resistance. Still, I would find ways to incorporate some elements of web-based communication by asking them to at least be online during our calls so that we could look at the same page at the same time. They started to see the possibilities and developed a greater level of readiness to take the next step.

You have to know your student population and how to introduce tools, train them on usage and interaction, and have the appropriate level of support to ease their fears and trouble-shoot the inevitable hiccups that happen at the most inconvenient times. The merging of technologies is exciting and creates enormous possibilities for instruction. But developments in technology often outpace our human ability to adjust. There are two things to keep in mind: "Focus on Function" and the continuum concept. Focus on Function tells us to identify what we want to *do* with a tool or technology and then get advice on the best match for our needs. The continuum concept reminds us that technology moves along a continuum from simple to complex, and human willingness to *use* technology also moves along a continuum from unwilling to enthusiastic. The best pairings of technology with users are the ones where the willingness to use the tools meshes with the complexity of the tools.

Right Tool, Right Place: A Few Sample Approaches

Still having trouble visualizing what your distance instruction toolkit might look like in practice? The following sample combinations of tools and instructional approaches may help you think about how best to use various tools in different situations.

Low-Tech, Low-Cost Professional Writing Workshop

Description: This is a 3-week workshop for a targeted group of professionals seeking to improve their writing skills.

Tools used: Email discussion list, teleconference, collaborative workspace, and private email exchange

Approach: The course begins with a teleconference in which the participants and instructor introduce themselves and discuss their personal goals for the course. The instructor uses the call to lay out the four key content areas they will cover with lectures emailed and posted to a collaborative workspace, email discussion, and peer-to-peer mentoring work. After the call, the instructor emails the first lecture (textual) and assignments, and posts them to the collaborative workspace. The participants conduct discussion via email on the topics in the lecture and can post comments directly to the collaborative workspace. They email their assignments directly to the instructor, who makes detailed notes on the assignments and emails them back. (One student has trouble viewing the comments; the instructor faxes a copy of the marked-up document for her review.)

Throughout the progress of the course, the instructor monitors discussion and directs students toward additional resources for deepened learning. New topics are introduced with emailed lectures and assignments, which are simultaneously posted to the collaborative workspace. The participants also work in pairs to review and edit each other's work, which they exchange via email. A second conference call allows the instructor to pull together the threads of activity and direct participants on a final project. Final projects are emailed to the instructor, as well as to the entire peer group.

Introduction to Marketing for Small and Micro-Businesses

Description: Small-business owners and one-person operations take part in a 6-week workshop on marketing strategy and tactics.

Tools used: Email, private online asynchronous chat with digest features, web-based conference, and synchronous chat

Approach: Following a launch meeting via a web-based conference, the participants interact primarily through a Google Groups AD space. The instructor posts threads to Google Groups for personal introductions, discussion topics, and questions. Lectures in core topics are posted to the group and also emailed to participants to ensure receipt and review. Participants discuss the lecture and assignments within the group; Google Groups automatically creates a daily summary document—a digest—and emails it to all participants.

Participants also email and call the instructor with individual questions on an as-needed basis. They complete a team project by meeting via

Skype every few days; an archive of each Skype session is copied into Google Groups for later reference and review.

The instructor is able to incorporate live links to other websites into the group, assembling an excellent online collection of business references, and participants can add on other resources. One assignment involves sending participants to several of these resources to conduct specific research tasks.

The final projects are presented by teams in a web-based conference. Prior to the teleconference, each team emails a presentation and hand-outs, but during the session itself, the entire group is able to view the same documents at the same time and share feedback via the platform's integrated chat features and through audio connections.

Leadership Development Program: Peer Training on Data Visualization Tools

Description: The research center of a management consultancy licenses content from a number of publishers that all provide powerful tools for data visualization and analytics. These tools enable analysts and consultants to perform complex queries on the company's financial and economic data, but most do not take advantage of these capabilities because they are not familiar with them. As the firm's information strategy is to empower end users to do more of their own analysis, the research department creates a voluntary 4-week "leadership learning" program to encourage analysts and consultants to master these tools.

Tools: Web-based meetings, video archive of examples, exercises based on actual client work shared via collaborative workspace

Approach: A senior researcher in the center takes ownership of the project and first reviews the 4 databases to document the similarities and differences in how their visualization tools are set up. She then creates the agenda for the first meeting, focusing her comments on the similarities and inviting participants to look for these features in the reporting and analysis functions of the tools.

Participants then submit the specs and requirements for actual projects to the collaborative workspace set up for the program. They share with each other, with some pushing from the research center staff, suggestions for approaches on addressing each project, based on the tools at hand.

Over the next 4 weeks, the research center staff record brief (2–4 minutes) screen-capture videos demonstrating how to use the advanced visualization and reporting features of each product. These are posted to the collaborative workspace, where participants can post questions for each video if anything isn't clear. The senior researcher also hosts four more web meetings: Each involves a closer look at the unique elements of each product under consideration—what makes it different from the others—and then walks through a use case based on the client work of one of the participants. All of these web meetings are also recorded and transcribed; both video and text are posted to the collaborative workspace.

To complete the program, each participant submits a final report, demonstrating use of the advanced analysis features of at least one of the products, with a brief description of how this work product differs from what her approach would have previously been. Peers comment on each other's work in the collaborative workspace, and the case studies are also added to the research center's intranet portal as training and reference tools for other employees.

After they have submitted the final project, participants are able to update their HR files to document their completion of a "leadership learning" credit.

As you can see, the combinations are limited only by your creativity, the willingness of you and your students to use the tools, and your budget. The tools will support almost anything you might want to try to implement quality instruction, and the functionality is available to make just about any distance learning program succeed.

A View to the Future

Distance learning builds upon the technological developments taking place all around us. What's possible today was hardly dreamt of 5 years ago, and the evolution is accelerating. I don't have a crystal ball, but I can offer perspective on what to watch for.

More Social Interaction

The encroachment of social tools into our lives is deepening every day and changing the way we think about relating with people, with ideas, and with organizations. The ease with which people can share through social tools makes them more likely to do so; in an instructional setting, this might start to translate into increased peer-to-peer learning.

More Mobile Tools

Apple released the first iPad in January 2010. While the digital world was already becoming more mobile with each new hardware release, the introduction of tablet computers fundamentally changed the place of mobile content in professional, educational, and personal lives. Smartphones, a wider range of tablet devices, ereaders and ebooks, and further development of resources specifically designed to be used via mobile devices are continuing this evolution. Watch for more mobile-enabled tools to deliver instruction and more students who ask for mobile-enabled versions of your distance learning program.

More Ease of Use

Tools are becoming more user-friendly with every iteration. Next-generation tools will be more intuitive and continue the trend toward graphic-driven interfaces that look and feel similar to software and systems that users are already familiar with.

Deeper Integration

As evolutions in technology continue, the boundaries between one type of tool and another will continue to be blurred and even erased. At the same time, technology tools will become a more seamless part of the educational experience; educators and trainers will find ways to deepen the learning experience by integrating tools like web-based collaboration, AD, and listservs into the "standard" curriculum.

Shorter Learning Curve for New Students

The pool of adults who have already participated in some form of distance learning is growing all the time; even those who have not participated in distance learning are gaining more experience with the technology that enables educational interaction at a distance. As we all gain more experience, the learning curve will no longer be overwhelming for new students. They will be adapting existing knowledge rather than engaging with an entirely new process.

At the same time, the youngest generation of adults participating in distance learning will have a greater presence in more classrooms. This generation is extremely tech-savvy and quite comfortable experimenting with tools to get them to work. As we see more and more of this generation showing up for educational opportunities, they will push their instructors to explore even more potential directions for their learning experiences.

Just-in-Time Learning

Here is where instruction will start to merge with knowledge management (KM); businesses in particular are looking for learning solutions that deliver the right educational experiences at the moment they are needed and in the most useful format. Course management systems can be tied into KM database systems, as well as into software designed to intelligently "discover" what a person is working on and suggest learning modules that can help.

If KM systems are populated with targeted learning modules, and if those modules can be accessed and uploaded to a course delivery tool in response to a user's query, I can think of quite a few enterprises that would be very satisfied by the result.

As our expectations of education shift to accept distance models as part of the norm, we'll be able to choose between tools much more easily, even unconsciously, similar to the way we choose today between picking up the phone, sending an email, or transmitting an instant message. Earlier in my career, sending an email (especially with an attachment) was a project; I usually had to call recipients to be sure they received the message and were able to read it. Today, I barely notice when I'm choosing one communication tool over another. One day soon, we'll feel similarly about choosing tools for distance instruction.

Worksheet 1.1 on the following pages will help you organize your thoughts about choosing distance learning tools. Visit web.freepint.com/go/research/learning to request a download of this and other worksheets and planning tools.

Worksheet 1.1   Needs and Readiness for Distance Learning Tools

Use this worksheet to help you determine what you may need in a distance learning tool and how ready you may be for technology.

1. Budget
Do you know your budget for a distance learning tool? Y/N
Budget is approximately: _____ per   course
                                                semester
                                                year
                                                student
                                                other: _____

What factors influence the budget?

2. Functional Needs
Which of these functions does your distance learning program require?

Functions: Communication and Classroom	No Need	Could Use	Must Have	Don't Know
Email				
Asynchronous discussion				
Synchronous discussion/IM				
Teleconference				
Webinar				
Collaborative online workspace				
Online whiteboard				
Blog				
VoIP				
Videoconferencing				
Multimedia (web-based)				
Multimedia (CD/DVD-based)				
Custom applications				
Other:				
Other:				

Worksheet 1.1   (cont.)

Functions: Administrative	No Need	Could Use	Must Have	Don't Know
Electronic gradebook				
Attendance				
Usage monitoring				
Secure payment				
Secure registration				
Student records access				
Instructor access to course controls				
Scalability				
Other:				
Other:				

Of the functions you have listed as "must have," which are the highest priorities?

What systems or tools have you used, demo'd, or observed in action?

Please rate your agreement with the following statements, where 1 = completely disagree and 5 = completely agree:

	1	2	3	4	5
I am comfortable learning to use new technology.					
I need to use tools that are extremely easy to get started.					
Budget is the most important factor in my decision about which tools to use.					
It is important that I choose a tool that does not require high-speed internet access.					
It is important that I not rely too heavily on technology.					
My students are comfortable learning to use new technology.					
My students have access to appropriate technology.					

When you have completed the worksheet, review again the information presented in Chapter 1 to determine which tools are most appropriate for your needs and readiness. Visit web.freepint.com/go/research/learning for a web-based tool that will make recommendations based on your responses.

Chapter 2

What to Expect When You're Expecting Students

When I work with businesses on developing an audience-focused approach to their marketing, I try to hammer one message home repeatedly:

It's not about you; it's about *them.*

The most common mistake most of us make is to create communications that focus on what the company or organization offers. Great communication shifts the perspective so that all materials put the customer first. It's always about them. It has to speak to them in their language and motivate them to deepen their relationship with the company or organization. It has to anticipate and adequately respond to the implicit—or explicit—question: What's in it for me?

A similar shift is necessary for instructors who are used to thinking primarily about what they offer rather than what their students may need. It has to be about *the students* for distance learning to succeed. In fact, the best educational experiences, distance or otherwise, are those built around what the learner wants, needs, expects, and is ready to try.

Under any circumstances, it's a tough challenge to develop and deliver engaging, effective courses focused on student needs and desired outcomes. In distance learning, the challenge is compounded by the broader range of students in terms of their skills, interests, backgrounds, and levels of engagement. And, as discussed in Chapter 1, the nuances of media and their uses will have a significant effect on how students encounter and work with the material, instructor, and each other.

Most instructors intuitively understand how students, individually and as a group, change the entire experience of teaching. After teaching even a handful of classes, you know that every class has its own character; you can teach the same material in the same way over and over yet create a different learning environment each time because of the human mix. For me and for many of my colleagues, the thrill of this experience is part of the pleasure of teaching. On the flipside, of course, are the disaster classes

41

where the chemistry just doesn't work. (Not fun for anyone involved—students, instructor, or the long-suffering friends who have to hear about it throughout the duration.)

Despite the fact that you will never have control over some elements of your classroom chemistry, you can create the conditions for success if you understand who your students are (or will be) and what they need, and then use that knowledge to plan and craft learning experiences that will bring out the best in them. You can build this knowledge in two ways. First, use the information in this chapter to develop a baseline understanding of the types of students you are likely to encounter, in terms of their expectations, learning styles, and how they will interact with you, each other, and the material. Second, identify the kinds of students—their characteristics and needs—you want to be working with and market your offerings specifically to attract them.

Understanding Adult Learners

This book focuses on instruction for adult students. Your students may be nontraditional college students, professionals seeking development and training, association members gaining industry knowledge, or leisure-time students pursuing personal enrichment opportunities. They may be on the cusp of adulthood, in their older teens or early 20s; they may be enhancing their retirement years with learning new skills. Distance learning students will come to you with all kinds of skills, experiences, backgrounds, and history as learners. They will have different equipment and varying degrees of comfort with it. I've worked with relatively recent immigrants from Asia and Latin America in the same class with second- or third-career learners pursuing a new line of work. While teaching through the University of Phoenix Online, I facilitated courses made up entirely of active-duty members of the military at various stages of their careers who are distributed throughout the world.

Despite the diversity, these groups of learners have some things in common. It's important for instructors to understand five key characteristics shared by most adult learners.

1. Personal History and Experience

Adult learners are not blank slates. They come into the classroom with the wisdom of experience. They have a personal history of and relationship with their own identity as students—the ones who loved school and excelled in every endeavor, as well as the ones whose experiences with formal education were, shall we say, more ambivalent. Most have some professional experience, which has a deep impact on what they want to learn and why. At the same time, they have a variety of interpersonal experiences, which impact how they interact with classmates as well as instructors. With adult learners, you get the whole package.

Within a distance learning context, adult learners also bring their history (or lack thereof) with distance education. Some may have experienced distance education, and they may bring certain expectations into your classroom of what the experience should be like. It's increasingly likely for most to have some experience in a distance environment. Your requirements and approach may come as a surprise. Even at the University of Phoenix Online, where instructors are trained to very specific program requirements, my students were frequently surprised by the approach *I* took to guiding them through the course. "My last instructor never …" and "My last instructor always …" were comments I heard all too often.

Of course, you may also have students with *no* experience in a distance learning environment. And they too will come in with assumptions and expectations about what it will be like. Often students expect their first distance learning experience to be relatively lightweight, compared with traditional classrooms. (In my distance learning programs, at least, they are soon disabused of that notion!)

Instructors need to take into account the way personal history and experience will color an adult student's perspective. Most of all, we need to respect these students' life wisdom and find ways to honor and validate that wisdom through our courses.

2. Preferred Learning Style

Every human being has a preferred way to encounter and master new information. Some are audio learners, absorbing information most effectively when they can hear it; others are textual learners who prefer the written word; still others are hands-on learners who need lab courses to engage their brains with the material. A basic understanding of learning styles is critical to being successful as a distance instructor. (It doesn't hurt in any kind of instructional situation, actually—including parenting!)

Later in this chapter, we'll explore learning styles in greater detail, including how to identify them and how to teach to them.

3. Additional Responsibilities and Demands on Their Time

Have you noticed that your adult students are often running just a little bit late, are suddenly out of commission because a family member is sick, or seem to be distracted by managing the details of their lives? The pace of most of our lives outruns our ability to keep up. Busy adults who are also pursuing education require instructors to understand the demands on their time. This doesn't mean making wholesale excuses for late or missing work, slapdash participation, or other kinds of sloughing off. It does mean, however, that an instructor might want to consider carefully the appropriate workload, timeframe, or technology for a course. For instance, the fact that I work with busy adults (and that I am one myself) is one of the reasons I almost always incorporate an asynchronous discussion (AD) component into my distance offerings; when I train students in the appropriate usage of AD, the tool lets us create a deeply collaborative environment for discussion and exchange, without requiring us to be anywhere at the same time. The flexibility of the tool is well-adapted to the needs of busy adults.

When I first plan out a class, I'm also careful to consider how much my students will reasonably be able to accomplish in a particular timeframe. I often find myself pulling back on the breadth of material I want to cover in favor of creating more in-depth, "sticky" learning on a narrower topic. The smaller chunks, covered in greater depth, enable me to deliver courses that require shorter time commitments while helping my students achieve meaningful results. This translates to ongoing and deepened motivation through incremental success.

4. Motivation to Learn for a Variety of Reasons

This brings us to another key characteristic of adult students: They seek out and participate in educational experiences with unique motivations.

They have a broad range of needs and interests that they look to learning to satisfy.

Understanding and capitalizing on an individual's motivation to learn are mission-critical skills for a distance instructor. Later in this chapter, as well as in Chapter 6, we'll discuss in greater detail how to leverage student motivation. For now, you should know that a student's motivation will tell you a lot about how to work with him or her. Every touchpoint between you and the student needs to push the student's motivational buttons.

5. Psychological Dimensions

Finally, adult students arrive in our classrooms with their egos, fears, and defense mechanisms in working order. Even the students who seem incredibly confident and competent may be harboring (or compensating for) secret fears about their ability to succeed.

No one likes to feel like a beginner, and adult students may be returning to formal learning after a long hiatus. For students who are used to traditional classrooms, the added uncertainties of distance learning can inhibit performance even more. Distance instructors working with adults need to help students feel confident and capable, even as they introduce new ideas and skill development.

Unlike children, who are wired to learn, many adults find learning a scary experience. After all, learning means change. Learning also means admitting one's own deficiencies. As a distance instructor, it's important to make room for the fears your students may be acting on, whether consciously or unconsciously. Always work on activating and projecting your own sense of empathy, subtly telling students that it's acceptable to feel whatever they're feeling.

Confidence Strength Training

How to make room for confidence building within the context of the course work was a regular feature of my writing and composition courses. Students in these classes would come to me with deep anxieties about their ability to write; teachers and even their parents at times had told them that they were terrible writers. If I ignored the psychological baggage they brought into the classroom with them, I'd never get them to write anything. My strategy, then, was to start by helping them reflect (in writing) on a positive experience they may have had with writing—perhaps a love letter or an assignment that seemed to flow without effort. Throughout the course, even when I was pushing them to practice difficult skills, I would refer to their positive experiences, pointing out that they were building on abilities they had never before recognized in themselves. By the end of the course, most of the students didn't necessarily love writing, but at least the disabling anxiety had been neutralized.

Attitudes Toward Education

If adult students share some general characteristics, they are also confoundedly individual. From overall attitudes toward learning to preferred learning style to generational differences and more, each student will come to you as a unique blend of unpredictable ingredients. Their variability is one of the reasons instructor-led experiences will always have a preferred place among educational models; the computers can't quite take over our jobs yet!

Beyond the shared general characteristics of adult students, I've found that there are two kinds of people in this world: perpetual students and outcome-oriented learners.

A perpetual student may have several academic degrees, a long list of continuing education credits, and a constant hunger for discovering the next intellectual mountain to climb. They can be challenging students, because they demand a lot of satisfaction from their educational experiences. At the same time, they are highly rewarding students to work with, since they need just a little light and fertilization to grow like kudzu. For these students, a good instructor is truly a mentor and guide along a path that they are bound and determined to follow. Perpetual learners often thrive on theory and are endlessly enthusiastic about discussion, exploration, dialogue, and debate.

The other broad type—and one who has turned up more frequently in my own distance courses—is the outcome-oriented learner. This learner is pursuing an educational opportunity because of a perceived immediate payback (e.g., acquisition of new skills, which can translate into better on-the-job experiences; higher pay; a promotion; entry into a new field; etc.). This kind of student wants to know that the time and resources spent mastering the material will result in the expected payoff. For these students, a good instructor lays out a clear path from Point A to Point B and draws explicit links between any theoretical components of a course and their practical applications. "Trust me, you'll be glad you learned this" is not an effective instructional technique for outcome-oriented students, who may even be skeptical of the value of education, except within the context of their immediate goals.

There are two *other* kinds of people in this world: those who think there are two kinds of people in this world, and those who know better. The perpetual learner and the outcome-oriented learner are flattened stereotypes—images reproduced with the contrast set way too high, eliminating the texture and character of the real individuals who turn up in our classrooms. If you have an opportunity to work with a group of learners over a period of time, you will likely discover that the boundaries between these two types are rather more permeable than not. Outcome-oriented learners may discover a latent love of theory and debate, while perpetual students, when bored or (worse) disappointed, may simply want to cut to the practical details in a course and move on.

Why present these types at all if they are such a poor representation of reality? Because, as types, they form an introductory understanding of the kind of student you may be working with, and, indeed, the kind of student you may be.

I am a perpetual learner; I'd be happy to pursue degree after degree for the sheer joy of it (my family is grateful that responsibilities such as earning a living preclude the fulfillment of that particular dream). However, the majority of the students I work with for professional development and in undergraduate degree programs are outcome-oriented learners. They have a particular personal goal in mind that usually involves advancement and improved professional skills rather than with the content of my course *per se*, let alone the joy of learning. For me, it was a process of trial and error to figure out why things that naturally motivated *me* were not working to motivate my students. I couldn't figure out why they weren't jumping into the online discussion and batting ideas back and forth, because that's what *I* would do. I had an inkling of why they were unwilling to slog through theoretical readings that formed the basis of the assignments, but I was absolutely baffled by their *refusal* to do so, given that the theory was so important to the work.

And then, after months of frustration, I started to realize that I had to motivate outcome-oriented learners on *their* terms in order for them to do what I wanted them to do. I had to be sure to make theoretical readings as grounded in practical reality as possible. I couldn't assume that once they had read the material, they would figure out the link, and I couldn't even assume that they had read the material simply because it was assigned.

With that insight, I shifted the way I designed my courses and laid out assignments. I rewrote most of my syllabi and lectures to motivate students in different ways. In creating assignments, I began to offer choices that would help perpetual learners come down to earth and push outcome-oriented learners toward a more systemic understanding of the material.

Know the kind of learners you are working with and craft your approach to hit *their* points of motivation.

Learning Styles

For most of us through elementary school, high school, and even college or post-graduate studies, we encountered little understanding or nurturing of our personal "learning style." Whether we preferred to learn verbally or visually, kinetically or collaboratively, we sat in classrooms, listened to lectures, occasionally worked on team projects, researched and wrote papers, participated in lab sections, and more or less sank or swam based on how well we adapted and responded to presentational education.

The science of understanding how humans absorb information and turn it into competence has come a long way in the past few decades. Many of these insights have already found their way into classrooms of all kinds—certainly, our culture's nascent understanding of multiple intelligences is beginning to achieve a certain "household word" status—but many of us who are now instructors were ourselves educated in a system blind to learning styles. As a result, our unconscious models of what it means to teach do not reflect the important insights into learning styles and how to work with them.

The research on learning styles indicates that styles are not static; most of us can accommodate educational situations that do not speak to our preferred style, as long as we can use our preferred style *some* of the time. Unfortunately, unique styles are difficult to accommodate in a traditional, face-to-face classroom.

One of the great benefits of distance learning is that it is easier for an instructor to help students customize the experience based on the preferences of the learner; thus, each learner can satisfy the needs of his or her preferred learning style more frequently than in the traditional classroom. An audio learner can access materials in ways that maximize these learning strengths, while a textual learner has options more suited to a reading-and-absorption style.

Most of all, distance learning allows for repetition of concepts or exercises that are particularly challenging, allowing learners to customize their experience even further. Students can review, repeat, and master the areas of study they need to work on most, while moving quickly through (or even testing out of) areas of study they have already mastered.

Three's the Charm

Instruction would be much easier if people naturally remembered everything they encountered the first time they encountered it. However, our brains do not absorb facts perfectly on first exposure. Some students will remember everything on one exposure; a larger portion of students will remember most information after two exposures; after three exposures, most students will remember most of the material. That's the rule of three.

The importance of repetition will come up again when we examine the craft of course materials in Chapter 4, as well as in the discussion of classroom management in Chapter 5.

Know Thy Style

What do you know about your own preferred learning style? It might tell you something about your unconscious expectations of what it means to learn. Just as I had to learn that not everyone was a perpetual student, I also had to learn that not everyone shared my preferred learning style.

There are a number of free, web-based tools that can help you identify and understand your learning style. Just for fun, try the following:

- What's Your Learning Style? (www.edutopia.org/multiple-intelligences-learning-styles-quiz): Collects information through a simple multiple choice interface and immediately generates a figure showing your results for eight learning styles; links to further information about each style
- Discover Your Learning Styles—Graphically (www.learning-styles-online.com): Measures a user's learning preferences in seven areas and presents results as a visual graph (Figure 2.1)

Interesting, huh? I've been asking students to complete one of these self-assessments and email me the results as part of the introductory stages of a course. The students are often intrigued by the way a learning style assessment identifies their strengths and weaknesses, providing key information that can help them succeed in my course and in others. And, as an instructor, I find the results of these assessments to be extremely helpful in getting to know the students and how I can best help them achieve their goals.

How to Work With Learning Styles

Entire academic careers have been built on the understanding of learning styles. This is a brief introduction to instructional considerations for working with different styles; you'll want to build these ideas into your course materials and include options that address different styles to be sure you are keeping students as engaged as possible and allowing them to learn effectively.

Learning Styles Graph

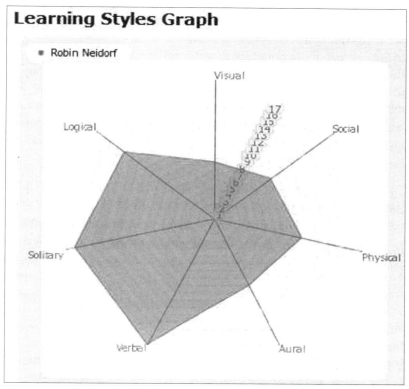

Figure 2.1   The graphical representation of my own learning style, based on the inventory at www.learning-styles-online.com: Don't put me on a learning team or ask me to repeat what I just heard, but you can give me a text to analyze on my own, and I'll happily get to work. [Used with permission from Memletics, Inc., owner of www.learning-styles-online.com.]

Verbal Style

Students with a verbal learning style respond to written and spoken language. They will have no trouble absorbing your carefully crafted written lectures or reviewing assignments presented to them in writing. You can maximize their use of distance learning tools and resources by adding elements to the environment, like a keyword glossary, verbal analysis of concepts, and even word games.

Visual Style

Students with a visual learning style respond to pictures and images. Add to their experience in your distance program by presenting information in the form of mind maps; link concepts to each other on the mind map or use mind maps to illustrate links between concepts and desired practical outcomes. Virtual whiteboard sessions are great fun for visual learners who can watch ideas emerge on the screen and even contribute to their creation. Well-designed web-based learning environments are great for visual students. You can enhance their understanding of key texts by marking them iconographically (e.g., placing icons next to particular kinds of texts so that they can visually tell the difference between a definition, an assignment, a team project, etc.).

Kinesthetic Style

Kinesthetic learners like to "touch and do." This style benefits enormously from recent developments in touchscreen technology. Offer projects and assignments that invite kinesthetic learners to build a model, draw or construct something, or observe changes in their own physical state while doing an activity. Anything that gets them moving will help them master the material you are presenting. Since kinesthetic learners are often primarily interested in personally experiencing an activity, computer simulations can also be good learning tools for them.

Social Style

Social learners want to do everything in groups; they will be active participants in your distance classroom and with their classmates once they get the hang of how to do it. In addition to team projects, some of the tools you can employ to stimulate social learners are role-playing exercises and group problem-solving assignments. This is a style that thrives in the new social web.

Solitary Style

Students with a solitary learning style resent the team assignments and need to feel confident that they aren't wasting their time with the team. They prefer to go off on their own to learn material. They may mistakenly believe that distance learning will mean little social interaction and will be painfully surprised to learn that they must interact in order to succeed. You can help the solitary learner by incorporating several elements into your course: Return regularly to the personal motivation of a solitary learner, so that he or she remains committed to the course. Role-playing exercises can also be effective for solitary learners, since they can take on someone else's persona for the duration of the project and distance their solitary nature from the immediate learning experience. Adding a personal, private journal for reflection can also help the solitary learner interact with the material in a way that honors this learning style while providing you with enough information to help the student make greater progress toward his or her goals.

Logical Style

The logical learner thrives on reasoning and systems. Logical learners are forever making lists and agendas; they can be a bit annoying on learning teams, but they do keep things on track! Stimulate logical learners by answering their constant query, "But *why*?" Provide deeper resources, readings, and exercises beyond the ones you assign for the course, to allow them to dive into the why's as much as they want. Simulations that enable them to test theories and work on a whole system rather than a single piece of it are great fun for logical learners.

Aural Style

The aural learning style is one in which the student responds best to sounds, rhythms, and repetition. Aural students often make up little rhymes for themselves to remember key information. Recorded materials, well-organized telephone calls, and even materials that integrate poetry and rhythmic language can help aural learners interact more intimately with the course.

Balancing Stylistic Needs

If you were to create style-specific pathways through every single course you created, you'd be so busy creating that you'd never have time to teach. The goal should be to offer at least some options some of the time that will appeal to a variety of learning styles. When I create a course, I never have trouble appealing to the verbal or logical styles, since I share many of their characteristics. However, I have difficulty thinking through offerings for kinesthetic and social learners; I've made it a point to put those options on my own "course review" checklist to remind myself to create options for them prior to launching a course.

The need to balance learning styles is another reason why creating distance learning courses in collaboration with others is so helpful. With a collaborative process, you are sure to be working with individuals who have different learning styles. Use their ideas and input to ensure you are creating materials that will stimulate the widest range of your potential students.

Generational Differences

Advances in healthcare and the trend toward the elongation of professional careers have created an environment in which four distinct generations are active, working, and learning together. The characteristics of those in their early 20s and early 30s today are very different—and make for very different kinds of students—than the characteristics of Generation X, the omnipresent Baby Boomers, and the Matures, who are still in the workforce and may be pursuing distance learning for professional or personal reasons.

As a distance instructor, you may work with students in any or all of the four generations, each of which has its own characteristics, perspectives, and expectations of the classroom environment (Table 2.1).

Matures

"Matures" are those born prior to 1946. The world events that have shaped their lives include World War II, the Korean Conflict, the Depression, and the New Deal. Matures grew up in a world where expectations and roles were clearly defined and values like thrift, hard work, and respect for authority were accepted as givens.

As students, Matures may need more time to acclimate to a new environment, regardless of the level of technology involved; they have decades

Table 2.1   Know Your Generations

Generation	Life-Defining Events	Core Values	Expectations of Classroom
Matures	WW2 Korean War	Dedication Conformity Respect for authority Adhere to rules Self-sacrifice	Clear hierarchy
Boomers	Civil Rights Women's Lib Cold War	Optimism Team-oriented Manipulation of rules "Live to work"	Discussion and creation of consensus
Generation X	AIDS Persian Gulf Latchkey kids Computers	Diversity Balance Self-reliance "Work to live"	Unimpressed with nominal authority; assign authority based on competence
Millennials	Oklahoma City bombing Columbine shootings Multicultural terrorism Internet	Optimism Civic duty Diversity "Edu-tainment" Collective action	Will cut-and-paste to create customized experience; technology is an enhancement to the process

Adapted from "Higher Education, Blended Learning and the Generations: Knowledge is Power—No More," by Charles Dziuban, Patsy Moskal, and Joel Hartman, Research Initiative for Teaching Effectiveness, University of Central Florida and Generations at Work: Managing the Clash of Veterans, Boomers, Xers, and Nexters in Your Workplaces, *by Ron Zemke, Claire Raines, and Bob Filipczak, Amacom, 2000.*

of expectations around what a classroom is like, and most distance learning programs will upset those expectations.

The importance of peer-to-peer connections may also be challenging for Matures. This is a generation accustomed to well-defined hierarchies. The idea that they are co-creating the learning experience may be a strange one at first.

Another consideration if your learning program will include Matures: larger fonts.

Boomers

What hasn't been written or said about the ubiquitous Baby Boomers? Boomers were born between 1946 and 1964; their childhood and adolescent years were characterized by confidence, prosperity, the rise of youth culture, and growing experimentation with alternative perspectives. Key events shaping Boomers' world view include the Cuban Missile Crisis, the Kennedy and King assassinations, the Vietnam War, and the sexual revolution.

As students, Boomers are often process-oriented and committed to building consensus. They can be extremely uncomfortable with open conflict. They are highly team-oriented and may be pleasantly surprised at the degree of interaction and kinds of relationships they can develop in a distance learning environment.

Boomers look to their peers for approval and direction. Applying a bit of positive peer pressure in the motivation department can be very effective for keeping them involved in a course.

Boomers generally want to have a clear idea of what they need to do to succeed; they are deeply committed to their own excellence.

Generation X

Generation X, born between 1965 and 1980, is the first generation to have grown up in a largely technological environment (though the impact is even more profound for the next generation). Critical events in the lifetimes of Generation X include the *Challenger* disaster, the outbreak and spread of AIDS, recession, and massive layoffs.

As students, Gen X-ers are cynical about authority, jealous of demands on their time, and committed to finding their own way through the material. Give them lots of options and help them feel that you respect their individuality, creativity, and ideas.

Gen X-ers are the first generation to grow up with the expectation that they would *not* have a single lifelong career. They do not expect institutions—or even their own communities—to look after them. Somewhere in the motivational system of most Gen X-ers is the sense that education, skills, and even personal enrichment pursuits could lay the path for the next phase of their multistage careers.

Millennials

The Millennials are the youngest generation currently in the workforce and in higher education. Born between 1981 and 1994, Millennials are fully digital and expect organizations to make technology available as a matter of course. Text messages, social media, and "always on" online presence are not "technology" to Millennials, any more than telephones are technology to Boomers. They are adept at cutting and pasting offerings to get what they want out of them, creating an entirely customized world for themselves in the process.

Perhaps a bit on the naive side in terms of information literacy and validating knowledge, Millennials as students are eager and willing to participate in team projects, although they benefit from clear direction and perhaps a few more seasoned individuals on the team. Of all the generations, the Millennials are the most comfortable and confident with change. They have high expectations of distance learning, and, because of this, they can be the hardest group to satisfy. Since this generation is only beginning to enter professional fields and join the ranks of our instructor-colleagues, we can be somewhat in the dark about what Millennials think and feel about us or the learning experiences we offer.

Not incidentally, the characteristics of this up-and-coming market are well-aligned with distance learning approaches. In the next decade, the possibilities and opportunities for distance learning—whether for professional development, academic advancement, or personal study—will no doubt explode as Millennials become a larger part of the potential market and bring their tech-orientation into the institutions they join and shape. Congratulations—you're on the leading edge of the trend!

The End-Game: Motivation and Learner-Centered Experiences

Developing an understanding of learner types, learning styles, and generational differences is an interesting exercise, but what do you as an instructor need to do with that information? Remember that it's not about you; it's about *them*. The more you know about them, the more you can choose and use effective distance learning models, write student-focused content, develop activities that deepen (and test) learning, and craft the learning experience to meet students where they are.

Most of all, you have the information you need to motivate your students. I can't say enough about the importance of motivation in creating successful learning experiences. All behavior, including learning, is motivated.

In traditional classroom environments, explicit attention to motivation is rarely part of the instructional equation. The student is assumed to be motivated by the sheer fact of his or her presence. In a distance learning environment, an instructor who ignores the motivation of the students and how to enhance and deepen that motivation is an instructor who experiences a lot of attrition, MIA students, and zero enrollments. Perhaps the key difference lies in the fact that the environment *is* distance; learning takes energy, and without constant pushing at the motivation button (which gets pushed, however discreetly, whenever a student walks into a traditional classroom), it's easy to get discouraged or even just distracted.

Motivation is the secret ingredient, the X-factor, in successful educational programs: no motivation, no learning.

In my own experience as a self-directed human being, the best motivation comes from the inside. Sure, I can do just about anything if I'm compelled from the outside to do it … for a little while. I can do a one-day training session simply because I "have" to. But commit to the challenge and energy-drain of a more in-depth learning experience? That takes positive, internal motivation to keep me going.

There's also a correlation between the amount of motivation a person needs to complete a task and the perceived difficulty of the task. Distance learning is perceived by many adults as difficult because it is unfamiliar. To overcome the perceived difficulty, students must have strong positive motivation.

Of course, motivation is a highly personal thing; what motivates one student will leave another completely cold. In interacting with individual students, a wise distance learning instructor will work to discover a student's personal motivational points and work to enhance them through the content of the course, feedback, and creating a meaningful, positive experience. (Chapter 6, which discusses instructor–student interactions, will provide specific tips on identifying motivators and maintaining motivation.)

Motivation can also be bolstered through the social nature of good distance learning programs. Interaction with peers does more than provide fodder for team projects and gripe sessions about the crazy, unreasonable instructor. Buddying up supports commitment, whether it's to an exercise regimen or a learning regimen. Creating formal or informal mentorship programs between more or less experienced students or students with complementary skills and interests can add to a dynamic where the students are helping each other succeed.

The literature on successful computer-mediated education indicates that the presence of a student lounge, where students can talk about anything and everything, contributes to the success of the overall learning environment. Even just a place to share news and blow off a bit of steam can help students feel connected to each other and create the potential for a bit of peer-to-peer coaching when motivation is running low. (Chapter 7, which focuses on creating a community of learners, will identify ways an instructor can use group interactions to support individual motivation.)

Culturally, we're all becoming more and more accustomed to casual, relationship-building interactions via social web experiences. The normalization of Facebook as part of regular interaction, for example, has trained many of us who spend significant time online to look for, expect, and manage a place in the digital environment where we can "hang out" and get to know others on a personal level. As an instructor, you can capitalize on this emerging skill to foster collaborative student relationships, as well as to learn more about what is going to motivate each individual you are working with.

Adult Learners Need ...

Put all this information together about attitudes toward education, learning styles, and generational differences, and the picture that emerges is both simple and complex. It's simple in that you can now understand your students first as human beings and relate to them compassionately in a way that allows their differences to enhance the learning environment. But it's complex in that humans and their interactions are inherently complex; we can't connect intimately and effectively with everyone.

I don't mind admitting that I'm somewhat starry-eyed about teaching. The instructor–student relationship seems to be the one that calls on me to be my best self and to encourage students to be their best selves. If I can create a safe environment for experimentation, a place where students recognize that they can learn from failure as well as success, an environment that makes me in some ways as vulnerable as the students themselves, then we all have a real opportunity to re-imagine the possibilities of our abilities and potential.

Instructors can create this kind of rich, creative, and rigorous environment by providing adult learners with the following:

- *A little TLC:* "Warm and encouraging" is always a good attitude to project. Care about your students as individuals, and communicate that caring. You don't need to fawn over them; just let them know you are a real human being who appreciates their own humanness.

- *Cheerleading and coaching:* Celebrate success and find the teachable elements of failure. Make it clear that you're there to help, not "out to get them." Know, too, that in a distance learning environment, you may need to do some cheerleading and coaching around navigating the course, as well as mastering the skills it covers.

- *Collaborative projects:* Teamwork pushes learning to a new level; in addition to mastering subject matter, students must also work with the material in a group setting. Together, they discover more about what they know and what they need to learn. In distance learning in particular, collaborative work helps cement the relationships that create a community of learners.

- *Flexibility:* Keep an open mind when learning about your students' needs for different learning methods, timeframes, or approaches to the material. In addition to the variations required by learning styles and busy schedules, you will likely learn something entirely new about great teaching strategies.

- *Practical usage:* Cut to the chase, as they say: Demonstrate the practical value of the knowledge students are gaining and allow them to apply the knowledge within the context of their own interests and experiences.

Not Working With Adults?

Even teenagers can benefit from this kind of approach to understanding the needs of learners. Although lacking in life experiences that are of critical value to adult learners, teens can thrive in an educational environment that helps them take charge of their learning, become more self-aware and self-confident, and create a customized path toward the learning objectives.

While you have their attention, it's also a good idea to plant the idea in their heads that their learning preferences may change over time. Today's teens will need to be life-long learners in order to make their way through life. Each instructor they encounter along the way has an opportunity to help them understand themselves as learners, as well as how their particular approach to learning can be an asset. Lay the foundation for formal and informal educational experiences by doing more than creating content-specific competence; teach the students, not the subject, and teach them something about themselves along the way.

Now Let's Build a Course

Who knew there was so much to know about the students before we even could start planning what to teach? No wonder so many educational programs focus on content—it's much easier to understand than students!

By now, you should have an idea of the kinds of students you may be working with, as well as the potential tools and technologies at your disposal. Complete Worksheet 2.1 on the following page to capture your ideas and knowledge about your student population. (A web-based version of this worksheet and other tools can be found at web.freepint.com/go/research/learning.) Now you are ready to tackle the actual creation of a course that will be appropriately tuned to the needs of your students and the capabilities of your chosen technologies for interaction.

Worksheet 2.1   Understanding Students

Use this worksheet to understand your student population and what their educational needs may be.

Which generations are represented among your students?

Generations	None	A Few	Many	Don't Know
Matures				
Baby Boomers				
Generation X				
Millennials				

What are the most common motivators bringing your students into the classroom?

Please rate your agreement with the following statements, where 1 = completely disagree and 5 = completely agree:

My students ...	1	2	3	4	5
Know they need what I am offering.					
Have clear goals in mind for pursuing education.					
Prefer environments in which they have a lot of choice and control.					
Prefer environments in which the path to success is very clear.					
Have access to technology.					
Live within driving distance of each other and of me.					
Are comfortable with technology.					
Take my class because they want to rather than because they have to.					
Are self-aware learners—they understand the circumstances that help them learn best.					
Have intense demands on their time, professionally and personally.					
Are under external pressure to succeed in my class.					
Believe in the value of classroom studies.					
Have taken distance classes before.					
Are confident in their abilities to learn.					

Other observations or insights about your students, based on your experience with them or with similar groups:

Use the information on this worksheet when you consider audiences in the instructional design process.

Chapter 3

Content, Part I: Instructional Design

Instructional design is an even more misunderstood profession than teaching. Just as subject expertise does not guarantee teaching skill, teaching expertise does not guarantee the ability to design and create effective learning experiences tuned to the desired outcomes of the teacher, organization, and student. Turning information delivery into instruction is the purview of instructional design.

What Is Instructional Design?

Instructional design is a process by which learning experiences are engineered, based on student needs, desired outcomes, and available tools and resources. Instructional designers need to

- Understand the student population

- Be familiar with the medium of delivery and interaction

- Sift through and organize content

- Select appropriate methods for creating the optimum learning experience

- Establish the environment for learning

- Assess results and outcomes

It's not enough to be an expert in your subject matter, proficient in choosing tools and technologies, or able to conduct ad hoc student psychological analysis; now you also have to be an instructional designer. (No one said the glory of being a teacher would come easily.) Prior to writing and developing actual teaching materials, exercises, assignments, and activities (which we'll tackle in Chapter 4), you must create an instructional framework for your course.

Think of the instructional design process as a kind of cartography. When you finish, you will have created a map indicating the various routes through the material, stops along the way for activity and interaction, and the destination you and the students will reach when successful. The instructional design process is invaluable for clarifying your thinking about what you want to share with students and coming up with creative ways to work with them across media and learning styles. Additionally, the design process serves as your guide to the actual content you need to create. After a few courses, you'll be able to eyeball your map and estimate how much time you will need to develop content for a new program.

The process and the resulting map have enormous collaborative value as well. Work through the design process with your distance learning team, and you create a shared understanding of the goals and requirements of the project. Or work through the process on your own and use the resulting map to brainstorm with your team as to the resources, approaches, tools, and technologies that best lend themselves to your course.

Don't discount the possibility of adding a trained instructional designer to your team, if you have access and budget. You can apply the principles of instructional design as laid out in this chapter on your own, but a trained designer draws on education, experience, and professional focus on understanding instruction from the learner's perspective. If you don't have time or budget for a designer as a working part of your team, it might be worthwhile to hire one as a consultant for a few hours just to get you started on the right path or to review your design prior to implementation.

Most of the principles of instructional design apply equally to traditional and distance learning environments. This chapter will first introduce the general principles and then examine some of the unique instructional design challenges of distance learning programs. Finally, the worksheets and process description at the end of the chapter will guide you through the draft of a design for your course, either on your own or in collaboration with the rest of your development team.

General Instructional Design Principles
Start With the End in Mind

You can't get where you want to go unless you know where that is. Start with the end in mind: What will successful students say, think, or do once they have completed the course?

Notice how starting from the end and framing the question this way immediately shifts your thinking from *what to teach* to *why the student needs to learn*. That's a crucial shift and one that many instructors are unaccustomed to making. Furthermore, this shift prepares you to think in terms of learner motivation; they *need* to learn, but do they *want* to learn?

Getting the Most Benefit From an Instructional Designer

Even if you are working with an instructional designer, don't skip this chapter! It will help you understand what the designer is up to, and it will put you on track to work in tandem with your designer to reach your goals.

Keep in mind that a designer does much more than translate your expertise into a syllabus and a test. Designers craft the learning experience so students can do what they're supposed to be able to do when they complete the program. A creative, collaborative relationship between you and your designer requires that you learn something about the unique value he or she brings to the table.

One caveat, though: Many professionals have become de facto instructional designers without a real background or training in the field. For instance, some software developers have been pushed into the role of instructional designer because they are the ones building an elearning interface. Be sure your instructional designer is actually designing instruction and not a website or presentation slides.

Different Settings, Different Goals—Same Process

When I taught college communications through the University of Phoenix Online, I had very clear outcomes in mind. My class formed the foundation of students' research and writing skills for other courses in their programs of study. At the same time, I wanted them to feel good about the writing process and their own abilities. But the bottom line was how well they could perform: Could they write college-level papers, or not?

On the other hand, my students in Creative Writing in English at the University of Gävle in Sweden had successful outcomes that were much more individual and amorphous. Every semester for 4 years, I worked with a dozen or so students, each of whom had a different genre focus, level of expertise, and distinct personal goals for his or her creative writing. A few were native English speakers, but most were not and wanted to work on their language skills. It was an enjoyable challenge to treat this class as a class and not as a series of mentored relationships. But if the participants were to benefit from being a group of learning peers, the other instructors and myself needed to have an instructional focus rather than simply responding to each student individually. Over time, I developed an over-arching instructional goal for my work with the class: No matter what kind of writing the students were doing or where they were in their own development as creative writers, my instructional goal was that they read literature and respond to it as creative writers rather than simply as readers. If I were to write a learning objective for this course, it might be this: Students will identify specific writing techniques found in literature of their choosing and apply those techniques in their own creative work. In other words, I was pushing them to see themselves and their work within the broader context of world literature.

These were two very different kinds of writing classes with very different kinds of goals. Yet in both cases, the presence of these goals provided me with a lens through which to focus my instruction. We were not floundering for something to do, and I was not simply reacting to what a student turned in. There is too much to know about writing to try to teach it without specific goals. The same is true for any area of instruction.

Learning Objectives

Instructional goals often translate directly into learning objectives. Learning objectives are succinct, learner-focused statements of defined, measurable outcomes for the course. In the planning and development process, learning objectives create checks and balances for me to use in reviewing a draft outline or an assignment for a course: Does this project satisfy the learning objective? Does this assignment give learners enough information and practice to subsequently achieve an objective?

Learning objectives need to be targeted, specific, and measurable. Here are some examples of learning objectives written to meet these criteria:

- Students will correctly identify and format the parts of a business letter.

- Participants will accurately apply the three steps of analysis to solve the problem presented in the case study.

- Trainees will operate a forklift under normal warehouse conditions while achieving a safety score of at least 99 percent.

Notice how these objectives are

- Action-oriented

- Measurable

- Learner-focused

- Grounded within a specific condition or context for action

Learning to write objectives is a little like learning to write haiku. "Condensed and specific" describes both art forms. The impact is also similar—both create a universe shared between reader and writer with the minimum number of words.

Keep in mind that you may have implicit or hidden objectives, as well as explicit objectives. For instance, whenever I teach a course comprised of students who are mostly new to distance learning, one of my objectives is that they successfully complete the assigned activities in all areas of the course. Whether I ever express that objective to students depends on the groups and our relationship, but knowing that it *is* an objective ensures that I monitor progress toward that particular goal.

Despite my appreciation for learning objectives, I feel that they are overused in course materials. Current standard practices suggest that learning objectives should be placed prominently at the beginning of distance learning materials so that students are prepared for what they are about to learn.

Words to Use in Learning Objectives

Verbs that result in an observable action are the best ones to use:

List
Identify
State
Describe
Define
Solve
Compare and contrast
Operate

Avoid verbs that result in actions that are difficult or impossible to quantify:

Know
Use
Understand
See

That practice can create problems. Read the following learning objective, and try not to roll your eyes:

After completing this course, you will be able to

- Place a caller on hold

- Activate the speaker phone

- Play new messages on the voice mail system

- List the three elements of a proper phone greeting

- Transfer a call to a requested extension

I know these are important skills (I've accidentally hung up on more than one caller when I was learning a new phone system), but from a student's perspective, it's impossible to take them seriously as learning objectives.

Just reading them, I feel slightly insulted—not a frame of mind that will lead to an enjoyable learning experience.

Learning objectives are raw material, not final content. Use them for planning, focus, and development purposes, but be sure you translate them into something a little more learner-friendly before you launch your course. Go back to motivation: Make the objectives clear, but also make them compelling. In Chapter 4, we'll look specifically at how to communicate learning objectives without alienating, insulting, or boring your students.

Scope of Content

One of the hardest parts of developing content for a course is editing. You have sophisticated knowledge of a subject, and you are eager to share that knowledge with learners who need and want it. It's hard to say no to anything that could add to the learner's appreciation for the topic. Yet learners are not ready for everything a topic expert knows; throwing too much at them (unless they are highly motivated and have powerful incentives to persist) will overwhelm them. The result? Attrition, poor motivation, confusion, dissatisfaction, zero outcomes (and then where's your funding going to come from?).

Sifting through areas of content to cover requires a topic expert to step back into the learner's shoes. Return to the overall goals: What should a learner be able to say, think, or do as a result of completing a course? More importantly, what does a learner *want* to be able to say, think, or do? Where's the pain that the learner is turning to education to try to assuage? The best content to choose is the material that will directly address that pain.

Throughout the learning experience, of course, a skilled instructor plants the seeds for a deepened engagement with the topic. "You think you got great results from *this?* Wait till you see what we can do once you've learned …" Aha! Now the learner is internally motivated to bite off a bigger chunk.

It's tempting to put in every possible objective, but you risk losing your students entirely by giving them too much irrelevant instruction. Sure, you may know that it is incredibly relevant, but the learner remains dissatisfied. Overstuffed courses or courses that are too far afield of the pain do not encourage deep interaction of the learner with the materials, instructor, or other students. Students have little chance to find much

---

How Many Objectives?

The number of learning objectives you need for any course depends on a host of factors. Clearly, a self-contained training module needs far fewer objectives than a semester-long college seminar. How much you break down large objectives into smaller pieces will also have an impact on the final number. Programs can be built on as few as one objective. Most of my college courses have between six and eight objectives; professional education, development, and training, which I usually teach in 5-week sessions, generally have four to six objectives. Single-session workshops tend to focus on one learning objective, two at the very most. If I find that I have substantially more than that on my working list, it's an indication that I'm trying to cram too much into a course.

---

meaning in the information, and so it remains in the "training" file, never to be put into action.

Or look at it as a kind of self-preservation: If you insist on covering *everything*, you will end up with a course that takes much longer than it should to prepare and deliver. Remember that adult learners are battered with competing time pressures; you're probably feeling a bit of that yourself. Be realistic or you are setting yourself and your students up for frustration. If, on the other hand, their learning experience is exciting and produces the results they want, they are motivated to take the next step and go more deeply with you and the material.

Have I convinced you yet? If you just can't help yourself, here are some tips to save your sanity:

- Create "deeper reading" and optional assignments that delve into critical areas that you don't have room for in the syllabus. Make these materials available after the end of the course, perhaps as a self-paced add-on, to support those who are motivated to continue.

- Review your entire course against your learning objectives; is there anything a bit off-topic? Consider making it optional or moving it to a different course altogether.

- Review the number and complexity of learning objectives; can you focus on a smaller number of objectives in this one offering? Can you simplify any of the objectives to reduce the amount of content you need to cover?

- Allow potential students to preview the courses and give their impressions of the appropriateness, complexity, time commitment, and focus of the course. Listen to their feedback!

- Ask an instructional designer, if you have one on your team or can corner one, to run a professional eye over what you are creating. Instructional designers have professional skill in matching content to expectations.

- Offer courses in a series, or develop an outline for additional courses that you could offer in the event of sufficient interest. Don't pour hours of your time into courses that your audiences aren't ready for yet—and possibly don't even know they need!

Eventually, you have to make your choices and live with them. Select the topics you will cover, based on your goals and objectives, the needs of the students, and the smallest portion of material you feel is necessary for the students to reach the objectives within the time frame of the program.

Events of Instruction

When I taught entirely in traditional classrooms or in one-on-one mentored situations, I never gave a thought to the mental processes required for students to learn what I was teaching. Once I moved into a distance environment, however, the necessity of planning *everything* in advance pushed me to learn more about what I needed to do to create readiness on the part of my learners and then maximize that readiness by delivering instruction.

Robert Gagne is known in behaviorist circles as the father of instructional design and training. (Did you even know there were "behaviorist circles"? There's a specialty for everything.) In his 1965 book, *The*

Conditions of Learning, Gagne first identified and described the mental conditions for adult learning:

- *Capture attention:* Directing and focusing the students' attention activates their "learning receptors."

- *Inform learners of objectives:* Students need to know what to expect of the learning experience; informing them of objectives sets their expectations and prepares them for entry into the learning experience proper.

- *Stimulate recall of prior learning:* By building on existing knowledge, whether tacit or explicit, students can prepare to encode new information in their short-term memories.

- *Present the content:* The instructor makes a selective presentation of material, filtering it for students so that they understand its context and meaning.

- *Provide "learning guidance":* By interacting with the material under the guidance of an instructor, students begin to understand its meaning and relevance to their needs. This step begins the process of encoding the information in long-term memory.

- *Elicit performance (practice):* Students practice or work directly with skills and concepts to demonstrate understanding, deepen the encoding process, and verify the accuracy of their understanding.

- *Provide feedback:* Instructors and peers reinforce performance by providing assessment and correction.

- *Enhance retention and transfer:* Students begin to generalize from their newly acquired knowledge and apply it to other situations.

Too often, instructors jump into presenting the content without attending to the earlier events. As a result, students are scrambling to catch up—or drop the course. At this stage in the instructional design process, make sure your design covers the entire continuum of instructional events: You have to capture students' attention and carry them through to generalization of their new knowledge. In Chapter 4, we'll be spending more time with the events of instruction as they impact how you create actual instructional materials.

Activity-Based Learning

Presentational instruction (e.g., standing at a podium and delivering a lecture, jazzed up, perhaps, with a presentation) is hardly an optimal model for education of any kind. Yet "talk and test" is a common enough model—one you may even be unconsciously mimicking. Adult learners need practical, results-oriented learning experiences. Activity-based learning can meet those needs while moving them along the continuum of instructional events.

As you review your topics and objectives, you should ask yourself one question over and over: "How could this be an activity?" Here are some answers you might come up with:

- Conduct an interview

- Role-play with classmates or other colleagues

- Conduct an experiment

- Participate in a survey and compare responses to an aggregated benchmark

- Respond to reflective questions in a private journal

- Respond to content questions in a public discussion

- Complete a simulation

- Fix a software bug

Don't worry yet about creating assignments or even figuring out how you'd get students to do the activity within the context of a distance learning environment. Focus on generating a long and interesting list of relevant, engaging activities that will help students move along the path to achieving their (and your) objectives.

Evaluation and Assessment

How will you know if your course is effective? The best test of effectiveness is the performance of the learners when they take their learning back to the real world. Barring an ability to assess performance following a course, most instructors resort to testing of some kind.

When students are earning credit for completing a course, either at a college or their place of work, evaluation becomes even more important. In such cases, it's extremely helpful to have evaluation tools that can help you review the work of individual students against a single standard of excellence. When grading essays for my University of Phoenix communications students, I always used a rubric in which I scored the paper in particular areas (see Figure 3.1); otherwise, grading a writing assignment could become far too subjective. For the students' sake, and for my own, I needed to work from an established standard.

Consider, too, what *you* consider to be a successful outcome for your course. For instance, if you regularly lose one-third to one-half of your students by the midpoint in the program, something is not working. That's a kind of assessment-in-action.

Distance Learning Design Particulars

Most elements of instructional design are common to traditional and distance learning environments. However, some elements have unique considerations in distance learning, as described in the rest of this chapter.

Nonlinear Information

In a traditional classroom, an instructor presents ideas sequentially, since the classroom is governed by the clock. An instructor moves in a linear fashion from one idea to the next throughout the classroom period as well as the term of the course.

In a distance learning program, you still have the option to move sequentially, but you are no longer bound by that model. You can present materials simultaneously, in concert with one another, in parallel or intersecting tracks, or just about any other way you can imagine. And your students will probably find ways to move through the materials.

One example of a way to break off from the sequential pathway can be found in some of the computer games my daughter likes to play. These games involve different problem-solving activities built around a narrative that takes the main characters through the environments within the

Checklist for Effective Writing (1 [low]–5 [high])

What is the point? (Content) _____ of 12 possible points
_____ Student accomplished the objectives of the assignment.
_____ Student clearly demonstrates understanding of the subject matter at appropriate depth.
_____ Ideas and information presented are adequate; data is not limited or missing.
_____ Paper is clear, focused, and interesting.
_____ Paper includes relevant material and conveys more than a general message.
_____ Adequate support is provided for assertions.
_____ The ability to link theory to practical experience is evident.

How well was the point made? (Organization) _____ of 8 possible points
_____ Organization emphasizes the central theme or purpose.
_____ Paper demonstrates a determination of audience and is appropriate to that audience.
_____ Each paragraph contains only one main idea, logically developed.
_____ Information is properly sequenced throughout the paper.

Is the paper professionally presented? (Format) _____ of 5 possible points
_____ Paper has been carefully edited.
_____ Paper is professional in appearance.
_____ Paper conforms to MLA/APA standards for format and citation of sources.

Was the writing effective? (Readability) _____ of 5 possible points
_____ Student used short words and sentences appropriately.
_____ Word choices convey the message in an interesting, precise, and natural way.
_____ Student selected an appropriate writing strategy and style.
_____ Sentences are well built, with strong but varied structure.
_____ Sentences are fluid.
_____ Student used powerful verbs, active voice, and appropriate vocabulary.
_____ Paper is not excessively wordy or full of redundancies.

Was the writing grammatically correct? (Grammar, Punctuation) _____ of 5 possible points
_____ No shifts in tense or voice are evident.
_____ Student avoids colloquial expressions and jargon.
_____ Pronoun referents are clear.
_____ Proper grammar and punctuation are used.

Total points: _____ of 35 possible points

Figure 3.1   This is a copy of the rubric I used for grading written papers. The rubric keeps me focused on learning objectives and specific areas for improvement.

game. My daughter can choose to follow the narrative, or she can jump to the particular activities that she feels like doing at the moment.

Similarly, a distance learning experience could be designed to enable a student to access any activity or area at any time rather than moving along the standard "narrative," the chronological progression primarily intended by the instructor. Such a design could be challenging to combine with peer-to-peer interaction, but an instructor could work around that challenge by requiring students to navigate the course with a buddy or two other students in small learning groups. In fact, game-based learning design has become one of the most interesting and innovative areas of instructional development.

Another example of a nonlinear approach is website design. The familiarity many adults have with navigating nonlinear websites enables them to work with instructional materials built on the same model. Although the instructor will have to find ways to boost the peer power of such a learning environment, it can be an effective approach, particularly for students who are more highly motivated in situations in which they have greater control.

Customization

Presentational instruction, such as that found in lecture halls, allows for little or no customization on the part of the learner. The instructor presents the material; the student takes notes and may have an opportunity to ask questions. Any customization happens outside of the main educational environment. Instructors may teach to the least able students, expecting that others will tune in and out as their attention is piqued; they may teach to those students in the middle, hoping that the bottom end will struggle to catch up or drop the course. Or instructors may just present whatever they want to present, without giving much thought to the abilities of the students in the lecture hall.

Move into a distance learning environment and customization becomes a more natural part of how students encounter the content, the instructor, and their peers, thus building their own learning based on their preferences and abilities. Students may access a page in a web-based course where they can opt to play a video, download and read an article or transcript, or view the original research that went into the video with the instructor's notes and comments intact. Students may receive an instructor's mailed feedback as handwritten notes, a marked-up PDF document, or an audio recording of comments. Students may call in for the teleconference, download the archived recording of the conference at a later date, access and search the file online, or even read a transcript of the entire call.

It's easy in distance learning to forget about providing options, perhaps because just getting the course pulled together and created is enough of a challenge. But students who can choose their learning methods, pick between activities, and access the material in a way that best suits their style are students who excel and leave satisfied.

Choosing Your Tools

Your choice of tools for distance learning has, of course, an enormous impact on your students, your development process, your budget, and the kinds of skills your team needs. If you are using web-enabled interactions for any part of your course, you need to work closely with the developers who design, build, test, and support the tools you use for interaction. Self-service forms of web-based interaction (such as Google Docs) have the benefit of your immediate hands-on control of the environment, but you may still want technical support to get the most value from the platform. If you are using designed documents (such as workbooks, whether in print or digital format) for your course, you need to find graphic designers with skill in creating instructional materials. Even if you are relying on email and telephone systems for delivering distance learning, you need partners or vendors who can support those functions and consult on your choices.

Many instructors don't have much choice of the tools they can use. Their sponsoring organizations have contracted with web-based course management providers, and they are required to use those tools to develop and deliver their courses. However, those platforms come with just about every imaginable feature, allowing you to choose which tools you want in your distance learning environment. You will still get to decide if you want to use the whiteboard, the chat room, the private journal, the learning groups, the glossary, or any of the other amazing functions that are literally at your fingertips.

Sometimes when you are working collaboratively with distance learning development teams, it may feel like you're speaking different languages. In fact, you probably are. Software folks think how software thinks, which may not be your particular cup of tea.

The best way to bring out the best in everyone's skill set is to focus the discussion on outcomes rather than functions. Tell your designer, developer, or overall tech guru what outcome you want to create. For example:

Not: Let's include a synchronous chat section.
But: I'd like students to have a secure space where they can have real-time discussions with access to the course readings.

Not:	I saw this cool multimedia thing in a friend's classroom; let's do that.
But:	I have video that I want to be able to play, stop and start, and enable searching. Students will need to access the video both during the real-time session and on their own. Oh, and I want some of the sections of the video to be linked to key sections in the glossary and reserve readings. What do you think we should use?

Be willing to try something new and experimental, but also be firm in pushing your partners to find the simplest solution to your challenge. Does it need a technology-intense solution, or can something low tech do the job? By moving to the lowest possible technology, you give yourself more room to maneuver. Costs and development times decrease, which means it is easier to make changes or updates. Furthermore, from the students' perspective, using the lowest possible technology makes the materials more accessible, physically and psychologically.

Putting the "Process" in the Design Process

By now, it's probably clear that planning and designing a distance learning course requires your brain to multitask. There are so many factors to take into consideration, and the enterprise is further complicated by the fact that many different individuals need to be part of the development process.

Worksheet 3.1 provides a format for group or individual brainstorming. Use or adapt it to ensure you are covering all the critical steps in crafting the design of your distance learning offering. If you are working in a group, use the worksheet to guide your discussion as you move from one section to the next. If you are working on your own, simply follow the organizational structure of the worksheet.

At the end of the brainstorming session, you should have a solid edited list of primary content areas for your course, as well as a long list of possible activities in each area. It's a good idea to come up with more ideas than you can possibly use; go for outlandish, as well as tried-and-true. Let your collaborative partners provide technical input into activities—

Worksheet 3.1   Instructional Design and Planning

Course name (tentative):

Description:

Who are the students? (Refer to Worksheet 2.1)

Where is their pain? What do they most want to get out of the course?

Course goals:

Draft learning objectives:

What are the challenges?

Topic areas:

Activities:

Verbs to use in learning objectives:
• list
• identify
• state
• describe
• define
• solve
• compare and contrast
• operate

your software developer may have a great idea for a virtual simulation, while your graphic designer may have brilliant insight regarding a workbook component.

Figure 3.2 shows what Worksheet 3.1 might look like when completed. Figure 3.3 translates the information graphically as a mind map. You'll see how this is already starting to look like a work plan for building a course, as well as a content outline you can follow to create your instructional content.

You will not hit on the perfect design the first time you try, any more than Henry Ford made it big with his first models. But getting it on paper, talking through the problems and opportunities with others, and working through a process will enable you to design a course that is both exciting and educational for you and your students.

Crafting a Topic Syllabus

The last step of the design stage is to craft a topic syllabus for your course. (Did you wonder if we'd ever get here?) The syllabus should capture all the main areas of the course and lay out the primary pathway through the topics, materials, and activities (see Figure 3.4).

Syllabi for distance learning courses are more complex than the ones you may have used for traditional courses. When I write syllabi for traditional courses, I usually include basic information like required reading, course description, my contact information, a run-down of topics, and time frames for completing assignments. I treat my syllabi for distance learning courses as a contract between the students and me. Everything from participation requirements to grading for specific assignments to an overview of netiquette (online etiquette) expectations goes in the syllabus. All that information makes for a long syllabus, and I also repeat much of the critical information in stand-alone documents that students can access on an as-needed basis. But the time and energy I put into creating detailed, comprehensive syllabi are more than offset by the value of having a single, controlling document to establish the parameters of the course.

For now, though, your draft topic syllabus serves primarily as your content development guide. It will surely change between now and the launch of your course, but at this stage of the process, it tells you and your development team what to write, design, build, and create to construct a distance learning environment.

Course name (tentative):

The "M" Word: What Rabbis need to know about marketing

Synagogue Marketing

Marketing as a Mitzvah

Description:

A five-week online workshop on the basics of synagogue marketing – what it is, how to do it, and what resources you already have so that you don't have to spend a fortune to get results!

Who are the students? (Refer back to the worksheet completed in Chapter 2):

Rabbis (?)

Synagogue staff

Volunteers

> *May have some marketing background; for most this will be the first online course ever*

Where is their pain? What do they most want to get out of the course?

They know they need to be doing something different, but they don't know what. Most think of marketing as equal to advertising – need to start to see it as about relationships and about current members as well as prospective members

They need practical tools so that the process isn't too "heady" or time-consuming. If it's too difficult, expensive, or labor-intensive, they will keep doing what they're doing.

Course goals:

Introduce concepts of strategic marketing

Reorient synagogue to audiences

Learn to tap existing resources

Write and maintain a marketing plan that is practical and measurable

Draft learning objectives:

- *List the three goals of marketing*
- *Identify and characterize internal and external audiences*
- *Apply the course templates to write draft press releases, flyers and notices*
- *Create a practical marketing plan with defined measures of success*
- *Identify existing resources for low-cost and no-cost marketing*
- *Compare and contrast print, electronic and word-of-mouth marketing methods*

Verbs to use in learning objectives:
- list
- identify
- state
- describe
- define
- solve
- compare and contrast
- operate

Figure 3.2   This example of Worksheet 3.1 completed shows what the instructional design team came up with in our initial meetings for Marketing as a Mitzvah, an online workshop to train rabbis, synagogue staff, and volunteers in synagogue marketing.

What are the challenges?
Use of a technology-based platform will be challenging for some participants
Time – everyone is overworked
Concept may be unsettling to many at first – think of synagogues as antithetical to "marketing"

Topic areas:
Definitions of marketing
Understanding Audiences
Public relations
Research and measurement
Copyright
Design
Web and e-communications
Low-cost and no-cost methods
Finding, training and managing volunteers for marketing

Activities:
- Evaluate current marketing tools
- Write a wish list for marketing tools
- Write a volunteer job description
- Research a public relations list
- Craft and implement a survey
- Compare and contrast marketing materials from different organizations
- Conduct a focus group and report back
- Run a brainstorming session on updating and improving the print newsletter
- Journal entries comparing expectations to new knowledge

Figure 3.2   (cont.)

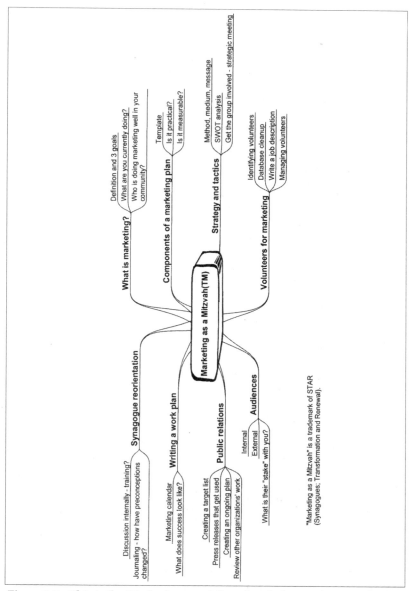

Figure 3.3   *This is the Marketing as a Mitzvah mind map showing the key topics for Marketing as a Mitzvah, as well as potential activities in each of the areas. The mind map also captures insights from our brainstorming session on the needs and characteristics of the audience and other considerations for the course.*

Main topics, with activity ideas for each topic:

1. What is marketing?
    a. List current tool and code for which goal each works towards
    b. Get member feedback via a survey on use of each kind of tool
    c. Gather and analyze marketing materials from other organizations
2. Components of a marketing plan
    a. Fill in a template
    b. Critique a draft plan – what looks like it will work? How can you craft a hypothesis around it?
3. Strategy and tactics
    a. Method, medium, message worksheet
    b. SWOT analysis
    c. Strategic planning session, with discussion guide – conduct the session and report back to the class
4. Identifying volunteers
    a. Database review and cleanup
    b. Networking – you know someone who knows someone
    c. Write a job description
5. Identifying audiences
    a. Review SWOT analysis
    b. Audience "tree"
    c. Member database analysis
6. Public relations
    a. Research media contacts
    b. Use template to write a press release
    c. Gather and analyze press releases from other organizations
7. Workplan and measurement
    a. Complete the marketing calendar
    b. "What is measurement?" worksheet
8. Re-orientation of synagogue
    a. Discussion guide – conduct internal meeting and report back
    b. Journal – how is this concept of marketing different from what you expected?

Figure 3.4   This is an example of a draft of a topic syllabus for Marketing as a Mitzvah.

Chapter 4

Content, Part II: Development

You've survived all that planning; now get ready for the flurry of activity that is content development. (Cue triumphal music.)

Not all distance learning programs will require that the instructor participate in crafting content. Some programs provide detailed content that an instructor must use to teach—lectures, assignments, and even a template syllabus. For example, when I taught at the University of Phoenix, the university had a system of course delivery that provided between 70 and 90 percent of the teaching materials. This approach helped standardize the curriculum across thousands of students and also enabled me to prep a new class in the minimum amount of time.

Many content management software providers also offer libraries of courses that instructors can access "off the shelf" or with minimal customization. Courses are available in a range of topics across the academic and professional spectrum. Some libraries are organized around "reusable learning objects," or RLOs, which instructors can plug into their courses or mix and match to create their course du jour.

Even when working with supplied course materials, however, a distance learning instructor should know what goes into crafting effective, targeted, and engaging content. First, the existence and availability of content is not a guarantee of quality; if you find something you like, you still need to be able to evaluate its quality for your purposes and be able to adapt, improve, or jettison anything that isn't up to your standards. Second, even courses that are terrific right out of the box require instructors to create a bridge between the material and the students—to be the human interface that enables learning experiences. When I taught University of Phoenix courses, I was required to use the course materials exactly as I had been trained to do, but I still had to write my own greetings, provide instructions about how I preferred to receive assignments, write feedback, add supplementary lectures where I perceived a need for more in-depth study, and respond immediately and appropriately to student needs.

So it is possible to be a distance learning instructor and have only a minimal need to create materials, but it's an extremely limiting position to put yourself in. If you have any desire to create unique courses based on your personal skills, experience, and interests, you will eventually need to be able to write and to co-develop the majority of the materials that students will interact with.

Creating content is a daunting task, but it can also be an exhilarating challenge (not entirely unlike writing a book). And the process is iterative: You'll write, teach, rewrite, and re-organize course content, based on what you learned the first time around. In that way, it's quite similar to what you may experience the first few times you teach any new course in a traditional format.

The critical difference, of course, is interface. Whether you are creating printed instructions or animated hands-on simulations, distance instruction means that you have to anticipate student questions and needs before they occur and build both questions and answers into the content itself. Additionally, you must be able to develop materials appropriately for the medium of choice and learn the right balance of textual, visual, and other kinds of information. At the same time, you have to keep in mind and work with the events of instruction discussed in Chapter 3: Capture attention, declare objectives, stimulate recall of prior learning, present content, provide guidance, elicit performance, provide feedback, and enable transfer of skills. And don't forget the specific needs and quirks of your student population, whether those quirks are generational, skill-based, or attitudinal.

You aren't creating the course content so much as you are creating the container for learning experiences, taking into consideration all the different elements that make up that experience. How do students encounter the material? How are their expectations raised? How are they prepared to learn? How are they invited to interact with you, the other students, and the material? How do they learn the criteria for success, and how are they motivated to perform? When I am working on the material for a course, I'm telling a narrative in my head—how Susie and Sam Student join the class, review and interact with the materials, and successfully perform to my rigorous standards.

It's much more complicated than developing a lecture, and it's utterly and completely different from writing an academic paper. Creating content for a distance learning course is more like assuming responsibility for building management (Is it too hot? Too cold? Locked when the students show up? Drinking fountain out of order?) in addition to prepping to teach.

Get It in Writing

Much of this chapter deals with written language for two reasons. First, I am a writer, so I tend to see most challenges as solvable through writing. (My graphic designer friends see most challenges as solvable through visual organization; we make a good team.) But more importantly, written language plays a central role in creating effective distance courses. Written materials, online or off, are a common point of interaction for instructors and students in distance learning.

Among the materials you may regularly be writing are:

- Course descriptions
- Lectures and explanatory materials
- Assignments and instructions
- Feedback to students
- Classroom commentary (in online discussion environments)
- Policy and procedure documents
- Syllabi
- Casual messages to students and colleagues

Writing isn't the only skill required for developing content and interacting with students, but it's one that is often overlooked—and any further development will always benefit a virtual team or distance environment.

Where to Begin?

The course map and draft syllabus you completed in Chapter 3 is the best place to start outlining and identifying the specific tasks and elements you need to create before you will be ready for students. Figure 3.3 shows the course map for "Marketing as a Mitzvah," a five-module professional development course I developed for Synagogues: Transformation and Renewal (STAR) for its work with synagogue professionals and volunteers. Figure 3.4 shows the results of the syllabus-crafting step of our design process, including ideas for activities and important considerations for a single topic within the course. The documents shown in those figures guide me in deciding what material I need to develop a course.

A Quick Peek at the End Result

Before we look at the step-by-step process for developing content, how-ever, let's take a quick look at the end result to see where we're going. (Good distance learning principle: Work with the end in mind!) This brief tour of the construction of the course will clarify how you can use the principles of instructional design, particularly the events of instruction, to develop materials. Instructional events are set in **boldface** throughout:

Figure 4.1 shows the welcome page for Marketing as a Mitzvah. The purpose of this page is to capture the students' **attention** and **inform** them of some of the expectations for the course. "Discussions" indicates that discussion will be part of their work, and "Resource Center" tells them that they will have access to resources. "Weekly Activities" tells them to check a page weekly.

Seem too obvious to be instructionally driven? Consider what might happen to a student who came upon a homepage that only said, "Marketing as a Mitzvah: Click Here to Enter." Who would be brave enough to enter into goodness-knows-what? Who would find the headline interesting enough to capture their attention? The course welcome page provides enough information to stimulate the first two events of instruc-tion while guiding the student into the content.

Figure 4.2 shows one page of lecture content for the same course. Now the events of instruction are embedded in the content itself. The graphic headline at the top of the lecture **captures attention**. The first paragraph is also written to **capture attention** as well as **inform** the students about the topic and objectives of this page. The content is placed in a univer-sally understood context, which **stimulates prior (if unconscious) learn-ing** about what it means to do marketing in a synagogue setting. Then, the text **presents the specific content** that I want to teach in this section

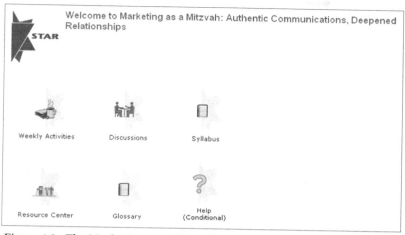

*Figure 4.1   The Marketing as a Mitzvah welcome page captures students'
attention and informs them of course expectations.* [Used with
permission of STAR and JSkyway (www.jskway.org).]

Figure 4.2   This is one page of Marketing as a Mitzvah's lecture content.
[Used with permission of STAR and JSkyway
(www.jskway.org).]

of the course. Near the end of the lecture, I provide the students with specific actions for how they can **"encode" the new information** in their memory and behavior. Finally, the **assignment reiterates encoding** and **elicits performance**.

But it doesn't stop there. After completing the assignment, students are asked to respond in the Discussions section with comments about their results. As a group, we discuss the outcomes of their efforts, **providing feedback,** as well as helping them **transfer and expand the new knowledge** to other areas of their work.

For each element in any course I develop, I consider carefully where it fits within the overall arc of the students' learning experiences and make sure I know where they are within the events of instruction.

Activities First

The path from course map to completed content is simple enough to navigate if you follow a process. (Note that "simple" is not the same as "easy"— this stuff stretches your brain in all sorts of new directions.) Because successful adult learning is predicated on learner-focused, practical, relevant *activities*, they are the first content element I create. Once the activities are in place, I can back up and reflect on what information, knowledge, or conditions students will need to complete the activity successfully.

Pull out those learning objectives. Is there a culminating activity that would enable students to demonstrate their mastery of most or all of the course objectives? Such an activity usually makes an effective final project. Again, consider what is practical and relevant for your students; if they come out of your course with a piece of work they can immediately apply to soothe their pain, you've hit the jackpot.

In Marketing as a Mitzvah, for example, the culminating activity is for the participants to write an actionable, practical, measurable marketing plan for their synagogue. Working backward from the culminating activity, then, I needed to consider what stepping-stone activities would help them complete the final project. Figure 4.3 lists possible activities for each topic area to develop knowledge and skills leading up to the final project. Notice how I've already struck a number of good ideas from the list. For instance, the whole area of volunteer recruiting, while critical to a successful synagogue marketing plan, is too much for this course; I make a note to create some add-on materials the participants could use on their own following the course to help them develop better practices in volunteer recruiting.

Back to Those Learning Objectives

Remember the list of objectives that told us we were going to learn to use the telephone? What do you do with those kinds of objectives to make them effective within your course materials?

You have to inform learners of objectives so that they can be prepared. Clearly communicated objectives also correlate with satisfaction; if students know what they're getting into, they're more likely to be happy with the results.

But you cannot and must not present goofy objectives (like "place calls on hold") to adults and expect them to respect you in the morning! The key to incorporating learning objectives into your course materials is to craft them in a way that connects with the student's emotional commitment to learning. Speak to the pain (ah, that useful pain):

"It's 9 AM on your first day at the job you've been dreaming of. You are set for your first meeting and have your notebook and pen all warmed up and ready to go. But the phone rings. The phone rings? No one has your number yet. You pick up the receiver and state your name with confidence. Wrong number, of course, but the caller wants you to transfer her to *your boss's boss*.

"Not to worry; you've completed the telephone training module, and you can transfer calls! Not bad for your first hour on the job."

It's a lot lengthier than, "You will be able to transfer calls and put callers on hold." But it's also more motivating and more emotionally engaging. Most importantly, it communicates the learning objective without boring the learner.

2.   *Components of a marketing plan*
    a. Fill in a template
    b. ~~Critique a draft plan — what looks like it will work?~~
      ~~How can you craft a hypothesis around it?~~
3.   *Strategy and tactics*
    a. ~~Method, medium, message worksheet~~
    b. SWOT analysis
    c. Strategic planning session, with discussion guide
      – conduct the session and report back to the class
4.   *~~Identifying volunteers~~*
    a. ~~Database review and cleanup~~
    b. ~~Networking — you know someone who knows someone~~
    c. ~~Write a job description~~

Figure 4.3   The revised topic and activity outline for part of Marketing as a Mitzvah lists possible ways for students to develop knowledge and skills leading up to the final project.

    Through a process of review, editing, comparison with the learning objectives, and head scratching, I came up with a final list of two or three activities for each topic area, leading up to the culminating project (Figure 4.4). The process is not perfect for any course, no matter the length or complexity; there are always areas of study I wish we would have time to cover and activities I know students would enjoy that are not directly relevant. My goal, though, is to end up with a final list that includes the right balance of activities to enable the participants to succeed.

    Since activities are where students "get busy," you want to design them to hit the appropriate events of instruction. Activities can help students encode new information, practice skills, and even get feedback, depending on how the activity is designed. One of the activities assigned early in my communications classes was an online grammar review; after completing the mini-quiz, students could immediately see which items they got wrong, as well as view an explanation of the grammatical rule governing the situation. Although I also provided feedback on grammar rules once the student submitted the results to me, the student received immediate feedback right in the context of the activity itself.

Main topics, with activity ideas for each topic:

1. *What is marketing?*
   a. *List current tool and goal codes each*
   b. *Write volunteer job description as an exercise in internal marketing*
   c. *Identify and develop enhancement plan for one low-cost or no-cost marketing tactic*
2. *Strategy, then tactics*
   a. *SWOT analysis*
   b. *Write an evite or web-based invitation*
   c. *Complete marketing planning worksheet*
3. *Understanding audiences*
   a. *Level of committed worksheet*
   b. *Information sleuth project—identify information repositories and come up with three new ways to use each*
   c. *Unaffiliated outreach—using levels worksheet to identify opportunities*
4. *Synagogue re-orientation*
   a. *Write an internal communication plan—getting the synagogue on board with marketing*
   b. *Write an external communication plan—getting the community and seekers to know who you are*
   c. *Journal—how is this concept of marketing different from what you expected?*

Figure 4.4   This is the final topic and activity outline for part of Marketing as a Mitzvah.

Core Content Development

With the activities established, I back up a little further. What information do participants need in order to complete the activity? Here is where I put the bulk of my time and energy—writing the lectures, finding the readings and resources, lining up guest presenters—to provide students with the knowledge they need to learn. I call this portfolio of material the core content.

When I wrote the first edition of this book, it was much more difficult than it is today to create, store, and stream video at a reasonable cost, and most core content was likely to be in the form of a written lecture. Today, many more instructors (perhaps even the majority) can and are incorporating video components—recorded "talking heads" lectures, demos, or recorded presentations—in their core content. Still, written lectures of 500 to 1,500 words are an important part of an instructor's portfolio because they are flexible, easily shared, and simple to change or update. Furthermore, for many instructors who are new to distance learning, written lectures are also a relatively comfortable place to start.

Tips for Writing Lectures

Writing lectures for distance learning is only nominally like writing lectures for traditional delivery. Distance learning lectures involve more than delivering core material; they are also the primary way students get to know the instructor. In a traditional classroom, students have a larger pool of data on which to make decisions about your competence; maybe your lectures are dense and convoluted, but you can really answer questions in a clear, cogent manner. Or you may talk in a monotone but make up for it with fabulous multimedia presentations. On the other hand, in a distance learning environment, if you bomb your lectures, you lose credibility, sink motivation, and make your whole job harder.

Telling Tales

The lessons of your lectures—and indeed of all your core content—will make the most sense to students when they are embedded in real-world situations drawn from your own experiences. Using narratives and anecdotes to draw readers in and illustrate the truth of your knowledge is an excellent way to engage students in the lecture material.

Lacking real-world experience in an area of study can be a stumbling block, but there are ways around it. Conduct and report on an interview with someone who has the experience; draw on mythology or allegory to illustrate your point; tell a story of a counterexample—a situation in which the target knowledge would have been helpful but wasn't present. Narrative is one of the fastest and easiest ways to get students emotionally and psychologically committed to learning what you present.

Short Sentences

If you do nothing else to your lectures, shorten the sentences: subject, verb, predicate. In most cases, students will be reading your lectures on a computer screen, whether you deliver them via email or within the context of a web-based course platform. Long sentences are difficult to follow, particularly on a screen. It's a stylistic challenge to find ways to compress your sentences, but it pays off by enabling students to wrestle with the meat of your ideas rather than with convoluted clauses.

Structure for Motivation

Remember that motivation is critical to success, so build motivation right into your lectures and other written content. Students may well be printing out and referring to your lectures regularly, thinking about them, and carrying the content into other areas of their lives. You can use your lectures to motivate, instruct, and inspire your students to keep going.

The following steps, when integrated into the flow of your documents, will spark and nurture motivation:

- *We are alike:* Motivational documents begin by establishing common ground between writer and reader. Make it clear that you can see the world from the students' perspective and that you've walked in their shoes.

- *Change is possible:* Bring home the idea that the status quo is not the only alternative. Remind students that the discomfort they feel in working with new ideas, skills, and concepts is the pain that accompanies growth.

- *The tools of change are available:* Immediately after reinforcing motivation by reminding students of the end goal, present the main concepts—the tools of change.

- *The outcome will be satisfying:* Don't leave the reader without pushing the motivation button one more time. Tell a story or demonstrate the positive impact realized when someone just like them follows through with a mastery of new skills.

Live or Die by PowerPoint

Presentation software (the most common of which is PowerPoint) is responsible for a variety of evils visited upon audiences. Slides packed with too much text, kitschy animated clip art, and poor choices of colors and fonts, as well as instructors who try to let the presentation do the instructing, are only some of the errors that turn a presentation into living death.

Effective presentation design requires professional skill, so if resources permit, get a designer to help. If you don't have access to professional help, however, you can still make important improvements to your presentations. Lots of sites offer tips and examples of effective slide design and are worth a bit of research to improve core content.

Lessons From the Copywriter

When I'm not doing one of the million other things in my professional life, I'm writing copy for a variety of professional uses. "Copy" was originally an advertising term, referring to the written text that appears in sales and marketing materials. These days, it's more common to hear writers talk about "developing content" rather than "writing copy," in part because advertising has a bad rap for being fluff at best and untrustworthy at worst.

I prefer the word "copy," however, because copy does something that content never can: Copy motivates a change in behavior, while content is static. Content is about the topic, but copy is about the reader. The motivational structure for lectures is just one example of how your words do more than communicate course information. Remember that motivation is at the heart of successful distance learning programs; write *copy*, not just content.

What does this mean in practical terms?

- *Use headlines:* Especially for material designed to be read electronically, headlines help break up the page and enable readers to identify key information. Readers tend to scan material, and headlines force their eyeballs to slow down.

- *Keep it short and sweet:* A two-column printed page can handle about 600 words without looking crowded. An email preview pane displays approximately 10 lines of plain text. A standard web screen looks clear and inviting with 200–400 words on it, depending on layout, typeface, and graphic elements.

- *Be real and accessible:* Work toward a written style that approximates your speaking voice (unless you are a naturally stuffy/uptight person; in that case, loosen up in your writing, and possibly in your life). Define words that your students might not be familiar with. Your writing should invite them in, not keep them out.

- *Involve the reader:* Use "you" and "your" and write as if you were having a one-on-one conversation with the person you are trying to reach.

- *Tell a story:* Humans are highly story-oriented; narratives are a great way to reach their emotions and get them committed to learning the material.

- *Write in active voice:* Avoid "there is" and "there are" constructions.

- *Pare it down:* Say what you need using the fewest words.

- *Be specific:* Use examples from your own experience that your students will relate to. (This approach also helps you "be real.")

- *Remember to motivate:* Sometimes subtly, sometimes with a sledgehammer, motivate your students to push forward because of the outcome they want to achieve.

- *Get feedback:* Share written materials with several people, preferably with members of the target audiences, and ask them to highlight anything that doesn't work for them.

Build on Core Content With Discussion and Activities

Since you are developing core content in direct relationship to the activities you've selected, you should find it relatively easy to draw direct links between core content and the activities. Place the instructions or an introduction to the activity in the same location as the core content and make the links explicit. Figure 4.5 shows an example of the end of a lecture and the start of an assignment for Marketing as a Mitzvah; this sample has the right amount of "bridging" information—perhaps more than you may think you need. Remember that you need to put all the information *in writing* that you might otherwise clarify verbally. Even if you are using a synchronous meeting or event to deliver the content and then explain the assignment, put the extra information right in the documentation.

Similarly, you will need to create discussion questions that build on the core content and make direct connections for students with their personal, practical experiences. For example, here is a sample discussion question I used in one of my introductory writing classes:

> Chapter 1 in *A Writer's Workshop* describes many different ideas and approaches to starting the writing process. Describe your own writing process—the steps you take when you sit down to complete a writing project. What works well for you? What would you like to change about your process? What is the hardest part for you? The easiest? What new ideas did you get from reading this chapter about how you could change or enhance your own writing process?

Discussion built around students' personal experiences, linked with the concepts presented in the core content, provide opportunities for learners to reflect on themselves within the context of the course materials. It also creates the potential for livelier discussions as students from different backgrounds and environments start to compare and contrast their experiences.

Instructional Events

Written lectures need to move readers through the events of instruction and prepare them to engage in the next event through activities. Lectures and other core content are the natural place to gain attention, inform the student about objectives, stimulate prior recall, and present content. When these elements are linked with activities and followed up with individual and group feedback, reflection, and synthesis, they carry the learner all the way through the instructional process.

Data Activation

Research can only benefit you if you act on what you learn. Information in a file or in an individual's head is not actionable! Start to make the understanding and use of information a regular part of your discussions around synagogue events and how you plan.

You have new programs, new events, new audiences to reach, existing relationships that you could deepen? what information would make it easier to do so? Chances are, you already have in place a mechanism or tool for getting and using that information.

Assignment # 3-2: Info Sleuth

This assignment takes a bit of sleuthing at the synagogue. Your mission: discover the ways your synagogue collects *and uses* information. Make a list of all your information-gathering opportunities in a table like the following (create your own table, based on this model):

Information gathering	Frequency	How it is used
Membership database	Annually, and as new members join	Mailings and voting, primarily
Program evaluation	Following every program	Planning upcoming events and gathering ideas for new events

Now pick one of these information gathering opportunities to think through creatively. How could it work harder for you? How else might you apply the information you gather through this method? Is there an opportunity to go deeper with this tool by adding a component like a focus group or a survey? Do your evaluations need a bit of tweaking? Should you add some fields to your membership database?

Post your ideas on how you can enhance and leverage at least one existing information resource in the Discussion classroom in the thread titled "Assignment 3-2: Info Sleuth"

Figure 4.5   The bridge from lecture to activity for Marketing as a Mitzvah is clarified in writing. [Used with permission of STAR and JSkyway (www.jskway.org).]

Challenges Unique to Distance Instruction

Much of the information presented so far would actually be just as helpful in preparing a traditional course as it is for a distance learning program. Many of us who have the privilege of teaching never received formal training in instruction. Having a process for identifying what to cover, how to structure assignments, and how to pace the progress provides us with a method for activities we've been largely doing by instinct. An ability to write for both instruction and motivation can be invaluable, even if you are delivering lectures orally before a live audience rather than at a distance. An emphasis on practical activities and learner needs helps us move beyond our expertise to focus on the experience of the students.

Yet distance learning does create its own requirements for content development. The rest of this chapter will lay out the special issues and opportunities associated with creating distance learning instructional materials.

The Expectation of Interactivity

In the introduction, I said it plainly: The core of learning is interaction. In creating materials for distance learning instruction, you have to build the expectation of interactivity directly into the content itself.

What does interactivity really mean? "Click here" is not any more interactive than turning the page of a textbook. Materials that are interactive change when a learner touches them. They're even better when they require learners to employ higher thinking to get the result they expect out of the interaction.

Getting students involved with their learning is the secret of success. When you create materials that raise the expectation of interactivity, you are setting the stage for further student involvement and commitment.

A simple yet effective model of interactive course material is a study guide that requires the user to fill in the blanks in a series of sentences based on information in the readings or in lectures. By writing down the information, students are forced to incorporate the message physically and visually.

Simulations and games are also great forms of interactivity, though they can be expensive and time-consuming to create. Similarly, and less expensively, online surveys or polling systems can engage learners and at the same time provide them with food for thought. For example, a leadership development program I consulted on used an online survey made up of yes/no questions on muddy topics in ethics, fundraising, and nonprofit management. The participants were forced to select a yes or no answer for situations that were definite maybes. When they completed the survey, they were able to view the aggregated responses of the entire class; what followed was a series of highly engaged discussions in the classroom as participants struggled together over the issues. Because of the way they had already interacted with the material, the participants turned what could have been a theoretical discussion into a highly personal one.

Single-Purpose Documents

The complete and unabridged syllabus (which we'll write before finishing this chapter) is the North Star for any course. With all the information relating to performance, deadlines, topics, assignments, and course policies in one place, I have a single place to direct students when problems or questions arise. However, as a communication tool, a syllabus of 50-plus pages is unwieldy. Much of the most important information, including participation requirements, deadlines, major projects, and netiquette policies, I also provide in stand-alone, single purpose documents.

Single-purpose documents are easier for students (and instructors) to find when needed. They're also a lot easier to absorb. Apply this same concept to other forms of your communication with students; if you email or mail instructions, keep to three or four items at the most. Find other tools within your learning environment (Posting classroom announcements? Your signature line in email communications?) to vary the ways you communicate with students. Variety, coupled with single-purpose documents, keeps students from tuning you out.

Repetition, Repetition, Repetition

"The assignment and the deadline were clearly listed in the syllabus. How come no one seemed to know how to do the project or when it was due?"

You will need to repeat information and instructions in a distance learning environment far more often than you might think necessary. For most of my classes, I include all assignment information right in the syllabus; I also highlight assignments in a weekly posting of What's New. A major or complex assignment will also be detailed in a stand-alone resource document, sometimes complete with FAQs. And I still expect to get several clarifying (or even totally clueless) questions in discussion with students about the assignment.

Why the repetition? Can't they read the syllabus?

Consider a traditional classroom with a term paper due midway through the course:

- The instructor puts basic information about the assignment in the syllabus.

- In the first class meeting, a student asks about major assignments for the course, creating an opportunity to highlight the assignment and talk about its requirements.

- During class discussion, a student mentions a topic she is considering for her paper. The instructor comments on the topic and reiterates the timeline for completion.

- Several weeks before the assignment is due, the instructor devotes class time to elaborating on the project and soliciting questions.

- A student emails the instructor with a question about another assignment; the instructor responds and asks how the research for the term paper is coming along.

That's a lot of repetition, with a lot of opportunities for give-and-take between instructor and students to clarify goals and requirements. An instructor has to create the same kinds of opportunities for repetition in a distance learning environment, taking into account that, in contrast with a traditional classroom, much of the information will be distributed either 1) in writing (and digitally delivered writing at that) or 2) over the phone, reducing the points of input in the exchange. You can't see the eye-rolling, glazed expressions, or naked panic. You have to find other ways to capture that kind of data about your learners so you can help them.

Nonlinear Approaches

Distance learning programs enable students to enter and move through the material in unexpected ways. Depending on the degree to which you want to encourage this kind of experimentation (with some audiences, you don't really have a choice—Millennials will do it no matter what you tell them), you need to keep student navigational behavior in mind when you create your content.

For example, be sure that key terms are always defined the first time they appear in *any* course document, not just what you think of as the *first* appearance. (You can minimize the hassle of this requirement, at least in an online environment, by linking key terms to a glossary database. That way, no matter where students find the term, they can always look up the meaning if necessary.)

Thinking about your information in a nonlinear fashion is a bit of a mental trick at first. After writing for websites for many years, I do it almost unconsciously. I remember that when I was first learning how to do work with information in a nonlinear fashion, I found it helpful to print out and shuffle my content, pick up a section at random, and see if I could locate myself within the material. If I had trouble, I knew that it was still too linear. I would rewrite the section so that a user entering at that point could make an informed decision about what to do next.

For most of my courses, I separate content into weekly modules that build on one another in a decidedly linear manner. Within each module, though, I aim to make each component stand on its own. I have a preferred path through the material, but a learner who chooses a different path, for whatever reason, will still be able to complete the work.

Customizable Pathways

Similar to nonlinear content, customizable pathways through the content enable learners with different learning styles, interests, and backgrounds to create the most effective learning experience possible. I often create two or more forms of an activity or an assignment—one that is largely text-based (remember, I'm a writer and a verbal learner) and the others to appeal to learners who prefer other kinds of activities. Since I've asked students to complete a self-assessment about their learning styles, they are equipped to pick the option that best suits their preferred style.

Another way to create customizable pathways is by considering a learner's background or existing skill set. My communications and creative writing classes mixed English as a Second Language (ESL) students with native speakers. I learned to develop additional materials and resources for the ESL students so they could tackle the material regardless of their language skills.

Marketing as a Mitzvah also has a subtle element of learner-based customization. The learners in this course are organized into teams of three individuals from each participating synagogue, usually a rabbi, a staff member, and a volunteer. Several activities and discussion topics were geared specifically for each type of participant—for instance, a reflective journal for the rabbi, a marketing budget project for the staff member, and a resource development challenge for the volunteer. This approach allowed everyone to get what was the most personally and professionally relevant from the course while still keeping everyone in the same workshop environment.

Reusable Learning Objects

Once you've started teaching a few distance learning classes, you may find that some introductory elements of your courses are more or less the same, regardless of the medium or the type of course you are teaching. Make life easier by creating your own library of reusable learning objects (RLOs). For instance, my "getting started with distance learning" document rarely changes, regardless of the particular offering; I almost always have some students who are new to distance learning, and even those who have participated in distance learning offerings still benefit from my introduction, which lays out *my* expectations for participation, assignments, etc. Similarly, my netiquette document is the same for every one of my online courses. As you prepare classes, consider which of the materials you are developing that may be applicable with few or no changes in additional courses.

No matter what blend of tools you are using to pull it off, distance learning requires a great deal of documentation to be successful. The written word becomes the primary connection among instructor, content, and students, whether it's an emailed assignment, a syllabus, or the contents of an online lecture or presentation. The words you use, your style, and even the layout of your pages or screens will make a difference in how well you bridge the distance between instructor and class.

Course Content RLOs

In addition to reusable introductory materials, you may find that you can reuse portions of your core content portfolio for other courses. Be cautious, however, about adopting a strictly "cut and paste" approach to RLOs. Course content created for one type of situation may not be directly applicable to another; if you change the types of learners, the medium of interaction, or the goals of the program, you may need to revise the content completely in order to satisfy the new requirements.

Even where you can't reuse course content verbatim (your own or that provided by a course library), you can save yourself a lot of time by adapting rather than starting from scratch. Evaluate course material for its reuse potential and enjoy the savings in time and cost that repurposing can provide. Just don't be surprised when even small changes in the audience or desired outcomes for a course demand significant shifts in the presentation of content.

Special Considerations for Digital Platforms

When I was researching the first edition of this book in 2005, the web was still emerging as a fundamental part of how organizations operated and how education was delivered. At the time, elearning guru Michael Allen shared this insight with me in an interview: "The web may be the worst thing that could have happened to distance learning. Eventually, it will be the best thing that could have happened, but for now, it's resulting in a lot of poor instruction. Developers are putting stuff up on the web that doesn't work for instruction and learning."

Web-based learning resources and practices have certainly improved, but there are always new complications. The current evolution toward mobile delivery of content means that hard-won knowledge about web-based delivery must be relearned for a mobile environment (e.g., smaller screens, different operating systems, and variable data capacity). If your content might be accessed via mobile device, as well as the web, you have a lot of additional considerations regarding format, length, style and delivery.

Even without these complications, the digital environment requires that special attention be given to its impact on content development.

Visual Content

The web is a powerfully visual medium, yet too often content is text-oriented. Reading web-based text is tiring for the eyeballs, and results in lowered concentration and reduced retention of the information. If your users need to scroll through more than two pages of material, you need to break it up more.

Online readers naturally scan material rather than reading every word. Write, design, and implement web-based material that students can scan for key information and then read more closely later to fully understand. Using headlines, icons, and other elements that stop the scanning process will give readers visual clues about where and how to enter and work with your content.

Screen Design

"Keep it simple" is a good motto for creating web-based classroom experiences. Overloading the page with information, action elements, graphics, and options actually taxes the learner's short-term memory and thus can negatively affect performance and retention.

Use a good-sized font, colors that are easy to view, and a consistent layout for each page within your course. If users are squinting to read the material or trying to re-orient themselves every time they view a different page, they're likely to become impatient and dissatisfied with the experience!

Presentations

The temptation is always there: Just take your presentations, which you've lovingly developed and delivered to rave reviews, and put them up on the web ... *voilà*, instant content!

Nope. It doesn't work. Presentations are not the same as digital learning materials. Wholesale copying from a presentation to the web is like filming an actor reading a novel out loud and calling it a movie version of the book. Content created for one medium needs to be adapted and changed in order to succeed in another medium.

If you are tempted to create or reuse presentations for online courses, consider what the learning outcome of that particular component is instead. Usually, there's a more elegant way to achieve it than by inserting something created for another environment.

Digital and Online Resources

Any class can incorporate digital and online resources into the learning experience, but elearning programs have a unique opportunity to turn the web into a virtual library, field trip, and scavenger hunt. The use of live links, online resource collections, and other web components can make your online classroom reach beyond itself. As you do so, though, be mindful of copyright implications; instructional materials on the web are not free tools you can use with impunity.

High Time for Collaboration

"Do what you do best and hire the rest." This is a basic survival technique of independent professionals. Sure, I *could* learn HTML and database management on top of developing, marketing, and teaching my courses, but when would I have time to do my other work, sleep, exercise, enjoy my family, or take the occasional nap?

When implementing a web-based course, I always work with others who can help me create content, think through the right web-based solution for a pedagogical challenge, and get beyond my own experience so I can better serve students. I simply don't have an interest in pursuing some areas; I doubt I could ever be good at others, even if I had all the time in the world to put into them. I'm fortunate to work with great professionals who care as much about software, web development, and course management as I care about teaching. Although collaboration can add yet another layer of complexity to a project, in my experience it always results in a better outcome.

Working With Tools

Course management systems like Blackboard and Moodle are designed to make it easy for online instructors to create, implement, and manage feature-rich distance learning courses. These environments offer variety, robust tools, references, and course materials. They also involve steep learning curves. When you teach on a course management system—particularly the first few times—allow extra time to learn how to master all those controls and options, not to mention time to get your materials uploaded to the tool, proofread, and tested.

It's also a good idea to create a learner's guide to the platform itself so that incoming students have a useful, course-specific reference to the features and applications within the system. The platform vendor may have a guide you can customize, so be sure to ask.

Take a Deep Breath and Jump

You will never be truly, entirely ready to create your first distance learning course. At some point, you have to simply take a deep breath and jump in.

By this point, your brain may be overloaded with plans, ideas, and questions. Take your topic syllabus and revise it based on what you actually created for content. Then fill in the rest of the syllabus to create the document that will serve as the contract between you and your students. Lay out exactly what you expect and what they can expect of you. It will be frighteningly long, and it will take about twice as long as you expected the first time you do it, but a comprehensive syllabus is a cornerstone of creating an environment of trust and clarity for you and your students. Worksheet 4.1 provides a framework for creating your syllabus.

Beta Testing

Just because you're jumping in doesn't mean you have to do it without a life jacket. Find ways to test and validate the course you've worked so hard to develop before bringing in the students. Invite a recent student and a prospective student to review the course and provide feedback. Recent learners are still in touch with what they enjoyed about their experience, as well as what they wish it had included. Prospective learners are the true test case—the ones who will let you know if what you've created will work for your target student.

Sometimes testing isn't possible, of course—you'll always run into situations with impossible deadlines. Your first students may also be your "beta testers." As you teach a course, particularly the first time, keep some working versions of all your content handy so you can make notes about what you want to change or enhance the next time around.

Worksheet 4.1   Complete Syllabus

Complete this syllabus worksheet to be sure you are covering all the critical areas for a distance-learning syllabus.

I. Administrative Information

Course Name:
Schedule:
       Dates:
       Synchronous sessions:
       Asynchronous access:
Instructor:
Contact information: (email)   (phone)
Availability (include time zone):
Alternative contacts:
Prerequisites:
Required reading:
Required resources:
Baseline technology:

II. Course Description

Narrative description:
Topics:
Learning objectives:
Successful outcomes:

III. Grading and Evaluation

Worksheet 4.1   (cont.)

Criteria:
Expectations for returning feedback:
Calendar for due dates:

IV. Course Policies

Class access:
Attendance:
Participation:
Netiquette:
Acceptable formats:
Late assignments:
Feedback:
Plagiarism statement:
Privacy statement:
Grievance procedures:

V. Group Work

Creation of working groups:
Group project requirements:

VI. Detailed Topics and Activities

[Create a section of the syllabus for each of your topic areas]

Topic:
Objectives:
Reading and prework:
Individual assignments:
     Activity descriptions and due dates:
     Instructions for completion and submission:
Group assignments:
     Activity descriptions and due dates:
     Instructions for completion and submission:

Summary of Deliverables for Topic:

Individual/Group	What?	Where?	When?
Indicate individual or group work	*Deliverable element*	*Where should students put completed work?*	*Deadline for full credit*

Budgeting Time

How much time does it take to prepare a distance learning class? This is always one of the first questions I'm asked when I'm talking with a new or prospective distance learning instructor. The answer, of course, is, "It depends." It depends on the format of the course, how much content you are covering, what the expectations of the incoming students are, the kind of delivery system you are using, the amount of existing material you can reuse and revise, and how much time you have, since projects will almost always expand to fill whatever space you give them on your calendar.

There's no doubt that preparing for a distance learning course takes more time than preparing for a traditional course, even if you are using low-tech or no-tech approaches to delivery. The checklist in Worksheet 4.2 may look a bit daunting, but it will help you organize your time and effort throughout course preparation.

On the upside, however, all this preparation pays off by freeing up your attention in the classroom so you can focus on the students. In a traditional class, I'm lecturing and leading discussions; I'm thinking as much about what I need to say next (and hoping I don't forget anything) as I am about what the students need. In distance learning programs, by the time I get into the "classroom," I've already said what I need to say; I can devote all my energy and attention to interacting with students, guiding them to the materials they most need, engaging them, motivating them, and responding to their questions and insights.

And that makes a great segue into the next chapter—what an instructor needs to do to actively manage the distance classroom, encouraging and guiding the learning process for the students.

Worksheet 4.2   Complete Content Development Checklist

- ❑ Complete instructional design process (Chapter 3)
- ❑ Draft topic syllabus (Chapter 3)
    - ❑ List potential activities for each topic (Chapter 3)
- ❑ Refine learning goals for course—what does success look like?
- ❑ Refine learning objectives
- ❑ Refine topic list
- ❑ Select and develop culminating activity for course
    - ❑ What do students need to be able to do before they can do that activity?
    - ❑ Select and develop "stepping-stone" activities
    - ❑ Make final list of 1 to 3 activities in each topic area
    - ❑ Cover range of learning styles with activities—check for the following:
        - ❑ Verbal activities
        - ❑ Visual activities
        - ❑ Kinesthetic activities
        - ❑ Aural activities
        - ❑ Social activities
        - ❑ Solitary activities
        - ❑ Logical activities
    - ❑ Compare to learning objectives
- ❑ What do students need to know in order to be able to complete this activity?
- ❑ Develop core content
    - ❑ Write lectures
    - ❑ Discuss multimedia and Web-based tools with collaborative partners
    - ❑ Develop timeline and budgets for materials that need to be developed externally
    - ❑ Identify other resources
        - ❑ Library
        - ❑ Web materials
        - ❑ Books
        - ❑ Articles
        - ❑ Guest speakers
        - ❑ Video
        - ❑ Audio
        - ❑ Other
- ❑ Write activity instructions and bridging material
- ❑ Evaluate content for nonlinear pathways and customization potential
- ❑ Write detailed syllabus, including final topics, activities, assignments, and policy information
- ❑ Write or pull and adapt standard and stand-alone documentation (e.g., welcome, netiquette, participation requirements, learning team instructions, etc.)
- ❑ Implement content (e.g., design and lay out, upload to Web platform, create digital files, etc.)
- ❑ Proofread and test content
- ❑ Review course for consistency, tone, usability
- ❑ Test with students, if possible

Chapter 5

Time to Go to Class

What does it mean to manage a classroom within the context of distance learning? It's as critical in distance learning as it is in a traditional classroom for an instructor to maintain gentle (and at times forceful) control over the formal learning environment. Perhaps even more so: Distance learning students are looking to their instructors to create order from what appears to be chaos and to help them feel as connected as they do in traditional classrooms. Students too are comparing distance learning to an expected norm. How the instructor manages their classroom experience makes an enormous difference in their willingness and ability to learn in a new environment.

But what are the parameters of a classroom when instructors and students are out of earshot? Where is it located? What are its requirements and character? The following definition is a helpful starting point for thinking about the instructor's role in the classroom, regardless of the medium of the course:

> **Definition of the Classroom:** The classroom is the designated space in which all three of the critical interactions of learning take place: interaction with peers, content, and instructor. The classroom is under the guidance and authority of the instructor, who is responsible for creating a culture of learning and exchange, risk-taking, inquiry, and collaboration, as well as setting and communicating the criteria for successful performance.

Some forms of distance learning (such as self-paced, self-contained training programs, tutorials, and the like) do not involve a classroom; they may involve instructors who respond individually to a student's input, but they do not require an instructor to manage the activity in a classroom environment. For such programs to have much depth or value beyond the development of discrete skill sets, however, requires extraordinary expense. In most cases, the cost-effective solution in which students need to expand beyond their own experience, think critically, and master concepts and skills is to create a classroom environment of some type—even a simple listserv, live webinar, or discussion board—and make it a central component of the distance learning program. Whenever that environment is implemented, an instructor needs to know how to manage it and maximize its instructional value.

One of the most common misconceptions and concerns of prospective distance learning students is that their experience will be impoverished by minimal contact with an instructor. Yet instructor contact can be more intimate and rewarding in a distance learning environment than a traditional environment, provided the instructor understands how to use the classroom to connect one-on-one as well as with the group.

Instructors too may mistakenly believe that distance learning requires little skill in classroom management. Especially in the wake of the hours of preparation prior to launching a course, instructors may expect (or at least hope) that the classroom can largely run itself. Early efforts in computer-mediated education tried to move in that direction, in fact, but the results yielded disappointingly poor learning experiences for students. Guess what? Students need instructors!

The classroom opportunity for interchange with a living, breathing instructor allows students to grapple on a deeper level with the content of a course. The give-and-take between instructor and students offers up the teaching moments when a good instructor can open up a whole new way of thinking for a student.

The idea of give-and-take is critical: Interaction between student and instructor means that you too will be learning from the exchange. This learning might help you enhance your course materials, or it may suggest a whole new area of study in which to begin developing a distance learning program. Interaction will make a resounding impact on how you teach, what you teach, and even why you teach.

What follows are key tips and best practices for managing the distance learning environment.

Strive for Predictability

Can you imagine how confusing it would be if your traditional class met in a different location every session and each location had a radically different atmosphere? If you met one week in a comfy coffee shop and the next in a sterile lab, what kind of expectations would you be creating for your students? Or imagine how your students would react if during one class session you were gregarious and outgoing, and the next you sat in stony, unblinking silence. Your students would probably clam up, waiting for more predictable cues from you as to what you were looking for from them.

Predictability creates the necessary conditions for learning and exchange. Without it, your students will put their creative and intellectual energy into figuring out your expectations rather than mastering the material. Until students trust you, they are unteachable; trust is predicated upon predictability.

You can create predictability in a number of ways. Detailed, sensible policies set out at the start of a class (about participation, deadlines, and other requirements) create predictability. You can focus on the consistency of your messages by the tone of your documents, the look and feel of your materials, even the organization of the course documentation. Does the font suddenly change from Times New Roman to Arial? Do the colors on your classroom webpage change from day to day and from page to page without rhyme or reason? Students may not even consciously notice these differences, yet they accumulate in the students' "perception banks." These perception banks delay the process by which students get to know the learning environment and settle down to do the work of learning. In your final edits (as noted in the checklist in Worksheet 4.2, at the end of Chapter 4), hunt down inconsistencies in the execution of your course content.

In the classroom, have and communicate a relatively predictable schedule for your own availability and involvement in the course. If you are highly visible and chatty for three or four days of asynchronous discussion and then disappear without a trace for a week, your students won't know what to expect of you or what you truly expect of them. Certainly emergencies come up, but when they do, you need to communicate with your students about what they can expect from you in order for the relationship—and the classroom—to work.

Life Happens

A couple of summers ago, as I was working on weekly feedback for the students in a communications course, I went
out early in the evening to walk down to the local convenience store. My daughter and I had our taste buds set for ice
cream. Somehow, stepping off the curb into the street, I
twisted my foot badly. Despite the shooting pain, I limped
down the block to fulfill our cravings before limping home.

Within an hour, the pain had intensified, and I was sure
I had broken something. During the two hours I spent in the
urgent care waiting room, I graded a few papers; two hours
later, I was home and icing a bad sprain.

Knowing that there was no way I could get detailed
feedback to students by my usual deadline, I posted a message to them in the classroom:

Subject: A funny thing happened on the way to the ice
cream shop ...

Just when you think you've mastered the art of walking, a
curb jumps in your face and trips you up. I'm back from several hours at the urgent care, with my ankle tightly wrapped
and a pile of half-graded papers next to me on the couch.
Please know that I am working as quickly as I can to complete feedback and grading on last week's work, but I will
not be able to return it to you for another 24 hours. I will
also be absent from the classroom during this period so that
I can focus on feedback. My apologies ...

P.S. We still managed to get to the ice cream shop and back;
a girl's gotta have priorities!

My students appreciated the note explaining the delay,
as well as the humanness of my message. Even the class
renegade dropped me a note to let me know he understood my predicament. I met my new deadline without
compromising the quality of the feedback.

Even when you're being predictable, you still have room to be flexible with your own schedule; some weeks you might feel like managing the classroom at 2 AM (Insomnia? Just fed the baby?) rather than your typical 10 AM time slot. Just be sure your students know about the shift so that they can adapt.

Be Prepared

More than half of this book deals with preparing for your distance learning classroom, and that's not accidental. Distance instruction requires hours of preparation. Still, in the classroom itself, you have to be prepared. Know your syllabus, your resources, and how to access your support system. Students will have questions about where to find materials and assignments, how to contact technical support, and where to find information for that assignment due next week (or the one due yesterday). Good familiarity with the nuts and bolts of the course will help you respond quickly so that you can all get back to learning.

If you recently developed the course you are about to teach, preparation should be pretty simple, since it's all fresh. However, if you are teaching a course that someone else developed, or if you are dusting off a course you haven't taught in awhile, take time before the students arrive to familiarize yourself with its requirements and components.

It's also a good idea to have someone else prepared to take over if needed. After years of self-employment, I've learned to have backup coverage for time-sensitive and critical projects. What happens to your class if, heaven forbid, you have an intimate encounter with the radiator grille of a school bus? It's like writing a will—no one wants to imagine *what if*, but you owe it to your students and your classroom to consider what options you have available if you are suddenly out of commission during a course period.

Plan for the Inevitable

If you are using technology to deliver your course, know this: Something will not work as expected. It might be as minor as losing access to email for an hour or two. It might be as major as a series of hurricanes blowing out all the phone and internet connections for your 10 students on the Atlantic Coast (been there, done that). It might even be something internal to the course: a bug that goes undetected in courseware until you suddenly have 50 students trying to access an activity. When technology is involved, even the most redundant systems can fail.

You have to think on your feet in a distance classroom, just as you would in a traditional one. When disruptions of this nature occur, your No. 1 resource is always your creativity and good humor. Screaming at the monitor will not solve the problem. Screaming at your web developer will only create a new set of problems. Don't get mad; get creative. You may need to:

- Send materials via fax or snail mail that were supposed to be available via email or the web.

- Extend deadlines or even the length of the course.

- Accept alternative, equivalent work from students. For example, you might allow them to complete a group project individually or turn an individual project into a team effort.

- Substitute different activities and learning experiences for the ones you had planned. For instance, turn an online research project into one that students can complete at a brick-and-mortar library.

For your own sanity and the smooth operation of your classroom, find a way to manage the technical hiccups without losing your sense of perspective or your temper.

Train the Students to Your Expectations

Because distance learning is a new environment for so many students, instructors need to attend to some basic training and handholding about expectations in the classroom. Prior to launching a class, be sure your policy documents and class guidelines are clear and comprehensive. Everything—including netiquette, assignments, deadlines, participation, and more—should be laid out in both your syllabus and in stand-alone documents.

It's not enough to simply give students these resources and documents, however. Chances are that one-quarter of your students will read them thoroughly, half will skim them, and the rest will ignore them entirely. Although my participation guidelines are described in my syllabi, detailed in stand-alone documents, and reiterated in the first few days in the classroom, I still have students who are surprised when I inform them that they haven't met the minimum requirements. Training students to understand and perform to your expectations requires a bit of creativity and persistence. Here are some methods you can try:

- *"Helpful hints" messages:* Incorporate an opportunity to provide brief instruction on some element of classroom life in a classroom posting, an email, or prior to leading a teleclass session. For example, when I led a recent teleclass component of a professional training program, I started with a brief reminder of how to access our online asynchronous discussion and asked two students who had been successful with the tool to comment on their usage (a nifty bit of peer-to-peer coaching and group bonding). For some classes, I include a statement in the signature block of my email messages that will help them with the course (see Figure 5.1).

- *Syllabus quiz:* Some instructors create a brief quiz on policies and syllabus guidelines for students to complete at the start of a course. The quiz, while fairly simple, reiterates the importance of the information in what is essentially a contract between instructor and student regarding the requirements and expectations of the course.

- *Introductory assignment:* Like the syllabus quiz, an introductory assignment helps students master the volumes of new information involved when participating in a distance learning class by incorporating knowledge of policies into an actual course assignment. This approach works well, more or less, depending on the topic of the course. For instance, it works very well with my courses in written communication, in which I assign a short paper on netiquette as one of the first assignments. By completing the assignment, students are forced to review netiquette policies for the course and reflect on their own contribution to a respectful, engaging environment.

Robin Neidorf
robin.neidorf@gmail.com
This week's office hours: Live chat via GChat on Thursday from 11 a.m. to 2 p.m., Central time.

Classroom tip: Use "reply all" to post to the thread or "reply" to share only with the original sender; trim your message so that only the relevant part to your reply is included.

Figure 5.1 I use a signature block for email communication in distance learning courses. Under my contact information, students can find a tip about using the classroom. I rotate the message every few days to cover a range of tips I want them to have.

What all these approaches have in common is that they involve "push" communication (instructor effort to bring critical information to the students) rather than relying on "pull" communication (static documents that students have to find on their own). The use of push in addition to pull enables the instructor to guide the students through the mountains of material to those items that make an immediate difference in the functionality of the classroom.

Be Responsive

Especially at the start of a distance learning course, students are likely to be overwhelmed by the new environment. They are absorbing a great deal of information in a very short period of time, and they are making new discoveries about their own preferences, needs, and biases in the process. Work with them to help them understand how to maximize their use of the distance classroom, and listen to their concerns. I make a point of monitoring classroom activity very closely at first, checking an asynchronous classroom every few hours, and interrupting my own progress in a synchronous classroom every few minutes to gauge whether I've lost or confused anyone.

In the first few classroom encounters, expect a lot of Help! and SOS! messages, which will need immediate attention to put your students at ease. Your immediate response, even if you can't solve the problem, will go a long way to helping skittish students relax.

When I taught at the University of Phoenix Online, students needed to access learning materials via the secure website, as well as through our newsgroup classroom. Sometimes, especially in high-volume periods right after new courses were launched, the site is slow or even inaccessible. Particularly with new students who were still trying to find their way around, seeing unavailable pages caused great anxiety; the students were convinced they were doing something utterly wrong. I could respond to their squeaks of fear by reassuring them: "It's not you; it's the system. It does this at the start of a class when everyone's trying to access it at once." My reassurance didn't solve the problem, but it did help students feel better about their learning environment.

Of course, sometimes you *can* solve the problem right away, which makes everyone feel better. I frequently coach students who are confused because they can't see their own postings to a classroom, listserv, or forum. When I can talk them through how to refresh their display or change their default settings so that they can see their own messages, they are delighted and reassured.

Beyond technical glitches (some of which are user-induced and others of which are truly technical), you'll find that responsiveness also helps in the ongoing struggle to encourage participation. In the early stages of any distance learning program, I am in close contact with students who seem to be struggling with participation or are altogether invisible. The student who seems to be lurking on the teleconference or in the webinar will get a quick email or phone call from me to learn more about his or her needs. The student whose messages come through with a particular tone of desperation will get a soothing email pointing out his or her successes to date and suggesting a few ways to make the acclimation process easier.

As I respond, coach, and interact with new students, I'm careful to use their posting errors as a teaching opportunity rather than a chance to show them who holds the gradebook around here and to "ding" them. (As a course continues, I expect them to overcome the learning curve, and I'm less likely to forgive consistent and egregious errors.) The student who never posts his or her comments in the right place gets a bit of gentle instruction, both inside and outside of the classroom. The student who submits the first assignment a few hours late gets a brief, "Everything OK?" message rather than an immediate reduction in points; that way, I can gather information about the particular kind of coaching that a student may need to be successful.

By consistently managing the classroom this way, you are demonstrating to the students that you are taking care of them professionally as their instructor. They will come to trust you more readily because they will perceive you as a partner in their learning process rather than an adversary—a surprise for many adults who may have had few nurturing relationships with their teachers, if any.

Points for Participation

Participation is one area in which I continually work to train students to adhere to my expectations. (Do I seem obsessed with participation?) In distance learning, participation requires conscious skill development in an area students previously have taken for granted—raising their hands and sharing a comment or question.

A common challenge is to route students' participation to the classroom rather than let them fall into the habit of directing personal communication to me. Part of the problem is that, in addition to the fear of looking like a fool in the public space, new students do not yet understand how their classroom participation co-creates the learning experience, for themselves and for their classmates. If their primary educational model has been test-and-tell, they are not prepared for active involvement in or responsibility for their role in the classroom.

Their course-related questions, in particular, tend to show up in my email inbox until I can train them otherwise. In asynchronous classrooms, I keep an active "questions here!" thread throughout the course, and in synchronous classrooms, I am sure to break up meeting times by soliciting questions. Still, even with prodding and encouragement, a lot of questions are emailed privately or phoned in to me. If I responded privately, then the rest of the class would not benefit from the questions or have an opportunity to come up with alternative solutions to the ones I present.

When I receive private questions that relate to the course, I present them within the activity of the classroom.

In an asynchronous classroom, for example, I post my own message to the thread for questions, along the lines of: "Several students have contacted me privately about research for their final projects ..." In a synchronous environment, I do something similar during the designated Q&A time: "I can't remember who came to me with this question, but it seemed like something that we should discuss together."

In reality, I may have received only one private question—or none at all. But posting or adding the statement never fails to encourage follow-up questions. It's a handy trick for training students to be more open about asking for guidance and clarification about what they don't know, and it reminds them that they are not penalized for asking questions and thus admitting ignorance.

On the flip side, I sometimes also have to train students to recognize that the classroom isn't the appropriate place for every discussion. Off-topic dialogues, while a welcome part of the community-building process, can make a distance learning classroom confusing and chaotic. Many times I've had to interrupt an online discussion thread with a brief "How about taking this to the chat room, guys?" or suggest during a teleconference that a particular line of questioning would make a great team project that can be discussed privately.

Hold Office Hours

At least once a week and perhaps more frequently in a short course or as circumstances warrant, make yourself available only to your students via phone, email, and instant messaging (IM). Let them know the day and time (include time zone) you are holding office hours. If you will be unable to hold your regular hours, schedule an alternate time.

Foster Dialogue

The classroom is the natural place to stimulate recall of prior learning, present content, practice and encode skills, assess performance, and exchange feedback—many of the necessary events of instruction. It all takes place through discussion and dialogue among classmates, as well as between instructor and student.

Dialogue means more than people talking to each other or posting messages in the classroom space. Rather, dialogue is an interchange that deepens ideas and awareness and is truly more than the sum of its parts. Dialogue requires conscious nurturing even more than it requires basic participation. (And you already know how I feel about participation.)

Keep in mind that the characteristics of adult students can be helpful in figuring out how to foster dialogue among them. Adult students bring their experiences into the classroom, and they learn best when they can apply what they are learning to their own world. Some of the ways to foster dialogue include the following:

- Build on contributions by sharing your own expertise and insight.

- Invite students to provide illustrative or contrasting examples from their own experiences.

- Relate a comment back to the core content or draw a connection between the comment and a new resource.

- Compare and contrast contributions from multiple students.

When a student adds to the richness of a dialogue, follow up in the classroom with praise by identifying the specific way the student added depth and meaning. This practice helps others learn what you are looking for. It also provides positive reinforcement and public recognition for quality contributions. Similarly, encourage students whose responses are scanty to probe more deeply by using examples from their work and life that support their ideas.

Repeat Yourself

I've mentioned the value of repeating information and instructions several times. Classroom management also benefits from repeating yourself. (What do you know—I'm repeating it!)

No matter how clearly you give instructions for an assignment, someone will have a question. And truthfully, we're not always quite as clear in our instructions as we think we are. Use the classroom environment to reiterate critical information, such as due dates, where to find the glossary and the class roster when needed, or your availability for private consultation. It can be subtle, like a breezily added comment: "This is a great idea to incorporate into the paper you're working on for next week."

There's also value in repeating the same kind of feedback and critique if you have several students who are making common errors in the classroom. I run into this situation regularly in my asynchronous writing classes, in which many students share the same difficulties with grammar (pronouns in particular give us all grief). Sometimes it feels as though I'm making the same comments over and over ("A singular noun requires a singular pronoun: *his or her* rather than *their* …"), but the repetition is good for everyone. For one thing, if I only comment publicly on the error the first few times it crops up, someone ends up feeling picked on. But more importantly, many students only read the responses carefully that I make to their particular contributions. If I want to be sure they get the instruction, I have to direct my comments to them. Finally, when it's an error a lot of students are making, it never hurts to repeat, repeat, repeat, so they become accustomed to spotting and then addressing the error.

In synchronous classrooms, too, repetition is important. In teleconference classes, students have limited input from you—only your voice. In webinar environments, they have more points of input but also more distractions. The email chime is like a cell phone going off in a lecture hall. When you repeat the material you are most committed to teaching, it has a better chance of hitting the mark.

Provide Timely Feedback

Feedback is critical to an adult's instructional experience. Your students cannot effectively complete the process without your feedback.

Feedback occurs individually, as well as in the classroom. If particular classroom assignments are due on a Monday, for instance, be prepared to respond immediately on Monday, at the latest, if only to the first few assignments that are turned in.

Until students become adept at discussion and engagement, you may feel like you are giving the same feedback over and over (which is good—you're repeating!): "Great comments. I particularly like how you described ..." or "Interesting. Have you also experienced ... ?" Slowly, though, as the students become more comfortable, they will start to give each other feedback. And then you know you have created a classroom environment that works.

Some Are More Equal Than Others

Even when students take on more responsibility for responding to their classmates, the instructor remains, in the words of one of my students, "The Queen Bee." As much as she appreciates what her peers have to say, she told me, "We're all waiting to see what *you* think of our work."

You can back off a bit once the students feel in charge, but you can never fully retreat. Interaction with peers, while wonderful for the learning experience and for creating a community of learners, does not replace interaction with the instructor.

Model Your Expectations

"Do as I say *and* as I do" needs to be your motto. If you expect students to adhere to professional standards of netiquette, then don't make offensive or inappropriate comments in your asynchronous classroom. If you expect students to complete assignments in a timely fashion, then meet your own deadlines for grading and feedback. If you expect students to participate with depth and intelligence in classroom discussions, then show them how by modeling the kind of participation you expect from them.

Frequent and clear communication on your part will set the stage for good relationships with your students and within the classroom environment. In the first days and weeks of a course, it is particularly important for you to be "visible" in the distance learning classroom, providing thoughtful and responsive feedback to your students.

Manage Conflict

Throw any group of adults together and eventually a conflict or two will bubble to the surface. In my experience, distance learning students generally bend over backwards to avoid offending anyone (which presents a different kind of classroom management challenge, since it can lead to milquetoast interactions), but someone, somewhere, somehow will spark a conflict. When it happens, you have to manage it in much the same way you'd manage it in a traditional classroom.

In the policies for my classrooms, I make it clear from the start that I do not tolerate unprofessional behavior, disrespect of students or instructor, foul language, or unwarranted attacks of any kind. The first infraction results in immediate response, gently in the classroom and bit more firmly in private. For instance, I might interrupt a cursing student on a teleconference by asking him or her to find more appropriate vocabulary for our discussion. I follow up with a private message, either on the phone or via email, thanking the student for changing his or her behavior and reiterating my policy. In the follow-up, I always emphasize the open and trustworthy environment we are trying to create in the classroom. Additional infractions result in a sterner warning and other kinds of consequences—reduction in credit, for example, in a credit course. If necessary, I will remove someone from a class, although I'm happy to say I've never had to resort to that measure.

I also try to steer dialogue away from hot-button issues, like politics, abortion, religion, and the like, at least until everyone has settled in and feels comfortable. These elements are most likely to arise in students' personal introductions, although they occasionally crop up unexpectedly in other places in our discussions. I'm not opposed to discussion around challenging issues, but they do not generally relate to the content of the courses I teach. When discussions of this nature arise, I ask students to take it to a private space because the classroom is for course work. (If your course is about politics or medical ethics, I wish you good luck!)

Every now and then, I end up with a class where two or more students are just plain hateful toward one another. What can you do? They are chronological adults, but sometimes they just can't control themselves. Often these explosive relationships erupt not in the classroom itself but in learning team situations—a smaller group setting where difficult person- alities are more likely to clash. But the impact is also felt in the classroom when students start giving each other the cold shoulder or trading insult- ing remarks.

If I can move them to different teams, I'll consider it. First, though, I contact them privately or respond privately to the one who comes to me first with, "I just can't work with so-and-so …" Unless behavior crosses a line of offensiveness, I ask them, and then *tell* them, to work it out.

In some classes, on the other hand, I long for conflict. It seems that every contribution from every student is cheerily positive. No one wants to critique anyone else's work, and no one wants to have a dissenting opinion. I want to shout at them, "How about a little passion, people?!"

Many students are downright afraid of conflict, even of the most minor variety. To liven things up and keep the classroom from going silent, I sometimes deliberately introduce conflict. Creating classroom exercises around debate and role-playing can be very effective for introducing pos- itive conflict; when students can dive into a role, they lose some of their inhibitions around disagreement. The resulting discussion pushes them further into the ideas we are wrestling with. Forced to defend a position, students think harder about the foundations of their logic or their approach to a problem.

Be Resourceful

Sometimes things just don't go as planned. An activity falls flat; the stu- dents are at each other's throats; the platform has a meltdown.

What do you do? Pull out your resources.

For every class I teach, I keep additional activities in my back pocket for each of the content areas. Field trips are always a good choice; anything that gets students out of the classroom environment is helpful when the classroom isn't running well. For web-based classes, field trips can involve sending the students out to find websites that meet certain criteria (e.g., nonprofit, certain budget size, focus of work) and then reporting back to the class on their findings. For any distance learning class, sending students out to visit a location in their area or interview another expert keeps them engaged and out of trouble for a little while.

Guest speakers can be equally distracting. A desperate call to a colleague, requesting 45 minutes to an hour of time, almost always moves a "stuck" classroom to unstuck status.

All the tricks I picked up in traditional classrooms for rerouting disappointing experiences apply to distance classrooms as well. And when all else fails, just know that this too shall pass—even if all your students don't.

Create Culture

When you put all of these practices and ideas together, you are creating a culture for your classroom—one that invites, prods, and urges students to interact with the material, you, and each other.

Of course, every instructor has to be true to his or her own character and style, but distance learning classrooms benefit from a surfeit of warmth and human appreciation. Ultimately, the students will participate and will perform beautifully, if they feel the classroom is a welcoming place and if they are eager to become part of the culture you have established. If "going to class" is a chore, they'll find plenty of other things in their busy lives to fill their time. On the other hand, if going to class offers a place to relax and get down to exciting work and if students feel appreciated and honored for their contributions, they'll find a way to participate despite everything else on their daily calendars.

Best Practices for Asynchronous Classrooms

Beyond the principles of classroom management that apply to all distance learning environments, there are some particular considerations for asynchronous versus synchronous classrooms. Asynchronous classrooms are hard to imagine until you've been in one. "But how does it *work*?" is the most common question I get from prospective students. Once you've taught in one, though, you quickly come to appreciate the wonderful features and benefits asynchronous systems offer.

Keep It Organized

It's usually relatively easy to keep an asynchronous classroom organized—once you know how to do it. (Aye, there's the rub!) Most asynchronous systems allow for threaded discussions in which replies appear below and indented from the original comments. Threads make it easy to tell who is responding to whom; you can follow a complete dialogue among several people simply by reading through the thread.

But threading is not exactly intuitive if you've never done it before. Listserv systems, in which the contributions are delivered to the participants' email inboxes, are notorious for creating confusion. Newcomers inadvertently hit Reply All when they want to respond privately to the contributor, and they soon find that their catty remarks about the instructor have been broadcast to the entire class. Newsgroup and bulletin board systems cause similar headaches when students swear up and down that they posted in the thread, but their contributions are mysteriously "orphaned" somewhere else in the space. Threads are also easier to follow if the participants change the subject line as the direction of the dialogue changes, but even seasoned users are apt to forget this detail.

Some days I want to tear out my hair in frustration as I try to get the postings where they are supposed to be. But then I remember that for most of my students, this is a new skill set, like learning to use a word processor for the first time. Then I'm grateful that they're attempting to participate at all.

Organizational problems are not limited to the discussion component of a platform. In a collaborative web environment, you might have students posting documents, adding a blog comment, or publishing webpages all out of kilter with your guidelines. It can make for an extremely confusing environment, and as a result, students become frustrated and their participation drops.

In the first week or so, when I find contributions and materials in the wrong places, I often follow them with a threaded reply or comment as follows:

Interesting comments, Xavier. I think you're on the right track. However, I'm going to ask you to repost this message in the designated thread. Threads help us stay on top of who is involved in the discussion, and they ensure that no one's contributions get lost in the shuffle of a busy classroom. Highlight the thread header, then hit Reply All to post in the thread; let me know if you have trouble. Thanks!

If I need to provide additional one-on-one coaching for a student who just isn't getting it, I can email, IM, or phone the student to review the steps of proper participation and my guidelines for interacting within the classroom environment. I can also record a brief demonstration and post the video or email it to a student who needs a bit of extra assistance. But the important thing is to provide guidance in a way that acknowledges the value of the student's ideas while instructing the student in how to use a tool. I also explain the value of the behavior I'm trying to encourage to the student because capricious rules bring out the rebel in many of us. If I focus entirely on the error or ignore the importance of the underlying reasons for a policy, I run the risk of insulting, embarrassing, or alienating the student—not a good move for our pedagogical relationship!

Use the Features

Asynchronous classrooms offer wonderful features that make any instructor's life so much easier. Want to know who has been participating and who hasn't? Set your viewing options to sort by contributor and date. Can't remember who made that thoughtful comment a week ago? Do a keyword search. Want to review classroom contributions prior to submitting final grades? Review them as thoroughly as you want, because every last comma is archived for you.

The features of the asynchronous classroom free me from the worry of remembering exactly what happened in class. I find that I can provide students with more accurate and unbiased feedback, because I am responding to what they said rather than what I remember they said. I also archive the entire class discussion on offline media following the end of the course; if, 6 months later, I want to go back to a previous course and apply something that worked there to a current class, I have the archive to help me do so.

The ability of an asynchronous classroom to accommodate many different dialogues and activities at the same time is also a feature I now find hard to do without when I go into a synchronous or traditional classroom. The multiple options mean that there's something for everyone; if one topic is dull or irrelevant to a student, there are three others they can dive into instead. In a synchronous classroom, it's one thing at a time.

Summarize and Send

The biggest downside to the asynchronous classroom is that it can mean a lot of reading and responding on the part of the instructor, and that means it's easy to miss the nuggets of great thinking amid the multitude of words. In a busy class of 10 or more students, it's not unusual to log in to class and find 85 new messages to read through. Even if you only respond directly to a handful of them, it's a lot of sifting and thinking, as well as crafting your replies.

Students experience the same kind of overload. As the instructor, you can help them deal with it by summarizing the key points raised and discussed in the classroom for each topic or week of the course. When you do so, invite the students to add to the summary: They can offer their own insights, including points you neglected to make, and their own reflections on how they will apply these key points to appropriate areas of their lives and work. By doing so, you accomplish several pedagogical goals. First, you filter the wealth of dialogue into digestible chunks. Second, you repeat the key takeaways that you want students to continue to work with. Third, you encourage the students to do some self-reflection and additional encoding of their new knowledge. Finally, you help them transition their new knowledge to apply beyond the classroom. How's that for hitting a few events of instruction with a single little assignment?

Keep an Eye on Everything

Instructors in asynchronous classrooms should have eyes in the back of their heads, virtually speaking. If you have meeting spaces within the classroom for learning teams, let them work on their own but monitor discussion in those spaces for appropriate, professional behavior; if interpersonal conflicts are going to arise, that's the most likely place.

Best practices for asynchronous classes call for us to create "chat room" space, where students can discuss anything they like. I usually keep a low profile in the chat room, so that students feel comfortable using it even to complain about me if necessary. But I also monitor it for language and appropriate behavior.

Finally, trust your instincts. If you sense that something is wrong (and it isn't just your own first-time jitters talking), follow up on it. Ask questions, probe for authentic responses, and ferret out the problems that may not be appearing in the classroom but are nevertheless affecting it.

Best Practices for Synchronous Classrooms

Maybe it's my age or natural inclination to written language, but I find it much more difficult to manage a synchronous classroom than an asynchronous classroom. When I'm leading a conference call, instructing through a web-based synchronous environment, or even just conducting an IM tutoring session with a handful of students, I have a much harder time keeping all the balls in the air at the right times. The word *multitasking* takes on new meaning when I'm leading a synchronous program; often I'm operating equipment, delivering a talk, trying to type a reply to an IM comment by a participant, and checking the time to see if I'm running over yet. It's no wonder I have more difficulty rerouting trouble when it comes up—trouble will just have to get in line for my attention! Such are the challenges of different media.

But (sigh), I know from my own experience that technology is mostly about becoming comfortable and not about the shortcomings of the tools. I run synchronous classrooms when necessary, and I become more comfortable with them all the time. Adhering to these practices helps a great deal.

Have an Agenda

The worst synchronous classroom experiences I've ever had were the ones where I said to myself, "Hey, I've presented this talk a hundred times. I can go into the classroom and practically do it in my sleep." No matter how often I've presented on a topic, I go into the synchronous classroom with a detailed agenda: so many minutes for introductions and "housekeeping,"

my opening attention-grabber, my first key points, my first question solic-
itation, and on through the final sign-off. I mark up the agenda with notes
on progress; for example, I need to be at Agenda Item 6 by 2:55 PM; if I'm
running late, then skip the second example.

The agenda is my lifeline. When I am instructing through a teleconference, the agenda keeps me grounded in instruction rather than simply
talking about what I know. It reminds me that I'm managing a classroom.
When I am instructing via web-enabled conferencing, the agenda keeps
me on topic and on track. Otherwise, I become too distracted by the tasks
of managing the interface.

I keep thinking I'll outgrow the agenda, just as I once outgrew the training wheels on my bike. Now I'm starting to think the agenda is more like a
safety helmet—the thing that will keep my brains together if my bike
should crash!

Break Up the Presentation

It's a challenge when instructing through a synchronous classroom to stay
focused on the students rather than the content. There's a lot of material
to cover (there's always more to cover than you really have time for), so we
tend to talk and talk and talk, and the students absorb maybe a third of it
all. When synchronous classrooms take on this character, they mimic the
worst elements of the traditional classroom while lacking the guilty pleasure of being able to see who's wearing cute shoes.

Break up your presentations, much as you would for an asynchronous
classroom. If you wouldn't make students read through five pages of a single-
spaced lecture (and you'd better not), then don't make them listen to you for
60 minutes straight.

Fifteen minutes is a good chunk of time to plan for each segment of
your classroom session. When you create the lesson plan, break up your
material into single-topic chunks that you can cover in these briefer periods. Between topics, offer opportunities for students to discuss their reactions, present brief case studies, and even engage in a game or two.
("Guess That Voice" is one of my favorites for a teleconference; it helps
everyone feel like we're getting to know each other as more than disem-
bodied voices.)

Yes, I know these activities are eating into your precious time for presenting content. But the truth is that you will have more success teaching

content if you break up your time and allow students to stretch their mental legs. (It's also harder for students to be secretly playing Angry Birds or checking their email if they know you'll be asking them to do something in just a few minutes.)

Keep to One Topic or Purpose at a Time

Synchronous classroom sessions should run between 60 and 75 minutes. If they run longer than that, I will bet you my gradebook that the students are not nearly as present as they may seem. Between getting started, breaking up a presentation with activity and discussion, and responding to interruptions or questions, you don't have much time to present material. When you include synchronous sessions in your course, plan them so that you can cover a single topic or purpose in a short time on each call or online interaction.

Keep Your Cool

One of the things I appreciate most about asynchronous classrooms is that I can think through my response before I send it. In a synchronous classroom, I lose the safety net of the delay. If someone pushes my buttons or violates the culture I've tried to create for learning and exchange, it's very difficult for me to respond effectively in a synchronous classroom. My immediate response is not always a well-advised or graceful one.

I've gotten better at keeping my cool, mostly by training myself to allow silence first before responding to just about anything. And truthfully, such situations have been extremely rare. In the interests of preparedness, however, it's good to have an idea for how you will respond if something goes awry.

Summarize and Send

As in the asynchronous classroom, students in a synchronous classroom benefit from the instructor's efforts to summarize the key points from a session and ask for additional input and reflection. It is a good practice to send a summary to all participants following the session, either via email, a post to a website, or even via snail mail. The summary and invitation to reflect frees students from focusing too much on note-taking during the session and helps them encode their knowledge and apply it beyond the classroom.

Rehearse

Truly the best thing you can do to ensure that your synchronous class-room runs smoothly is to rehearse. Run the first session with colleagues or friends; this gives you a chance to run through your materials, practice using all the tools and interactions you have planned for the session, and time how long different elements take.

For any session that includes a guest speaker or panelists, have additional rehearsals. Increasingly, I find that topic experts are being called upon to provide their expertise in distance learning environments—professional development webinars or online workshops, either for credit or certification or simply for the skill development of the participants. In every program I've been involved with, these instructors are eager to share their experiences and at the same time are quite apprehensive about presenting and working with students in this new environment. The time we spend in rehearsal makes an enormous difference in their confidence when the live session takes place. They can get over their jitters in the rehearsal and, in the session itself, focus on instruction.

More than one of these instructors has noted that more live events could also benefit from rehearsal opportunities: If you teach or organize teaching primarily in live classroom or workshop environments, consider adding rehearsal time to your planning period.

Beyond the Classroom: Accept Feedback

Educational programs are notorious for limited assessment of their outcomes. Part of the reason for this is that it is confoundedly difficult to measure whether someone has "learned" something. Indeed, sometimes it's even difficult to determine what it means to learn.

The ability to assess a program's success is predicated on the assumption that you have an idea of what success looks like. What should a student be able to say, think, or do as a result of completing the program?

Depending on the topic and type of program, successful outcomes might include the following:

- Succeeding at particular tasks, such as writing a professional letter or operating a piece of equipment with a specific degree of accuracy

- Applying new knowledge to achieve an increase in revenues, volunteers, students, donations, and so on

- Completing a novel or collection of poems and submitting the manuscript to a targeted list of at least three literary publishers

If these look like learning objectives, that's not a coincidence. One obvious place to look for desired outcomes is the list of specific and measurable learning objectives you crafted in Chapter 3. It may not always be possible to assess whether your students have achieved the learning objectives until they have a chance to apply their knowledge in the field. That's why testing for knowledge serves as a substitute for true outcome evaluation in many educational situations.

But assessment isn't about just what the students learned; it's also about how they encounter and handle the experience of learning. Sometimes students learn due to our best efforts; sometimes our best efforts fall on sterile ground. To evaluate the outcome of a distance learning program, it's also important to gather information about student attitudes, opinions, and reactions to distance instruction, particularly in the classroom.

Assessment can be a scary thing, which is why so many of us fail to do it. What if the outcomes tell us that we are not being effective instructors? As painful as it can be to receive disappointing assessment results, the overall outcome is worth it; how can we ever improve if we don't know where we are failing?

When I taught at the University of Phoenix Online, the students were asked to complete a substantial end-of-course survey, which instructors could review without identifying details attached. As a result, we instructors had a sense of how many of our students considered us to be "informed and professional" about our areas of expertise and how many felt they would or would not recommend our courses to others. In Creative Writing in English, which founding instructor William Males used as a laboratory for experimenting with online platforms and processes of teaching creative writing, students completed a brief evaluation monthly, as well as a more extensive assessment at the end of each term.

It can be a humbling experience to review those end of course surveys, and I always do so with a sense of perspective. The student with whom I butted heads for 5 weeks about the consistent lateness of her assignments and the erratic placement of her punctuation may ream me in the end-of-course survey. At the same time, I've found that these anonymous tabulations of strengths and weaknesses, covering content, interaction, and my teaching skills, have helped me become motivated to learn more about how to teach and how to help these students who want and need my help.

The end-of-course surveys and other kinds of student assessments keep me focused on improving my own performance and understanding student needs in my classrooms. For example, several items in the end-of-course survey ask for student input on how well I create a professional and friendly atmosphere in the classroom. The first time I read that, it got me thinking: What *do* I do to create a professional and friendly atmosphere in the classroom? Similarly, the items regarding how much care and concern I showed for individuals' needs and progress made me more aware of this issue from the students' perspectives: What was I doing every day in the classroom so that each student would feel cared for and attended to?

On the research side of my consulting work, I'm often explaining to clients that conducting research or an assessment is about creating awareness as well as gathering data. By naming the variables on which you will be assessed, you create greater awareness in yourself and your students of the importance of those variables. Asking your students to assess your performance in the classroom gives you all an opportunity to reflect on what goes into effective instruction and classroom management.

Easy Does It—and Enjoy!

Lead gently in your distance classrooms, even while you push your students forward. If you are enthusiastic and genuinely concerned for your students' learning experiences, you can enjoy the process and invite them to enjoy it, too. Keep a copy of Worksheet 5.1 handy throughout the course; it will remind you of ways to maximize the classroom experience for you and your students.

In the first few classes, it may seem as if you are mollycoddling recalcitrant students. But over time, you'll find that the handholding, repetition, and confidence building actually results in students who are more in charge of their learning experiences. You are providing them with, and training them to use, the tools they need to succeed in your classroom and beyond.

Worksheet 5.1   Checklist: Practices for the Well-Run Distance Classroom

Prior to course launch:

- ❑ Review and edit (if needed) any classroom documentation
- ❑ Prepare all documentation for delivery to students
  - ❑ Post to asynchronous classroom
  - ❑ Email copies if necessary
  - ❑ Snail mail copies if necessary
- ❑ Post instructor bio or send instructor bio via email
- ❑ Set and communicate schedule for office hours

First day of class or initial classroom encounters:

- ❑ Greet all students on arrival
- ❑ Request bios from all students
  - ❑ Ask them to post to asynchronous classroom **or -**
  - ❑ Email to instructor for routing
- ❑ Assist with classroom usage issues
  - ❑ Call-in problems
  - ❑ Webinar connection problems
  - ❑ Access to web-based space
  - ❑ Use of asynchronous discussion—threading, editing replies, etc.
- ❑ Respond to bios with probing questions about goals
- ❑ Make notes to student files on goals and personal details

During class (asynchronous):

- ❑ Review all postings
- ❑ Respond to deepen thinking and elicit discoveries
- ❑ Send positive feedback for substantive comments
- ❑ Watch tone to create encouragement, warmth
- ❑ Identify any potential difficult issues or personalities
- ❑ Post easy-to-find "questions" thread
- ❑ Monitor participation
- ❑ Summarize and send summary, at least weekly

During class (synchronous):

- ❑ Plan for presentation in 15-minute intervals
- ❑ Break up presentation with Q&A opportunities and group activities
- ❑ Focus on students not content during presentation
- ❑ Identify any difficult issues or personalities
- ❑ Monitor participation
- ❑ Summarize and send summary following presentation

Following class:

- ❑ Complete detailed feedback in a timely manner
- ❑ Archive class contributions for later reference
- ❑ Make notes for changes or additions for next time
- ❑ Conduct evaluation and request feedback

Chapter 6

Individual Learners

During the 15 years I've taught professionally, I've experienced a tremendous range of emotions in relation to my students and the class experience: excitement, fear, collegial good humor, maternal-like protectiveness, boredom, annoyance, and more. There have been classes where I adored every one of my students; there have been others where I could barely control my irritation over every last question.

Over time and with a great deal of soul-searching, I've learned that students reflect my own strengths and weaknesses in ways that are by turns dismaying and encouraging. Whether they bug me or thrill me, they are teaching me about the limits of my power—and my potential—to influence others. The one who is pushing my buttons is the one who reflects something irritating back to me about myself (usually, ego). And the one who takes my instruction and raises it to the next level of insight is the one who validates, humbles, and inspires me. The relationships I have with individual students are what keep teaching interesting. There is always something new to learn about myself!

Adult learners, as we discussed in Chapter 2, bring their histories and experiences into the classroom. They have firm ideas in their heads about who they are as students. They tend to see themselves as primarily flawed or primarily outstanding, depending on how they experienced formal education while growing up. (Ours is not a culture that emphasizes balance.) I'm sorry to say that the majority of the students I work with tend to focus on their flaws at the expense of their talents. (I blame insensitive educational practices for this sad state of affairs.) As a result, members of this majority are insecure, anxious, and defensive—not a state that primes them for intellectual adventuring.

Students typically enter my classes with far more than one piece of carry-on baggage. Before I can help them learn anything, my first job is to get them to stow that baggage. Luckily, the process for doing so also helps me create personal relationships with them. Through these relationships, I can respond more appropriately to the particular learning needs of each student. I think that's what's known as a win–win situation.

It's All About Them

When we first looked at the idea of students as the center of the learning program in Chapter 2, I shared my mantra with you: It's not about you; it's about *them*. The same principle is at the heart of building relationships with individual students. Learner-centered instruction means that it doesn't matter how expert I am in my field; it doesn't even matter how much work I've put into preparing an effective course. What matters is that the individual learner achieves a successful outcome. The learner is the purpose. I am only an instructor when I am in relationship with a student.

Being in a relationship means that I need to expend as much energy, or even more, on listening as I do on presenting information. Within the context of distance learning, listening involves careful attention to explicit questions, comments, and the implicit information students share every time they contribute.

In a traditional classroom, the personal relationships I develop with many students are gravy—a nice benefit of our shared experience. In distance learning, on the other hand, I find that these relationships—and the work I put into cultivating them—take on a much more central role.

Why the shift? Probably because of the wider range of roles I play with distance students: cheerleader and mentor, as well as instructor. Remember the model for inspirational writing I presented in Chapter 4: The first step is common ground—we are alike. Until I know how we are alike, it's difficult for me to inspire. Once I know how we are alike, a relationship is inevitable.

Getting to Know You

In traditional classes, I usually start things off with a quick round of introductions. By the time we finish going around the room, I'm lucky if I remember most of the names and a salient detail or two about their interests and backgrounds. Little else sticks in my overstimulated brain, especially since I'm already worrying about what I'm going to say next.

Most of my distance learning courses start the same way. I ask everyone to provide a brief introduction—name, geography, interest and background in the course topic, perhaps where they are in a longer program of study, and any other details they want to share. I post my own introduction to start things off.

Since all my distance learning courses involve some online component, even if it's just an email exchange, I always make sure introductions
are shared through that medium. Even if we kick off the course with a teleconference and do quick introductions on the phone, I ask students to do
it again online. The benefit, of course, is that we have a written record of
all those details, right down to the number of pets they have and the age
of their kids in many cases. It's much easier to work from documentation
than from my faulty memory.

From these introductions, I get a lot of information, both explicit and
implicit. I get personal details—who is expecting a baby, who breeds
German shepherds, who is planning a cross-country move, and who has
finally returned to formal education after dreaming of it for years—that
help me connect in a human way to the individual students. A short comment like, "How are the dogs these days?" dropped in at the end of a message can help a nervous student remember that there's a living, caring
human at the other end of the communication.

I also get a lot of information that the students don't even realize they're
providing. With a scan of my eye, I can tell who will benefit from additional coaching in grammar and sentence construction to support effective written communication in all contexts—in my class and beyond. I get
an immediate sense of the student's mastery of English (also important
when I'm working with ESL students). I can even tell from the student's
use of paragraphs and line breaks how accustomed each of them is to
electronic communication; those who are most comfortable with digital
connections write with line breaks and formatting that are easier on the
eyes—they've unconsciously mastered the creation of scannable material.
Students with online experience also write sentences that feel more confident and natural—they've found their "evoice." (I don't have data to support this particular insight, but I have yet to peg someone as a newbie who
has actually done a lot of online work.)

Perhaps most importantly, I learn from these introductions how ready
and prepared each student is to learn and to work in partnership with me
to get what he or she needs out of the course. Who is receptive? Who is
defensive? Who is distracted by a recent move or a tangled divorce? All of
these impressions get filed away in my notes—a spreadsheet in which I
record all of a student's grades, performance notes, and tidbits of information that will be helpful when I communicate with the student.

Tip for Managing Introductions

As helpful as the introductions are, I usually try to keep them out of our main classroom, which I reserve for course-topic discussion. For instance, when I taught at the University of Phoenix Online, I would ask students to post their introductions in the chat room—the "anything goes" student lounge. This practice encouraged everyone to use the chat room for other kinds of networking and casual dialogue while keeping the main classroom organized.

If a separate space isn't available, I work to contain the introductions in a single thread or a single set of emails. If our "classroom" is based on simple email exchanges, I often ask students to send their introductions directly to me so I can manage their distribution and control the flow of data, and make sure that everyone gets the information. (Reply and Reply All remain confusing to so many email users, particularly at the start of a course—did the introduction go to everyone or just to the last person who sent one?)

Being Proactive and Reactive

When I spot potential challenges (and they are always present), it's my choice whether to be proactive or reactive in response.

Some challenges require a willingness to react to what unfolds rather than an attempt to accomplish an immediate fix. For instance, a student who seems defensive and upset by the newness of the environment may just need a little practice to become more comfortable. If you immediately respond with a message offering assistance, you might in fact reinforce the idea that the distance learning environment is scary and difficult to master, and requires special help to make it successful. By sitting back and letting students build their own confidence through practice, you let them naturally find their own coping and adapting abilities.

Other kinds of challenges, however, demand that you respond proactively:

- *Antisocial behavior:* Inappropriate language and disrespect of any kind get an immediate response informing the student of the ground rules for netiquette. Subsequent problems require even more forceful action. It's impossible to establish an environment of trust with a loose cannon in the classroom.

- *Severe difficulties with written English:* Students whose initial contributions indicate serious trouble with written English require a "fact-finding mission" at the minimum. I usually contact the student privately to find out more. If I want to know whether English is a student's second language but the student does not volunteer the information, I might make my contact via telephone to listen for an accent. In most cases, once I've learned more about the student, my initial suggestion is simply for some additional grammar exercises or tutorials. Other times, I probe tactfully for underlying learning difficulties I need to be aware of. This is a sensitive area, but if I can help a student tell me the nature of a special need, I can assist and accommodate within the parameters of the course.

- *Inadequate preparation:* If a student enters a course with dramatically inadequate preparation, it creates challenges not just for the student in question but for the functioning of the entire classroom. If it seems a student may have a hard time with the complexity or pace of the work, I try to work with him or her to create a remedial plan. Very occasionally, I end up with a student who just isn't ready for the work. While I'm rarely able (for a variety of contractual or political reasons) to ask a student to drop a class, I make a point of providing the student with particularly detailed and objective feedback, comparing his or her performance to the criteria for success. For everyone's sake, it's best when an unprepared student bails out.

But truly, the fun and pleasant discoveries about new students almost always outnumber the red flags. They all have interesting hobbies and histories; they tell funny stories, and they ask great questions. They may be wary about this newfangled distance learning thing, but they are also curious, excited, and comforted by a warm welcome.

Pairing Up

Learning style information is helpful in coming up with fruitful pairings or team assignments for students. Suggesting to experiential or kinesthetic learners that they might get more out of the course by working in partnership with a text-oriented learner creates the conditions for success and satisfaction. In most of my distance learning classes, I require my students to read and absorb a lot of textual information; I know that this emphasis will be frustrating to a kinesthetic learner. But a text-oriented learner will thrive and, together, the odd couple will succeed.

Enabling Customization

By the end of our first interaction, I know a distance learning student far better than I know many of my traditional students at the end of an entire term. When I receive the first optional assignment—the completed learning styles inventory—I know my distance learning students even more intimately.

The learning styles profile, for the students who choose to do it, immediately turns what could be a content-centered program into a learner-centered program. When I receive the profile, I respond immediately with some tips on the best way for the individual to use the course, based on the techniques best suited to each learning style (see Table 6.1). I also let them know which activities may be most effective for them, as well as areas to watch out for. For instance, I always comment to solitary learners that the learning team component of a course may be challenging for them. I take the time to explain the pedagogical reasons for learning teams, along with some of the specific skills they will develop by participating.

Motivating Your Students

By getting to know students as individuals—both who they are and what they are doing in your classroom—you gain an opportunity to motivate

Table 6.1   Learning Style Advice: What I Communicate to Students

Style	What you will probably enjoy	What may be challenging for you	Strategies to try
Verbal	Reading lectures Reading class discussion (asynchronous)	Holding web-based conferences and other synchronous events that cut down on text-based information Dealing with graphic orientation to materials	Conduct a verbal analysis of anything that is challenging Use a keyword glossary Pair with a visually oriented student
Visual	Using video, graphic presentations of information, whiteboard sessions (team or class), and mind maps	Reading text-only lectures and classroom discussion (asynchronous) Holding web-based conferences with little or no visual information	Create your own mind maps of information Draw links between ideas, activities, and desired outcomes "Visualize" success
Aural	Listening to streaming audio Holding web-based conference and webinar sessions that deliver information orally	Reading lectures, content, and class discussions	Record key information and play it back for yourself Discuss concepts with a classmate or colleague
Kinesthetic	Doing activities that relate to the desired outcomes	Holding web-based conferences unless they have a strong interactive component Text-based content presentations (written lectures)	Pair with a verbally oriented student Suggest alternative projects and pathways through the course that speak to your learning style
Social	Participating in group work Participating in discussion Using social media components	Doing independent projects	Form informal study groups if formal group work is not part of the course
Solitary	Working on individual projects and reading assignments	Participating in group work Participating in dialogue in the classroom	Role-play Identify specific pieces of group work that particularly interest you and work at your own pace within the context of the group project
Logical	Analyzing and pulling together ideas Using whole-system simulations	Having discussions that run to superficial	Go as deeply as you are compelled to go with the material Probe in classroom discussion for more depth from classmates and yourself

them in ways that have long-term effects on their success and, indeed, on their lives.

Many students move from class to class without having a clear idea of what they are working toward. Without personal clarity and strong motivation, students get distracted, amass a body of credits and knowledge without knowing what they're truly for, and muddle aimlessly along. Focus and motivation work together. You can help enhance their motivation by working with them to:

- *Clarify their goals:* Successful students identify specific reasons for choosing to be in a course or in a longer program of study and can describe what a successful outcome looks and feels like.

- *Internalize their goals:* Committed and self-aware students believe in their goals from the inside out. "My boss wants me to take this" or "A degree is just a piece of paper, but I can't get ahead without it" are not internalized goals. Students need to be internally committed to the stated goals in order to stick with the course when things get tough. If the goal hasn't been internalized, over time students will become resentful of the pain and sacrifice of getting there.

- *Identify and achieve incremental success:* Motivated students set and achieve interim goals that move them toward their dreams. Completing a single course, or even a single assignment within a course, is an incremental success. Motivated students also recognize partial success as success; completing a course with a less-than-ideal grade does not need to suck away all of their motivation.

For most of us, motivation is not a fixed state. We move along a motivational continuum, some days feeling completely charged up and ready to take on the entire dream and other days feeling a bit more sluggish and unsure of ourselves. In getting to know your students, you'll get an idea of their motivation in general, but know that some days it may spike or plummet, possibly in remarkable sync with your cycle for returning graded assignments!

When I respond to student introductions, I often ask directly, "Tell us why you are taking this class. What are your goals?" I review their responses carefully for the balance between self-directed statements and external triggers. I also look for proactive motives (e.g., preparing for a new career or promotion) versus reactive motives (e.g., was told to build skills because of on-the-job deficiencies).

Finally, I pay close attention to the students who don't seem to have goals; they don't really know what they're doing in the course. The kinds of things goalless students talk about include:

- Vague plans of "getting a better job someday" (with no idea of what that job might be) and as a result being able to spend more time with their families

- A spouse, friend, or colleague who is taking classes and seems to be making progress

Or they don't answer the question at all. The students without goals are the ones I need to work with most to identify, clarify, and internalize motivators. They are the most at-risk for dropping out of educational pursuits without having an opportunity to figure out what they want in life.

Multiple Motivators

Even with a clear motivation in place, it never hurts to have another. With multiple motivations, students are able to reinforce their commitment to the course work.

When I was working with students at the University of Phoenix Online, I would often see the need to build additional points of motivation. Since I worked with them early in their course of study, they were fresh off the recruitment and enrollment process and still fired up about the fact that they were going to be able to get the college degree they once thought was out of reach. Yet the workload of my class was a surprise, and the degree was (usually) quite a long way in the future. I needed to help them develop additional motivators that involved closer, more tangible goals to get through the intense challenges immediately in front of them; the long-term dream of a college degree was too far away to keep most of them motivated through the pain and uncertainty of their first college research paper.

Strategies to Identify and Deepen Motivation

Since each student is unique, it's important to have a number of tricks up your sleeve to identify and deepen motivation (see Table 6.2). You never know what's going to be the most helpful for the student until you are in relationship with a particular individual. The following learner profiles, which are based on composites of students my colleagues and I have discussed (ad nauseum) regarding their motivation and learning quirks, demonstrate multiple ways in which you can work with students with different points of motivation.

Learner Profile: Alissa

Alissa is a 35-year-old student at an international online university. She immigrated to the United States from the Dominican Republic nearly 10 years ago and is becoming more confident with her English skills while pursuing a degree in accounting. She also works full-time at a small accounting firm, where her innate math skills and can-do attitude have helped her advance. Alissa began her studies in part because her husband and boss talked her into it, but over time she has discovered that she really enjoys the process and is accomplishing a lot.

Table 6.2   Motivational Cue: Making It Work

Cues I get from student	Strategies to try to enhance motivation
Can't keep up with the work; too busy	Identify most important activities for each topic and prioritize with student on the basis of student's personal goals.
Lack of interest in topic(s)	Find ways to link topics with personal interests; customize assignments to allow student to adapt them to personal interests; link work to outcomes desired by the student.
Perceptible hostility	Call—personal voice-to-voice connection often helps; relax pressure on student to allow for acclimation; identify (if possible) root cause(s) of hostility and try to distance the cause(s) from the classroom environment.
Unprepared for complexity/focus of course	Suggest remedial resources, reading, and activities; pair with a "mentor" student, if possible.
Course isn't what student expected	Focus on desired outcomes—can student still get personal and professional value from the course? Link activities to individual goals.
Reluctance to participate in group projects	Emphasize importance of distributed teams in modern workplace; highlight moments when insight comes into the classroom because of interaction; identify motivation (solitary learning style?) and suggest ways to accommodate teamwork.

Alissa's motivation has shifted from largely external to internal. The instructor can build on this shift by helping her identify some specific directions she would like to take in her studies. She is enjoying college now, but naming and mapping out several short-term and long-term goals that are meaningful to her will help her over any bumps in the road. At the same time, Alissa needs to continue to build her English skills. The instructor provides specific feedback relating to English structure and usage, as well as links to online resources for ESL support.

Alissa concludes the writing class with a C+ average, in part because she has more trouble with formal written English than with informal or spoken English. In the final feedback to Alissa, the instructor reiterates the progress she has made and emphasizes that completing the course is still a step toward her long-term goals.

Learner Profile: Mike

Mike, a 32-year-old student at an online university, is returning to formal education after 13 years. He is picking up where he left off when he stopped taking classes at his local community college to build his full-time career as a computer technician. He is extremely successful and knowledgeable as a technician, but he has hit a ceiling for pay and advancement because he lacks a college degree.

Mike is skeptical that college can offer him anything of value; he knows he is talented in his profession and feels that a degree is little more than a piece of paper certifying that he knows what he knows. In addition to a series of testy contributions to the classroom discussion, he responds angrily to the critiques in the first detailed feedback he receives from his instructor.

The instructor recognizes that Mike is not truly motivated to learn or in a state of readiness to learn; he is defensive about any feedback he receives and does not trust the instructor or his classmates. To help him get past his defensiveness, the instructor calls Mike just to get to know him a little better. They chat for several minutes, not about the course, but about Mike's own career goal. A few days later, the instructor emails Mike an article from a business journal about the exploding opportunities in his field. The instructor is also careful, in all feedback to Mike, to draw clear connections between the class material and Mike's personal career goals.

Over time, Mike thaws slightly. He selects a research topic for one of the course assignments that enables him to discover new potential opportunities for his skills in fields that he did not previously know about. He also develops a close relationship with a member of his learning team who calls him for advice about a recalcitrant computer system.

Learner Profile: Janet

Janet is a 52-year-old director of adult education at a large synagogue in the Midwest. She is learning marketing skills and investigating the possibilities of developing education programs via distance learning at her synagogue. She is excited about the opportunity to develop skills, but she is also buried in the administrative details of her organization. Furthermore, she has a difficult time feeling fully comfortable with the distance learning format of the course.

After her initial introduction and greetings, Janet disappears from the classroom for nearly a week. The instructor first emails and then calls her to see if anything is wrong. Janet is fine, but she's distracted by a new series of adult education classes that has just begun at the synagogue; she's been trying to stay on top of enrollment changes for days, plus her assistant is on vacation. The instructor reviews the two most important activities that Janet needs to complete by the end of the week.

Janet completes one of the activities and enjoys it thoroughly, but she doesn't have time to complete the second. She participates enthusiastically with her learning team and makes several new friends while they work together.

The instructor monitors Janet's progress closely. When she has time to do the work, Janet does exceptionally well; she is clearly mastering the concepts, and several of her activities turn into actual marketing campaigns for her synagogue's programs. But the instructor and Janet become discouraged by the difficulty she has balancing the course work and her job. By the end of the course, Janet has completed a little more than half of the assigned activities. She keeps the remainder of the activities in a "to-do" file but wonders when she'll ever have time to get to them. In the final feedback, her instructor notes that Janet has gained value from the course, even if she didn't complete all the work. She has gained practical knowledge and broadened her professional and social network.

Learner Profile: Daniel

Daniel, a 42-year-old active-duty soldier, is preparing to leave military life within the next 3 years. Throughout his military years, Daniel has worked as a medical technician. However, his lifelong dream has been to teach elementary school. He is pursuing an associate's degree through a military program that will enable him to translate military education and experience into civilian credits.

Although his long-term dream is clear, he is unsure of what he wants from the associate's program other than to get through it. It's taken him a long time to work through the required courses so far because the subject matter has not been terribly interesting to him.

The instructor contacts Daniel after reading his introduction and suggests that he organize all of his work for the course around learning more about elementary education. Together, they talk through how to adapt the assignments laid out in the syllabus to fulfill the requirements of the course while enabling Daniel to study and learn more about his dream job. Although some assignments, including learning team projects, cannot be adapted, the majority can.

Daniel becomes more engaged with the course since he has a customized approach to the assignments. But he is less active in the learning team. He participates with the team, but he puts his full effort into the individual assignments. Daniel's contributions to the classroom are refreshing to everyone because he has a unique perspective on the course content—he relates everything to preparing for a teaching career. The contrast between his responses and those of his classmates help deepen the dialogue among the participants.

Learner Profile: Clint

Clint, a 31-year-old desk researcher for a global investment bank, is very skilled at his job, but his opportunities for advancement have stalled because of workforce reductions. In his most recent performance review, his supervisor suggested that professional development in project management, leadership, and strategic planning could help position Clint for additional opportunities. Clint also figures that additional training will help him in finding a new job elsewhere if need be.

Through his professional association, Clint finds several online courses and webinars that match his objectives. Because he wants to document his progress for job-seeking purposes and for his employment file, he contacts the instructors of each session ahead of time to make sure the course offers what he needs and to request that the instructors provide him with a letter of completion to add to his professional portfolio.

Although none of the courses offer formal certification or course completion documentation, several instructors are impressed enough with Clint's proactive approach that they offer to review and respond to a reflective paper or short project that Clint will prepare after the sessions to demonstrate his mastery of the material. In fact, two of the instructors bring the concept to the professional association as a way for future courses to be certified, and another instructor offers the same opportunity to other registrants and, in doing so, creates a de facto learning cohort of peers.

Clint finds that the sessions are not always as targeted to his needs as he'd like, but he uses the individual projects at the end to go a bit deeper into the concepts. Luckily, his supervisor supports his professional development efforts and lets him complete some of the tasks during working hours. It helps that two of his projects directly relate to supporting his department: one on research budget management and another on creating an external communications plan to create broader awareness of the research team's capabilities.

The small cohort of peers turns out to be a useful addition to the experience. The students share work with each other and even make plans to have drinks together at the next association convention. Clint and his cohorts are each self-motivated but become more motivated through each other's encouragement. In this case, the students' enthusiasm further inspires their instructors rather than the other way around.

The Time It Takes

If it seems to take an immense amount of time and effort to focus on individuals and their needs, you are reading this chapter correctly. Because effective distance learning is learner-centered, an instructor can have a solid idea of how to instruct only by having a detailed understanding of the learners.

Over time, it becomes easier to identify what the learner's trigger points may be. You can review their introductions and their first few contributions to the classroom and have an immediate sense of a good approach for helping them. You'll also know just how far you can stretch your content and curriculum to meet learner needs without distorting your program beyond recognition.

Being Resourceful

No matter how comprehensive your course is, your students will have questions and needs that go beyond its scope. While it's not your job to be all things to all people, you can be a hero by providing your students with additional resources that meet their needs and move them toward their goals. As you learn about your students, be ready to pull out and offer resources that address what they need—you'll enhance their satisfaction with you and the course, as well as push that motivation button!

For example, I maintain files with articles, web links, and books that address the most common questions and knowledge gaps among my students. My files are heavily weighted with grammar and communication resources because I see so much need among my students for improvement in these areas. I have also created a guide for college students on web-based research and information literacy, which includes links to reputable sources and a step-by-step introduction to effective use of the web for research. At first I provided that resource only on an as-needed basis, but I soon learned that "as-needed" really meant everyone. Now it's part of my standard toolkit.

For my nonprofit marketing courses, I refer students to online discussions and listservs that they can access to pursue specific lines of thought or expand their work beyond the scope of my courses. Annotated bibliographies of journals, books, tools, and assessments are also in the file; rather than simply provide a laundry list of titles, I describe each item on the list so that students don't have to search everything to figure out what will be the most helpful to them.

The team component of distance learning is challenging for many students, so providing them with additional resources on the how's and why's of team projects helps them work together effectively. Teams need to be able to create team standards, set agendas and deadlines, identify skills, and assign roles. Resources and instructions on doing so help them get off the ground. (Chapter 7 provides more information on the team toolkit.)

My own goal in working with individual students is never having to say "I'm sorry, but I can't help you with that." If I can always provide some sort of answer, even if it's just a referral to someone else who might be able to help, then I am putting the needs of the learner at the center of our relationship and digging into my resources to meet those needs.

Providing Feedback

Individual feedback, both in the classroom and in private communication, can offer the biggest immediate impact in the learning experience for students. In feedback, you respond in writing to specific assignments and contributions of the individual, place the individual's work in the context of the course overall, and compare the performance to the student's own goals and the established criteria for success. Feedback bridges all the elements of the learning experience and translates it into actionable information for the student: Where do I go from here? What's working? What could I be doing differently to enhance my own learning and performance?

Crafting substantive feedback is the most time-consuming part of instructing an active course, which is another reason it is so important to have additional resources at the ready that you can point students toward.

Every word is worth it, though. Feedback is one-to-one instruction, the meeting of the minds, the jelly next to the peanut butter.

Written feedback is preferable to oral feedback; even if you provide oral feedback during a formal conference, put your ideas, reactions, and suggestions in writing, too. Written feedback becomes the tangible document for students—something they can refer to over time to continue the learning process. Sometimes you provide guidance, for instance, on a skill or a task that the student isn't quite ready to fully absorb; if it's in writing, there's always the chance that it will emerge again when the student is ready to make that step.

Writing also forces us instructors to think through the instruction embedded within the feedback. Instead of simply telling a student, "This isn't working," we have to think through why it isn't working and come up with some suggestions for resolving the problem. I often tell my writing students that the process of writing doesn't just record thoughts; it also clarifies them. This is certainly true when I write feedback. I'm forced to support my ideas about the student's work. As a result, the student ends up with real information and personalized instruction on which to act.

The Feedback Sandwich

No one likes to be judged. Students experience a range of emotions—gratitude, anger, confusion—when they receive written feedback from instructors. Constructive critique and correction can be swallowed more easily when they are embedded in a "feedback sandwich"—a critique comment slipped in between two positive comments. For instance, I might comment on an essay turned in by a writing student:

> You've clearly given this topic a lot of thought, and you care deeply about the quality of on-the-job training at your office. It seems to me that a better organization of your ideas will help the reader follow the logic of your discussion—lead us from Point A to Point B and so on to the natural conclusion. (Revisiting and revising your outline will probably help, now that you've clarified what you want to say.) This is the kind of project you can definitely take to your supervisor when it's done and actually see change happen as the result of your analysis—let's get it ready for her!

Feedback includes specific positives as well as places for improvement. It even highlights an approach to improvement that builds on what the student has already done. The "sandwich" is completed with additional praise. As you develop more trust with your students, you can back off a bit on the sandwich approach and serve it "open-faced," with only an introductory positive comment before focusing on areas of improvement. But always lead with what the student has accomplished rather than what still remains to be done.

Sometimes building the sandwich is tough, especially when there is little to be positive about in the completed assignment or exercise. Still, it's worth the effort to serve sandwiches rather than humble pie if you want to keep your students motivated and involved with their own learning.

Which brings up another important point about feedback: The job of the instructor is not to "correct" the work but to provide guidance on how it can be improved as well as what is working.

Grading

If your program or course involves formal grading, your course materials must clearly communicate the criteria for grading. It's also a good idea to repeat the grading criteria for all major assignments when giving out the assignment. Standards should be consistent and, to the extent possible, objective. Create a process for yourself that will allow you to review a student's work, perhaps comparing an assignment to a checklist of excellence;

apply the process for every student. Every now and then, I'll spot-check myself by regrading an assignment a day or two later, just to see if I give the assignment the same grade again (within a small margin of error).

Do not mistake grading as a substitute for substantive feedback. There's a huge difference between telling a student the work has earned a B+ and giving the student detailed information about what works in the assignment and what could have been done better. The grade should reflect the feedback, but the feedback is where the instruction happens.

Grades are important, of course, but I also try to emphasize that the process and learning experience are what truly matter. (I'm a fine one to talk, of course—I used to have fits over tenths of a point in my GPA.) One of the best students I ever worked with ended up with a C- at the end of his written communications class; he just didn't do much of the work in the first half of the class. Over the course of our work together, though, this student developed an entirely new approach to writing and revising his essays, and he discovered a latent gift. After I sent him his final feedback for the course, he wrote to me saying that he knew he'd earned that C-, but he also knew he learned far more than the grade reflected. A year later, he was applying to journalism schools.

Grades can mean everything and nothing. When all else fails, they can be useful in stoking up motivation; more than once I've found that explaining exactly how a student could move from a C+ to a B put that student back on track in a course.

Respecting Privacy

Throughout the course, the relationship you build with each student is private. For the sake of trust, keep detailed feedback between you and the individual. In the classroom environment, feedback should never get too personal.

For example, I never correct a student's grammar and punctuation errors in an asynchronous classroom; I focus instead on ideas, comparing and contrasting responses, and providing additional guidance and insight on different lines of thought emerging in the discussion. I've found that correction of language errors is just too embarrassing for most students and causes them to clam up. In my private feedback to them, I go over the most common errors in detail, encouraging them to use the resources available to practice new grammar and punctuation habits.

Privately, I can also push students harder. It's not unusual for students to start a class with great energy and enthusiasm, overflowing with dreams, but then they may fade into the virtual woodwork when they can't immediately perform to their internal standard of excellence. The distance between current reality and dream just seems too great. In private feedback and communication, challenge them to work toward those dreams in spite of whatever disappointments or setbacks they may be experiencing. Return to their motivational points; remind them that each tiny step brings them closer to where they want to go.

It's Not Easy to Have Relationships

Despite the distance between us, I find that the relationships I have with individual students are highly personal, enriching, and satisfying. Unlike traditional classes, in which I might get to know a handful of students, distance learning requires me to make an effort to get to know them all.

It doesn't always work, of course. Sometimes it's downright impossible to learn much of anything about a student except an email address and a habitual sentence pattern. No matter how you try to nurture it, no relationship blooms. In such cases, you just have to fall back on doing the best you can by teaching the content rather than the student. On the whole, though, I usually have a few authentic human-to-human interchanges with every student who shows up in my distance courses. Those interchanges form the core of our relationships.

Make no mistake, though: Being in a relationship with individual students does not mean you have to like everyone. In fact, one of the ways distance learning brings out the best in me as an instructor is that it enables me to work more effectively with people I don't like.

The "distance" in distance learning allows me to step back from the characteristics and personalities that I find off-putting and focus solely on the student's work. In a traditional classroom, it's easy to fall into the habit of avoiding eye contact with the student you dislike; in a distance classroom, you don't even have to pay attention to who is contributing a particular idea. When I'm leading teleconferences, I have a hard time distinguishing voices; in the online classroom, I may not even notice who posted a message until after I've read it. I've learned that a little willful ignorance allows me to respond to the work product rather than get sucked into unproductive personality clashes.

I learned a profound lesson in the positive elements of distance learning after the completion of an Introduction to College Composition class I taught early in my career as a distance learning instructor. After I had sent my final feedback to the students, one emailed me back, thanking me for my honest assistance with her rather shaky writing skills. The student went on to tell me that she is a paraplegic—something she had not mentioned in her introduction or at any point during our interactions over the 6-week period. What she most appreciated about her experience in this class—her first as a distance student—was that she knew she was evaluated based solely on the quality of her work, really for the first time in her educational career.

I thought about my interactions with her, and I realized that she was right: Lacking information that I would have found very difficult to ignore in a live classroom, I was able to focus solely on her work product. That was the moment I realized that the tradeoffs of *any* instructional environment offer benefits as well as challenges.

That's not to say it's always easy. I've had plenty of students who seem to go out of their way to challenge my ability to stay calm and focus on the work of the student rather than on that student's personality. I do find, however, that the physical distance enables me to create emotional distance. I have time to consider and modulate my responses; I can think before I reply. I take advantage of that reflective pause.

My role is to help *all* of my students find their own voice, even if it's a voice I disagree with. A student information log (see Worksheet 6.1) allows me to record observations that may be helpful in working with students as individuals and reminds me of the unique characteristics that each brings to our relationship. I complete a worksheet like this for each student in a class. I can use the worksheet to record participation, performance, and any notes I want to be sure to include when I send detailed feedback to the student.

As difficult as it can sometimes be to pull back from personality and focus on the work, it's harder still to get the students to do so. Yet it is critical for them in building their own community of learning that they hone in on teamwork and achieving a successful outcome. The next chapter looks at ways instructors can help that magic occur.

Worksheet 6.1   Student Information Log

Name:
Email:
Other contact:
Location:
          (time zone:)
Bio information:

Stated goals:

Observations:
(language skills, attitude, needs, preconceptions, unique potential)

Sent learning styles inventory? Y/N
          Learning style:

Team assignment:

Notes:

Chapter 7

Creating a Community of Learners

Private correspondence courses or mentored relationships rely solely on the educational value of interaction with materials and interaction with instructors. A good distance learning class, on the other hand, broadens and enriches everyone's experience by introducing a multiplicity of opinions and personalities into the mix through the third type of relationship in the distance learning model: interaction with peers.

Building community is hard work. It may be the most difficult element of creating effective distance learning programs. Learning communities face the same challenges as other types of communities: conflict, personality clashes, warring agendas, differences in work ethic, cultural missteps, and more. Add to these challenges the difficulty of working across time zones and with technology that puts many of us at a communication disadvantage, and it may sometimes seem easier just to forget the whole thing. Let the students interact with the material and the instructor, and leave the group stuff alone ...

While this option is tempting, it means ignoring a piece of the process that can make learning especially engaging, relevant, and enriching. For all its difficulty, the work you put into cultivating a community of learners will pay off for you and your students alike. To make it happen, you will need to provide clear, explicit, and practical guidance to students on the right steps to take to become a community. (Yes, I know that I've said that just about everything needs clear, explicit, and practical guidance; it's a running theme in all distance learning where *nothing* can be taken for granted.)

Logistics and Psychology

"How are we supposed to do group work?"

I frequently hear this question during the first days of a distance course. Although this query is usually emailed to me, the whine comes through loud and clear.

To be honest, I'm pretty sympathetic to the whine; sometimes I whine, too. The whiner doesn't really want to hear about instant messaging (IM) sessions, phone calls, email discussions, or dedicated web space for project-focused discussions. The whiner knows these tools exist. What's really motivating the question—and the tone—is fear. The usual fears include:

- What if I get stuck with a lame team?

- What if I can't keep up with my team?

- How will we ever have time to do this team project when we need to use these awkward tools to communicate?

- I'm not even comfortable with this distance environment. Who are these yahoos I have to work with? Do they know what they're doing?

My stomach knots up just reading these words. These are real fears that could strike any of our hearts. The last thing Fear wants to hear is Logic.

In coaching students to work toward building a community of peers, my best resources are a willingness to let them air their concerns and my own experience with how, why, and to what end community works.

I let them complain. If I don't, they never get over it. But I also let them know I used to share those fears and have come to appreciate what team projects bring to the learning experience. (Sounds a little like the inspirational structure again, doesn't it? "We are alike.")

Psychology aside, the logistics do work. Groups find ways to work at a distance for all sorts of projects. Collaborative online workspace, conference calls, IM sessions, email exchange, and file sharing, as well as dedicated online asynchronous discussion space (when available), are all viable options for teams that want to meet, share ideas, and make progress toward goals. However, unlike offline teams, distance learning teams require a bit more foresight and planning, and you'll need to build enough time into the project calendar to account for the extra time that communication may take. However, these are increasingly important skills in all types of 21st-century work environments—the effort you and your students put into learning these skills will pay off far beyond your classroom.

Face to Face?

Is it easier to build community when we can see each other's faces? Probably. But that doesn't mean it's necessary—or even always a good idea—to add a face-to-face element to a distance learning offering.

Blending distance and traditional approaches to education offers instructors a chance to combine the best of all worlds—a few physical meetings or class sessions for real-time, live discussion and instruction, combined with the features and flexibility of distance learning. When blending is done to enhance the overall experience of the learners, it can be a wonderful way to build community while retaining the benefits of distance learning.

Lacking the wherewithal to create an actual, live meeting, an instructor can turn to video-over-internet solutions to create opportunities to "put a face with the name." It's gotten easier to incorporate video into web-based meetings, and judicious use of web cameras can build closer connections among group members. But I think I should tell you that my own experience with webcams is somewhat spotty; in my experience, they slow down transmission times and often create problems when communicating with more than one or two people at a time.

An alternative to using video is simply to ask all participants to post to a site or email relatively small digital photos of themselves.

But I want to make it clear that face-to-face elements—from the photo on up to the live meeting—are options, not baseline requirements, for achieving community. In many of my distance learning programs, I don't even ask students to share a photo. Yet we successfully create a sense of shared purpose and culture that supports our educational work together.

Building on the Classroom Environment

Community begins right in the classroom. The classroom management techniques and tips covered in Chapter 5 begin the process of building a community of learners with the classroom as their "home base." If we think of a community as a location, as well as an abstract collection of individuals, the distance learning classroom serves the purpose of locating the group in the universe, just as a traditional classroom creates the logistical parameters in its own context.

When students enter the distance classroom, whether by visiting the online course platform, opening the email discussion files, logging in to the webinar, or dialing in to the conference call number, they need to know what to expect and what is expected of them. They need to know what the community culture is, no less than what material you will be covering that day in class. The organization, protocols, and consistency you build into their classroom experience will go a long way toward helping them build community.

Still, even with the most organized classroom possible, an instructor will have to work overtime (particularly with a new group) to maximize the community-building potential of the classroom itself. Students are unsure of what to post, whether their questions really "belong" there, or whether they will be violating some unspoken rule that everyone knows about but them. Expect to do a lot of coaching and provide positive feedback for using the community space as a community resource.

Here's a typical problem: I am facilitating an online discussion forum that is serving as the classroom for a program I developed for a client. I started a new thread recently for discussion, questions, and ideas relating to an activity I'd previously asked all the participants to do at work. A few hours after I posted the message, I received a private email from one of the participants: "I didn't know about this assignment; what are we supposed to be doing?"

I laughed. I cried. It was so typical of how nervous students ask questions privately rather than using the public, community space. I emailed her back with a quick "Stay tuned" and then followed up my own initial forum posting with a reminder about where to find the assignment and what they were supposed to be doing. Then I followed up privately with her again, asking that she post a message in public asking for additional clarification. She did; I was thrilled. I thanked her in the forum, even as I responded to her question. A trickle of additional questions from other students followed. Everyone benefited.

I am quite sure that this individual was worried about asking something publicly that "everyone else" clearly knew. But of course, she was not the only one who had forgotten about the assignment or had questions about its execution. (Repeat, repeat, repeat!) At the same time, I don't want to be in the position of constantly "running" the classroom. Particularly when teaching adults, we have to create an environment in which they can take some ownership of the dialogue. Our goal is to help them become willing to post their questions and contributions without worrying that they will be judged negatively as a result and to see that their questions are actually the real purpose of the whole classroom enterprise.

Figure 7.1 illustrates how this very typical interaction plays out as a little one-act drama about community building. Community starts to put down roots when the instructor first creates guidelines and communicates expectations for participation. The instructor must also create opportunity within the classroom for community needs to be met, such as a designated place where students can put their questions and know they'll get answers quickly. Then the instructor has to step back and let the students choose to participate in the community. When private queries come in, the instructor can respond privately with encouragement but still direct the students to the designated community space. With specific coaching to help everyone contribute and public, positive feedback for success, the instructor can lay the groundwork for students to see the value of shared resources for themselves.

Group Work

Interaction within the classroom is an important step in building community, but it's only the first step. When all group interaction relates to classroom discussion or asking for clarification on individual assignments, you

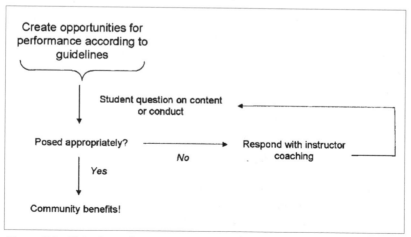

Figure 7.1   *This chart shows nurturing progress toward community formation.*

run the risk of having a more or less superficial discussion of the "I agree; let me tell you what happened to me along the same lines" variety. While valuable as a social experience, this kind of dialogue does not naturally enhance the learning experience.

Another risk in the classroom arises when you are working with a large group, say more than 15 students at a time. Many instructors and organizations get excited about the idea of distance learning because they think it will allow them to reach enormous numbers of students with minimal resources and time. For community interaction to happen and for instruction to be effective, however, small groups are necessary.

My Creative Writing in English (CWE) course regularly registered between 40 and 50 students. I divided them into working groups of about 14 students. A handful of students usually disappeared after a month or two, so the working groups eventually averaged about 10 members each. Similarly, the undergraduate classes I taught at the University of Phoenix were designed to enroll up to 20 students. I divided them into learning teams of four to six members to do projects together throughout the course, and the students came to rely on their teammates as a "community within the community."

Going beyond classroom interactions and getting students to work collaboratively on assignments has a profound impact on learning. When learners have to combine their ideas, skills, and experience and jointly create a product, they do more than master the material: They also learn about their biases and assumptions, strengths and weaknesses, and their ability to help others succeed. Again, these are essential skills for long-term success in the 21st-century workforce.

In a recent communications and writing class, I introduced a new team project I had never tried before. The students were each given a worksheet with a long list of statements. Each statement was a fact, an opinion, a value statement, or an assumption. I asked the students to first work independently to code each statement according to what kind of statement they thought it was. Then, as a team, they were to compare their responses and discuss any they disagreed on. Finally, the team had to turn in a completed worksheet with their aggregated answers, along with a few paragraphs describing the results of their discussion.

The outcome was fascinating, for them and for me. The team discussion was particularly lively over the differences between opinions and value statements. In the end, they correctly identified all of the statements on the worksheet, but the most important element of the learning experience was the dialogue. All team members were forced to examine their assumptions closely about different types of information. Had they simply turned the worksheets in as individual assignments and gotten them back with my corrections, I doubt the assignment would have had nearly as much impact. Because they had to mull it over together with peers, they were able to teach themselves and each other in a lasting way.

Of course, team projects are sometimes disastrous. In almost every class, I get complaints from at least one team that so-and-so never contributes. Sometimes I'm refereeing personality clashes, feeling as though I'm separating the 3-year-olds from the toy chest. Occasionally, I gently inform a student that he or she really *does* have something to learn from peers and that his or her skills aren't so far above the others that the teamwork would be a waste of time. In one way or another, I have to work to convince them that the team component of the course isn't just a way for me to make their lives miserable.

Occasionally, team environments create serious problems. In one team situation, a participant plagiarized her section of an assignment, endangering the entire team's performance on the project. Although she owned up to her actions and accepted the consequences, her team responded by freezing her out of subsequent discussion, making it impossible for her to gain any additional value from the team component of the class. On one hand, I couldn't blame them; on the other hand, I was stuck with a classroom management problem. I reminded the team that conflict resolution was a team responsibility, and they managed to get through the rest of the assignment together.

More frequently, clashes arise when one member of a team tries to take over the process, or worse, when two members of a team each try dragging it in different directions. Private counseling with the warring factions is sometimes helpful, sometimes not. These are common enough situations, not just in a classroom but also in a business, organization, or community. When I get complaints from team members who are caught in the middle, I remind everyone that the ability to work through conflict and collaboratively create a product, despite the challenges of distance and communication, is a life skill. Learn it now or later, but ultimately, it's not optional.

Getting Them Talking: Stages of the Teaming Process

An ounce of prevention, I've heard it said, is worth a pounding over the head with a gradebook. If teams can get off to a good start, they have quickly built a teeny-weeny history of success. Any good experience is something to fall back on when individual personalities, fears, and egos start spicing things up. Just as I launch a classroom by creating a culture within it, I encourage and coach students to create a culture within their teams.

The first stage of team formation is known in the organizational development field as "storming." This is the stage in which everyone is bubbling with ideas and offering their time, skills, and expertise to help the team reach its goals. Storming is also the "getting to know you" phase when team members start to share information about their preferred learning and working styles and to see how they fit together as a group. Finally, storming can also be a bit of a panic stage when the team first takes a look at the project it has to tackle and is overwhelmed by its scope and challenge.

Following storming comes "norming," the stage in which teams start to get a sense of who they are as a working group. The team members begin to establish regular systems and protocols for working together. They become used to the idea of being a team, and they can break down a large task into component parts to build a workable plan. Norming is when teams learn that they can function without too much pain.

Finally, teams reach the "performing" stage, when the team members no longer think twice about how they will work together and simply do the work. It's like the final phase in learning a new dance—it comes naturally and effortlessly, even if the dancer is perspiring like crazy when the music stops.

Teams move through these stages, whether or not they have a process in place to help them do so. Unless they blow up for some reason in the storming or norming phase, teams will make it to performing. To help them get there more quickly and more effectively, a distance instructor needs to give team members a tool to create a community-based understanding of what they are trying to do, how they will do it, and the resources they have to accomplish their goals. This tool is known as the team charter.

A charter is essentially a descriptive document that lays out the team purpose, its members, the specific skills and resources each member brings to the project, a process for leadership selection and conflict resolution, guidelines and policies for meeting and progressing on the work, and criteria for success. Worksheet 7.1 shows a sample charter, but any format works as long as the team members can use it to structure their work and interactions with each other.

Worksheet 7.1 Sample Team Charter

Course:

Team members:

Name	Phone	Email	Preferred contact and time zone

Team projects (review syllabus):

Project	Due date

Requirements for completing projects:
List skills needed, coordination of tasks, interim deadlines for reviewing work product, etc.:

Skills of team members:

Process for group work:
Describe plans for meetings, project leadership, criteria for individual assignments within projects, etc.:

Conflict management and resolution:
What potential conflicts may arise in the course of doing team work? How will the team identify and address conflicts?

Successful outcomes:
What will be deemed a successful outcome for our team work? (Focus on output rather than grades.)

All members of this team have reviewed the contents of this team charter. Our names added below signify our agreement to this charter.

In most of my classes, creation of the team charter is the first project I assign to teams. By creating a charter, teams accomplish a number of things that help them move through the storming and norming stages and get to performing:

- *Collective agreement on the nature of the task(s):* Team members discuss as a group what they think they are supposed to be doing. They create a shared understanding of the scope and nature of the project(s) at hand. If they find they disagree on what the project is supposed to be, they can contact the instructor for clarification (and I get a chance to see where my instructions still need a bit of editing).

- *Appreciation for and acknowledgment of unique skills:* In listing each team member's unique skills and resources, teams have an opportunity to see the richness of experience they have at their disposal. If they also share learning style information with each other, they have yet another lens through which to view the different ways they can approach a problem and solve it together. Reviewing the aggregated skill list can also be comforting to team members who are afraid that they'll get stuck doing a whole project on their own or that the project is too big to complete in the time frame allotted. A shared skill inventory helps teams begin to see themselves as a community that together can take on more than an individual can handle.

- *Process creation:* Charters help teams break down large projects into discrete, manageable chunks and create a process by which they will complete them all. Even if the team does not follow its process exactly, having it helps members identify when they are moving off track. Psychologically speaking, having a plan takes some of the panic out of large projects.

- *Strategies for conflict resolution:* At the start of most team-building exercises, most teams feel that they will be the exception to the human rule that conflict is bound to happen. With the optimism they have at the start of a journey, they are sure that since they are all good people, they will naturally (and with great maturity) deal with any minor disagreements along the way. My advice is always to believe in the goodness of your teammates but also to have a plan for dealing with the inevitable. Putting conflict resolution into the charter forces team members to recognize that they will likely disagree somewhere along the way; they have a chance while they're all still on cordial terms to work out how they will resolve those issues. If they wait until it's a crisis, conflict can be crippling.

- *A picture of what success looks like:* Finally, the team charter helps members share and combine their ideas about what a successful outcome of their work together might be. There's nothing worse than getting three-quarters through a team project and realizing that you've been working on a presentation while your teammates have been working on a full-scale model. Shared understanding of the outcome not only clarifies what everyone is working on; it also helps teams budget their time and avoid wasted effort.

The chartering process results in a document to which teams can refer along the way. It also gets them talking to each other and communicating on a very practical level about what they want out of their participation in the community of learners and what they bring to that community. At the same time, chartering emphasizes self-reflection. Individual members must think about specific actions they need to take in order to contribute to the success of the team. They cannot be passive on teams, and the charter helps them identify the unique contribution they can make.

No matter how well you support the formation of teams or working groups, you will experience resistance from some students. Many individuals have not previously considered their peers to be an integral part of their learning experience. They may prefer to be in the classroom, where authority is clearly held by the instructor, rather than in the team room, where authority must be shared. They may resent having their own performance depend on someone else's work. Chartering is not a panacea for the ills of team work, but it does help even the most skeptical student feel that there is a route to success.

Peer Evaluation

Showing students how to accept evaluation from their peers helps members of a team become more reflective and less reactive. When they know that they will be giving and receiving feedback using a formal peer-evaluation process, they take their teamwork more seriously. It's no longer something they're just doing to please the instructor or meet the requirements of the course; peer evaluation also serves to make the team members more invested in creating a functioning work group.

Peer evaluation also gives team members a way to begin talking about conflict while avoiding a personal attack. They can use an evaluation form to provide a team member with feedback that may be difficult to say directly. Asking a team member, "Why didn't you contribute to this phase of the project?" creates an adversarial relationship. On the other hand, providing a team member with an evaluation that states, "So-and-so did not contribute to the best of his abilities to the completion of the project," has more potential to open the door for dialogue about the situation.

I let students know, however, that I do not consider peer evaluations when I complete my own feedback and grading; I try to create my own impressions of a team dynamic without relying on the peer evaluations to keep me informed. Instead, when I review students' evaluations of their teammates, I turn the questions around:

- What could you have done differently to elicit optimum performance from your teammates?

- What did your teammates help you learn about yourself and your contributions to success?

- What worked well in this team environment?

- What will you try with your next team to achieve the results you want?

Thus, peer evaluation also turns into self-evaluation—an opportunity for students to understand themselves as a part of group solutions.

Making Magic

The mysteries of human relationships and community never fail to intrigue me. Chemistry can allow the oddest collection of individuals to come together and create something none of them expected. When personalities, learning styles, and tasks really mesh, it's absolutely magical. The group members come together and have fun, learn the material, turn out a great work product, and may even develop a few lifelong friendships.

An instructor can only do so much to elicit magic, of course. The final ingredients have to come from the participants themselves. But you can create the right environment for the transformation to happen.

One of my favorite tricks is to ask groups of students to do a small project together without informing them ahead of time that it's coming. For instance, if I have two learning teams responding to discussion questions, I'll ask members of each team to do a brief critique of the other team's response. The unexpected mini-assignment pulls them out of whatever dynamic they may have created in crafting their own response. It also throws them back into brainstorm-and-analysis mode, shifting them out of production mode. I've often found that these unexpected summonses (combined with an opportunity to do a bit of peer review) bring out the best in work groups. They know how to perform together, and they discover they can have fun doing it.

Counterforces to Black Magic

If the magic in your community is of the darker variety, you have to do what you can to neutralize it. The plagiarist is one example of how badly things can turn, but there are countless others: the student who irritates everyone within emailing distance; the little dictator; the "whatever you want to do is fine with me but I'd better get a good grade" freeloader; the perfectionist who insists on doing every step of the project alone, even if it means redoing everyone else's work.

Communities at a distance require a high level of communication skills to be truly successful. And let's face it: There are a lot of poor communicators out there, and even those of us who make a living in communication could always use some improvement. Emotions can run very high within group-based projects. If you mix intense emotion with unskilled communication in a pressure-cooker situation in which everyone is struggling with new knowledge, the resulting dish can be pretty hot.

Sometimes the best thing an instructor can do is let everyone back off for a few days. If the problem is within a small working group or learning team, I will even consider mixing up the teams to see if a new configuration of personalities may smooth things out. If explosions have taken place in the classroom, I devote classroom time (remember, this is *my* environment, too) to discussing the problem as objectively as possible. I ask everyone to focus on what action we can take, not on what has happened.

Finally, I communicate, individually and to the dysfunctional team, that it isn't a question of whether they like each other. Rather, the objective is to be able to achieve the community's goal: project output and successful completion of the course. It isn't much of a trick to achieve results when everyone is passing around the warm fuzzies. It's much harder to achieve results when we have to deal with opposing ideas, different ways of working, and competing approaches to the problem. If we can learn to listen and work around interpersonal conflict, real change—in class, in community, and in the world—is possible.

Communication x Time x Outcomes = Community

If you have the luxury of working with a group over a period of time, or if you have a class made up of students who are moving through a program of study together, you have a wonderful opportunity to build community that will exist beyond the parameters of your current course. Most courses I teach last between 3 and 8 weeks, which isn't much time for laying the foundations of community. Students gain terrific benefits from the group orientation of these courses, but they are unlikely to continue most of those relationships unless they are compelled to do so.

Time and continued progress are the differentiating factors between course-based community and long-term community. A "cohort" of distance learning students who work together over 6 months or more get to know each other more intimately. As they learn to function more and more efficiently, they can take on bigger projects and challenges, which also deepens their commitment to their community.

Instructors are also changed by the experience of belonging to this remarkable distance learning community. Because distance learning puts us into relationship with so many types of people, it's a great arena in which to discover our own biases, soft spots, and assumptions about people. I have had many of my own subtle prejudices dismantled because I've participated in these communities. The revelations and personal growth that I gain as a result of these interactions are what I've come to love about distance instruction. I can learn more about all the different ways there are to be a good person, to be a thinking human being.

The most dramatic impact that participating in distance learning communities has had on my own attitudes has come through my work with students who are on active duty with or recently retired from the military. Before working with these students, I didn't think much about the reasons young men and women chose military careers. In the past few years, I've worked closely with military students around the world and learned more about what it means to them to serve. I've had students keep up with course work despite a last-minute deployment to Iraq; I've had students use my assignments to write, for the first time ever, what they saw and heard, thought, and felt while serving on missions in Haiti and Bosnia. Their perspectives, ideas, and words never fail to shake me out of my cocoon of ignorance with respect to what's going on in the world.

Not every course results in the blossoming of community, just as not every student enters into relationship with the instructor. But by the end of most courses, the students are usually cheering each other on. They come to believe in each other, and the strength they gain from earning the confidence of their peers means just as much as the individual instruction they get from me.

Community building may never be easy. Students come into distance learning with an intuitive understanding that they will need to interact with content and interact with the instructor. Interaction with peers is less intuitive and needs to be proven through usage and results.

The amazing thing is that interaction with peers is the one element students can most easily take with them. Content and instructor are only available for the duration of the course. The more students come to see their peers as learning resources, the more they can continue to take charge of their learning beyond your classroom experience.

If you're lucky, they might even invite you to their reunions.

Chapter 8

Beyond the Formal Classroom

I did not pursue formal education to become an instructor. In fact, none of the skills I use professionally are ones I gained through formal education. In today's professional world, I do not think I am that unusual. Most career paths today require an attitude of continuous development, and the more ways we give ourselves to access education, the more likely we are to thrive in a quickly changing world.

My employer, FreePint, Ltd., publishes a range of professional development resources to support the way professionals interact with information—everything from how to do research online, to better management of sensitive records, to integration of social media into information work, to tips on how to share complex information as effectively as possible. These are all information skills that knowledge workers desperately need to know. But how and where to get the training?

FreePint subscribers use its resources internally to develop and deliver a range of practical and focused training to their employees on these skills, right at the point of need: the desktop. Furthermore, FreePint offers a professional development series called FreePint Webinars (web.freepint.com/go/research/webinars), in which topic experts share their knowledge with others scattered around the globe, both in live sessions and via recorded and archived versions. Subscribers, participants, and FreePint's entire global audience rely on FreePint to keep abreast of fast moving changes in the world of information; FreePint's users trust the contributors and editors to keep them informed of the latest trends. These users then apply their learning directly to what they're doing at work that day, sometimes even that hour.

FreePint is only one of the myriad sources for training and learning opportunities that go beyond formal classrooms and into the realm of targeted, as-needed instruction. Many professional associations have created effective educational programs aligned to the changing needs of their members, helping them stay competitive in the marketplace and, at the same time, keeping association membership relevant and valuable. Large organizations have internal training departments that manage career development needs, and identify and address gaps in the knowledge of their workforce to keep the company competitive. Independent training and/or consulting companies have developed and deliver extensive curricula in every imaginable niche and industry. Regulatory and licensure boards for professions like law, medicine, engineering, and social work that require continuing education deliver education that meets those requirements, as well as certify the offerings of others.

In each of these instances, career-long learning is essential, and distance education can play a critical role. For instructors, organizers, and students alike, informal distance instruction meets today's needs for:

- *Flexibility:* Busy adults need access to learning on their terms and schedules. Often the barrier to training is the time it takes away from doing other activities, more so than its cost. Distance instruction enables greater flexibility. Using tools like asynchronous discussion, archived materials, and self-paced programs, instructors can create more flexible environments for their students.

- *Relevance:* Distance learning provides customization in choosing materials, adapting assignments to learning styles, and applying the content directly to the students' needs. By doing so, distance learning also builds innate relevance into the offering. Busy adults seek out educational opportunities that are directly relevant to their needs, which is something distance learning can deliver.

- *Practicality:* One of the advantages of distance learning is that it fits more easily into the regular workflow or lifestyle of the student. Students can access learning from their offices or homes, engaging with new ideas in the environments where they will need to use them. The ability to use new ideas right away helps the learning stick.

- *Efficiency:* Distance learning eliminates travel time and water cooler talk, making the time devoted to learning more efficient. Working people may not always be able to justify days away from the office for workshops or conferences, but they may be able to make the case for an hour or two of professional training that doesn't even require them to leave their desks.

- *Cost:* The cost of attending live learning events these days can exceed tight corporate travel budgets. Many professionals who may have had leeway to attend two or three professional development programs in the past no longer have the option to do so, or they may have to select a single event to attend live and manage the rest through professional reading and distance learning. Even organizations with larger travel budgets may find that, in practice, professionals simply cannot afford to spend a full day or more away from their offices. Even if a distance learning program and a live event cost the same, the real cost to the student (or the student's employer or sponsor) will be lower for the distance program, thanks to less of an impact on productivity.

- *Reduced risk:* Live events are risky for organizers; anything from bad weather to traffic jams to poor logistics can turn a well-planned event into a disaster. Distance learning programs reduce these risks (although the risk of technical failure is still present). For participants, distance learning may also represent reduced risk. Participants who are dissatisfied with a particular event can easily reduce their time commitment by logging off; however, if they have traveled to an event, the time is simply wasted.

- *Scalability:* Live events and learning environments are dependent upon capacity—only so many people can fit in a room, and instructors can only teach so many sessions in a given week. Distance learning truly enables you to teach beyond your reach, allowing you to instruct more students, fill more sessions, and expand capacity to reach more learners. Distance learning scales more easily than live events and provides a more flexible format that can produce learning quickly around a variety of topics.

Informal Learning Opportunities

For me, teaching is one of the most rewarding elements of my life. I get great satisfaction in helping others improve their skills and in helping organizations succeed through the better education of their workforce. I love to share what I know and to help others facilitate sharing what they know; at the same time, I learn as much from the students as they do from me.

Informal learning opportunities enable me to be an instructor far more often than I would otherwise be able to be. However, informal learning requires an adapted approach to instructional principles. A brown bag lunch session does not demand the same level of preparation as a semester-long course or even a half-day workshop. Still, applying good instructional principles ensures that everyone's time is well-spent. You can make the most of these flexible, on-demand, casual learning options if you keep in mind the concepts and practices presented throughout this book.

Consider the following informal distance learning opportunities, any of which may present a chance to practice your skills and share knowledge directly at the point of need.

Communities of Practice

Communities of practice bring together professionals to provide networking, peer-to-peer knowledge exchange, and pooled know-how to support a business or project. Multinational organizations use communities of practice to connect staff with their counterparts in far-flung offices around the world. These staff members may never (or rarely) meet face to face, but they connect regularly via teleconferences, web-based meetings, intranet portals, listservs, and other communication tools that are common to the digital office and the distance learning environment.

Other communities of practice have been built to support social or cultural change, such as formal or informal networks of grass-roots political organizers, volunteers, professionals in nonprofits, and mission-based organizations. Since more of our social and cultural world has a digital component these days, it's easier than ever for informal connections to spring up via tools like blogs, Facebook, and Twitter.

Professional association discussion groups are a kind of community of practice. When email communications first became more commonplace, many associations started listservs to generate private discussion among members. Often, these email discussions provided great value to members by enabling close connections between professionals with common aims and offering a way to share ideas despite geographic distance. Many of these listservs continue today, but others have migrated into social media, such as LinkedIn. LinkedIn Groups is a common place to find active communities of practice on almost any professional topic.

As an instructor, consider any communities of practice to which you belong as a potential platform for ad hoc teaching. These communities exist because the members are personally invested in knowledge exchange and are already using the tools of distance instruction to create that exchange.

For example, you might simply apply some of the best practices for managing asynchronous discussion to support the community of practice. A good one to keep in mind is "summarize and send": Lots of excellent ideas are shared via asynchronous discussion, but they can get lost in the threads. Invest a little time periodically in summarizing key points for the community and publishing them to the community for further reflection.

It's also possible to integrate a subtle learning arc into the communications and discussions of a community of practice. Whether via intranet portal, listserv, or email exchange, plan and implement a series of reflective questions to pose to the group that build upon each other. I used this approach to support the learning of a community of practice devoted to nonprofit marketing. I didn't want to create a formal education module for the community, as it was developing its own character nicely. However, I did want to be sure that members had an opportunity to reflect on and interact with some key ideas about marketing over a 3-month period. Using links to reference material and examples, I posted a total of six questions to the group, one every 2 weeks. Some of the questions generated dozens of responses, while others only garnered two or three. By the end of the 3 months, I knew that members of the community had absorbed some of the key ideas that I wanted them to carry forward into their work, and it was accomplished without interrupting the regular flow of their dialogue and without formally introducing an education module.

Functioning communities of practice are fertile grounds for adding informal distance learning; they comprise motivated adults, already interacting effectively at a distance. All you have to do is fold in some instructional ideas and stir gently.

Frequently Asked Questions

Most websites host a Frequently Asked Questions (FAQ) page, which is the perfect place to provide information about an organization or a product line, as well as "how-to-use" resources or materials. FAQs are a basic requirement for digital environments. And if you think about it, they are instructional materials designed to be used at a distance.

Many FAQs, however, are poorly developed. They are too frequently written from the perspective of the writer, not the reader. Apply the principle of "It's not about you; it's about them." Turn FAQs into real instruction by keeping the needs of the learner in mind when crafting them.

Consider, too, the value of meeting the needs of alternative learning styles. FAQs do not always need to be text-based. A brief demo video of a feature or function might make more sense and be easier for the learner to absorb.

Any time visitors access FAQs, they are seeking knowledge. Turn the visit into an informal distance learning opportunity by giving FAQs the same attention you'd pay any reusable learning object.

Awareness Campaigns

A critical challenge facing organizations of all sizes is building awareness among employees, customers, and other stakeholders around any number of topics. For example, organizations may launch awareness campaigns to get employees to focus on green initiatives, knowledge sharing, or new resources that are available.

Marketing and communications departments often take control of awareness campaigns—and it makes sense that they do. This is their specialty. But add the expertise of an instructor to the mix, and the project may become a lot more effective.

My best experience with applying instructional principles to an awareness campaign occurred when I was helping a multinational consultancy build awareness for its new knowledge portal. Key staff had been working with the knowledge portal for several months, ensuring that it was full of meaningful and compelling information, as well as connections to the company's clients and resources. Now it was time to open the portal for broader usage, and we had to make the employee population aware.

We created many of the expected introductory materials, such as internal newsletter items, demo sessions, testimonials from users, highlighted content, and success stories. We were already adhering to many distance instruction principles while we did so—multiple learning modes, repeating information, and learner-focused materials, to name only a few.

As with my approach to communities of practice, we added more deliberate but informal learning objectives to the campaign. Within the project team, we defined two critical learning objectives for our "student population" to master:

- Name the four benefits each worker can gain from interacting with the knowledge portal.

- Successfully post new material to the portal and comment on items already in the portal.

The objectives were never articulated to the employees, but these goals drove each stage of the campaign. Over the 9-month period from launch to first full assessment, the project team released materials and gauged responses by measuring them against these objectives. To the "students," the campaign probably seemed similar to any other internal marketing campaign they had encountered; to the project team, we were delivering instruction to distant students who were each accessing the materials in their own time and in their own way.

Adapting Your Style

You already know that when moving from a live classroom environment to a distance learning environment, you have to adapt your instructional style. When moving from a formal distance environment to an informal distance environment, you have to adapt once again.

Many of the adaptations are ones you will already be familiar with, such as knowing your audience and working within the medium. Other adaptations are more specific to informal learning environments. Certainly a more informal instructional "voice" sets an appropriate tone. In asynchronous discussions in which you participate, for example, you may straddle a line between participating and leading, particularly if the other participants are your professional or social peers. You may only apply instructional principles at the start or end of threads rather than throughout. In these informal settings, it's more important than ever to keep your social antennae highly alert to the reactions of the rest of the group, so that you do not inadvertently disrupt the natural flow of interaction.

The major differences between formal settings and informal settings for distance instructors relate to the shift in relationship among the three interactions of instruction: content, instructor, and peers. Figures 8.1 and 8.2 illustrate this difference. In formal settings, the instructor truly drives the process—creating the content and actively fostering the interactions. In informal settings, interaction with peers forms the foundation of the experience, next is interaction with content, and *last* is interaction with the instructor. In Figure 8.1, the darkest shaded circle (interaction with content) represents the place where you are likely to put the most planning, development, and effort in a formal environment, and also where you have the most control over results. The circle with no shading (interaction with peers) is the area in which you have the least amount of control.

In Figure 8.2, the darkest shaded circle (interaction with peers) represents the area in which natural activity already takes place in an informal environment. The circle with no shading (interaction with instructor) is the area that simply will not happen without your intentional focus.

Thus, your role in this cluster of interactions is quite different than it is in a formal distance learning setting. Successful instruction in an informal setting requires a gentler and more subtle approach. All of the tools you

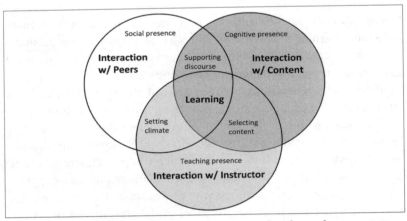

Figure 8.1   *The darkest shaded circle represents the place where you are likely to put the most planning, development, and effort in a formal environment, and also where you have the most control over results. The circle with no shading is the area in which you have the least amount of control.*

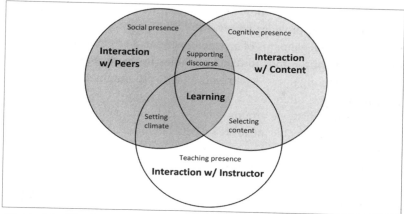

Figure 8.2   The darkest shaded circle represents the area in which natural activity already takes place in an informal environment. The circle with no shading is the area that simply will not happen without your intentional focus.

have developed as an instructor are critical: tuning instruction to the needs of the learner, focusing on learning objectives, giving attention to different learning styles, fostering healthy interaction, triggering motivation, and so on. But you must wield them with a lighter hand than in a formal setting.

Why Bother?

You've got enough to do in your busy life, including planning your formal distance learning opportunities. Why bother applying instructional principles to informal distance learning?

Some of us just can't help it; I'm one of them. We see opportunities to help people learn and improve, and we want to support them. We feel like we have something valuable to share. By consciously applying instructional principles in these situations, we create the best chance for success.

There are other, less altruistic reasons: Informal settings are all around us. By applying instructional principles in these settings, you have the greatest chance of reaching the greatest number of learners—even those who are not aware that they might need learning and may not be inclined to register for a formal program.

As with any skill, the more you practice, the better you get. Informal distance learning provides you with a multitude of venues in which to practice different elements of instruction and to do so in an environment in which one of the most difficult variables in the distance equation—interaction among peers—can resolve itself with minimal effort on your part. In fact, I've often found that the observations I make about what helps informal distance groups succeed in building community are the very insights that enable me to create better community in my next formal distance classroom.

Finally, there's no better way to demonstrate your competence than by using it. In today's world, workers must constantly hone their skills and position themselves for the next opportunity (whatever that might be). You create career resilience by demonstrating how well you perform. Offering your skills as an instructor in informal learning opportunities raises your profile and builds your credibility, no less than your CV.

Offer to contribute your knowledge as an instructor, without regard for territories or project ownership. At the minimum, you will contribute to successful outcomes and an improved learning experience for everyone. At most, you may create for yourself a whole new world of opportunity.

Avoiding Common Errors

Informal distance learning opportunities are all around us, and the errors that organizers, participants, and instructors make in these settings are equally ubiquitous. Your conscious avoidance of these errors will contribute to successful learning experiences and outcomes.

Phoning It In

Informal settings tend to encourage off-the-cuff interactions because they are, well, *informal.* Certainly you want your instructional approach to match the environment. At the same time, your approach to the events of instruction needs to remain thoughtful and informed by experience.

A very common error in informal distance education is for instructors to pay less than careful attention to the quality of their instruction. Just because you are in an informal telephone meeting of peers doesn't mean you can "phone it in." If you are treating the experience as an instructional opportunity, have an objective, use best practices, focus on the audience—and shut down the online Scrabble game while you're at it.

Covering Too Much

When I finished a 30-minute presentation at a conference recently, a colleague approached to thank me for the session. He compared it favorably to many of the others he had attended over the previous day, mainly due to one important characteristic: "You didn't try to cover too much," he noted. In a 30-minute session, my instructional goal was limited to a single learning objective, supported with three key points from my research. Had I tried to cover more (as so many presenters apparently did), it would have no longer been about the audience and what they could get out of it; it would have been about the content and jamming as much of it into the time allotted as possible.

Whether invited to present at an in-person brown bag lunch session or an informal community of practice web-based meeting, use the same principles of paring down your curriculum that you would use in editing your topics and activities, as we learned in Chapter 4. In fact, informal distance settings need even more editing than formal settings. As noted, in informal settings, the emphasis is on the interaction with peers; interaction with content and instructor take a secondary role, and your expectations for what you can cover must be revised accordingly.

Assuming "If You Build It, They Will Come"

Many organizations want to inspire and foster effective and meaningful informal interactions. Sponsoring organizations can achieve great benefits by doing so. Professional associations create value for members. Conference planners extend and deepen the relationship delegates have through digital discussion and interaction before, during, and after an event. Corporations foster a more effective, connected workforce, and an easier way of sharing knowledge. Professionals of all kinds tap a broader network and reach of expertise.

Sponsors of informal distance interactions commonly make the same assumption: Implementing the mechanism of interaction is the same as fostering interaction. This is wrong. Creating a discussion space, a portal, a series of web conferences, or a "comments" feature on a site does not automatically engender meaningful interaction. Building it is no guarantee that they will come.

In these situations, your abilities and experience as an instructor can make the difference between the failure and success of an initiative. You are the one who understands participant motivation and how to capture and maintain interest, activate prior learning, and create engagement. These are the essential ingredients in early stages (or faltering periods) of informal distance connections.

It might be a LinkedIn Group having difficulty developing meaningful discussion, a community of practice experiencing drop-off in participation, or any kind of informal distance network with the mechanisms of interaction in place but lacking motivated contributors. These are opportunities for you to collaborate with the organizer or sponsor to create something more meaningful and valuable. Help the sponsor identify its goals. Learn about the audience to better identify and focus on the potential motivations of its members. Propose and then develop content (provocative questions, compelling resources, engaging presentations or demos) to capture interest and draw in participation. Then manage—gently and subtly—to nurture motivation and achieve those goals.

As with any distance instruction, informal distance learning requires careful thought, planning, execution, and reflection on the outcomes, and it requires collaboration (the subject of the next chapter). Believe me: It's all worth the effort.

Chapter 9

Distance Learning as a Collaborative Enterprise

Learning occurs as a result of interaction. A learner encounters material, works with it, and in the process transforms it into new knowledge. Watch an infant or toddler for any period of time, and you can observe the process in action: Any interaction with the material world leads to experimentation, exploration, and natural learning.

Effective distance learning programs are built on a foundation of carefully designed interactions. The most powerful distance learning programs capitalize on three kinds of interaction: with content, with the instructor, and with peers (see Figure 9.1). In this distance learning model, students are not passive recipients of information; rather, they are the active center of their own learning experiences. To master new skills and knowledge, they must engage with the content of a course, interact with an instructor who can help them make personal meaning of the material, and validate and deepen their new knowledge through peer dialogue.

Before any of these interactions can occur, however, a different kind of interaction needs to happen: interaction among the collaborative partners who design, develop, and implement the program. Even the simplest and least technically dependent programs benefit from collaborative design and engineering. Because interaction is critical to the eventual success of a program, an interactive approach to development builds that orientation right into the foundation. You can't interact in a vacuum, nor can you create interaction from inside a vacuum.

The collaborative work that goes into planning, building, and implementing a successful distance learning program has requirements similar to those of other kinds of collaborative projects. Individuals who are part of the collaboration must have:

- Clear roles and responsibilities
- Shared understanding of goals
- Appreciation for how each contribution fits into the big picture

- Awareness of challenges

- Tools and processes with which to overcome challenges

- Ability to communicate

- Orientation toward problem solving

Roles and Responsibilities

Students and instructors are the primary actors in the distance learning drama, but there are plenty of supporting parts to go around. Some roles and the tasks associated with them occur in sequence, while others can occur simultaneously. All of these roles and tasks have elements that support both the instructor and the student, although some may have greater direct impact on one than the other.

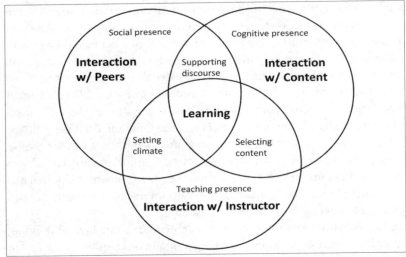

Figure 9.1   *The three kinds of interactions—with content, instructor, and peers—are what co-create an effective learning experience.* [Used with permission from Karen Swan, "Learning Effectiveness: What the Research Tells Us," in *Elements of Quality Online Education: Practice and Direction* (Needham, MA, Sloan Consortium, 2003), www.sloanconsortium.org.]

How to Use This Chapter

This chapter is designed to be a stand-alone resource that instructors and their development partners can use to establish a shared understanding of their projects, roles, potential challenges, and desired outcomes. Worksheet 9.1 (on page 195) can help team members define their roles and understand the full scope of talent and resources involved in the project. Worksheet 9.2 at the end of the chapter can be used as a discussion guide for team meetings or as a worksheet for each team member to complete prior to meeting. For further information and tools to support collaborative development of distance learning programs, visit the companion site for this book at web.freepint.com/go/research/learning.

Figure 9.2 overlays the roles and work of the different members of the distance learning partnership with the interactions that comprise the learning experience. Depending on the size of a project, the nature of the sponsoring institution, the budget, and the course platform, each role may be taken by one person, or some people may play multiple roles. For instance, in many cases, the instructor is also the topic expert and sometimes the instructional designer as well. An administrative department or individual may serve as project manager while supporting the back-end needs of students and instructor alike.

The unique way each distance learning project team comes together can create challenges if members of the team are not entirely clear on what their specific responsibilities are. Teams run the risk of launching a project while missing critical skill sets if they do not start by establishing a clear understanding of who is at the table and what tasks each will be performing over the course of a project. To mitigate these risks, teams should complete a job description for each of their members (see Worksheet 9.1). Comparing the aggregated job descriptions with the overall project plan provides an opportunity to identify any gaps or overlaps that could cause delays or communication challenges during the project.

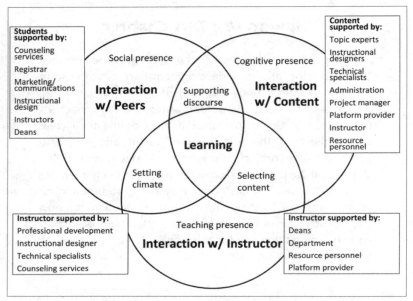

Figure 9.2   This figure shows the roles and responsibilities needed to create interactions.

Content Roles

Prior to the launch of a course, a distance learning team must first design, create, and test the content for the course. During and after delivery of a course, the team must assess the efficacy of the content, its usability, and its practical value to students and instructors.

The following team members are responsible for the content of a course:

- *Topic expert:* Individual(s) with expertise in the material students will be exposed to during the course

- *Instructional designer:* Individual(s) with expertise in the design and craft of instructional experiences based on learner needs

- *Instructor:* Individual(s) who will present the content and help students interact with it to maximize their learning

Worksheet 9.1   Team Member Job Descriptions

Name:

Title:

Essential role:

Skills required:

Timing:

Reports to:

Contact information:

- *Development expert:* Individual(s) responsible for packaging the content so that it is accessible to students and instructor during the course

- *Administrator:* Individual(s) charged with the task of overseeing content development and implementation tasks, maintaining overall quality and consistency standards, reporting on progress, and identifying process components that need to be improved, changed, or enhanced

Administrative and Support Roles

Before the course is launched, team members in administrative and support roles document and market the course offering, handle registration, and arrange for access to the course. During the course, administrative and support individuals manage any technical support or access issues that arise, monitor attendance and grading if relevant, and gather and compile all formal feedback regarding the course. Following the course, the work of administrative and support personnel includes recording grades and credit, performing any course shut down (including archiving) required, and distributing course feedback to other members of the team.

The following team members are responsible for administrative duties and support:

- Academic counselor

- Registrar

- Faculty or instructor development specialists or trainers

- Dean (or equivalent)

- Communications or marketing specialists

- Information technology specialists

- Student support services specialists

- Department chair (or equivalent)

Shared Understanding of Goals

With so many individuals participating in the collaborative work of building and launching a distance learning course, it is critically important for everyone on the team to have a shared understanding of the overall goals for the project. Each project will have its own specific goals, but distance learning programs must include these among their primary goals:

- To create learning experiences that are **relevant, engaging, and challenging for students**

- To enable student **interaction with content, instructor, and peers**

- To foster student learning so that students can **achieve the learning objectives**

It's easy, in the midst of the myriad tasks that occur during a distance learning development project, to forget about the students and their learning experiences. Keeping these fundamental goals in mind makes the difference between courses that work and those that have terrific content and fabulous interfaces but fail to make a difference for students.

Beyond the fundamental goals, a distance learning team must have a shared sense of the specific goals of its immediate project. Developing goals requires knowledge of the student population: What do they need to be able to say, think, or do as a result of completing the course? What are the specific challenges the learner population may face in completing the course? What outcomes would be perceived as success by the sponsoring institution? The team may want to consider the following questions:

- *Research:* Is there a need to conduct additional research about the needs and interests of the students before developing the course?

- *Enrollment:* Does a successful outcome involve a specific level of enrollment? Would the course be considered successful if five students completed it? If 25 students completed it?

- *Capacity:* What scope of course complexity and student population are you equipped to handle?

- *Use of distance methods:* Are there particular methods and tools you are required to use to build and implement this course? Are there methods and tools you would like to try? What additional information do you need in order to be able to make sound decisions about your methods and tools?

Establishing goals for the project on the front end enables the team to evaluate its own success. Without knowing what you set out to accomplish, it's impossible to know if you achieved it.

The Big Picture

Once you have established a shared understanding of goals, as well as the range of skills and perspectives represented on the team, you can assemble a holistic view of the distance learning project and how each member of the team contributes to its success. Table 9.1 illustrates the interrelationships of tasks and events along the timeline of a development project and how those tasks and events contribute to the goal of successful learner-centered instruction.

Recognize the Challenges

Any collaborative project will face challenges—timing, budget, communication, technology, contrary needs, and perspectives. Team members have

Table 9.1   Tasks and Events on the Development Timeline

	Stage of process						
	Pre-concept	Concept	Planning	Development	Testing	Course delivery	Evaluation
Administrative roles		Establish budget, parameters, and resources for course		Market course		Provide support resources during course	Review course evaluation
Student support roles	Conduct enrollment; provide counseling	Gather input on need for course			Test with potential students	Interact with content, instructor, and peers	Complete course evaluation
Content roles			Research resources and identify content experts; create instructional designs	Write/develop content and evaluations		Monitor during delivery and troubleshoot any emergency problems	Archive and document course
Technical roles			Brainstorm tech needs; review requirements	Build and implement technical elements of course	Test and tweak		
Instructor support roles	Provide faculty development	Develop concept for course	Provide input on design and content	Provide input on content, evaluations, and technology	Complete training on course and platform	Interact with students; provide feedback; manage classroom; report any problems	Review course evaluation

control over some of these challenges but not others. At some level, the budget cannot be budged; the technology can be manipulated only so far; project deadlines often have external triggers, such as the date that the new class of students is scheduled to show up and expect a functional classroom.

To be truly collaborative, distance learning projects require that all members of the team approach the challenges with a problem-solving orientation. No one is allowed to get hung up on a problem! The creative brain power of the entire team is ingenuity enough to get through just about any challenge as long as the members of the team perceive themselves as a team and not in competition for limited resources, budget, or prestige.

When in conflict or just plain stuck on an intractable problem, return to the fundamental goals: relevant, engaging, and challenging learning experiences that meet the needs of students; everything else is secondary. With that priority established, reconsider the problem using the following questions:

- Does this problem interfere with the fundamental goals of the program? If not, is it really a problem?

- Is this problem under the control of a member of the team? If so, how can that team member resolve it? If not, how can the team as a whole neutralize its effects?

- Is there something missing that would mitigate or eliminate the problem?

Communicate

Team approaches to challenges can only be successful if team communication is successful. Clear and open lines of communication enable members of a team to access each other's creative resources when needed. At the same time (and not incidentally), good communication keeps a project on target for deadlines while helping a team *feel* like a team.

Enable communication by establishing protocols for the use of email, teleconference, shared online workspace, and other resources that draw members of the team closer together. Over the course of a long project, meetings for periodic updates keep everyone feeling connected and provide opportunities for group brainstorming around any challenges or issues that have arisen.

Be a Network

Distributed teams don't get the full benefit of teamwork if members do not have direct access to other members—if, for instance, all communication is routed through a project manager or other intermediary. For a team to "know what it knows," it needs to create direct access opportunities between members. The project manager (or other central communicator) can be added to the communications loop.

It's difficult, however, for members of a large team to have working knowledge of all of the resources at their disposal. Network behavior is such that we tend to know our networks up to two steps removed from our own spot in the network: the "I know someone who knows someone" phenomenon. A point person, whose job is (put it in the job description) to know the depth and breadth of the team's skill set, can be the pivot that enables everyone else on the team to access each other. Figure 9.3 illustrates how this network model can help resolve a question or challenge that comes up in the development process.

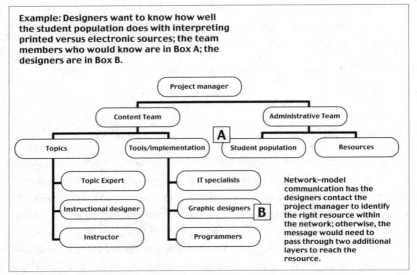

Figure 9.3   This example of a network model can help resolve a question or challenge from the development process.

Distance Learning Is in Beta

Over the past several years, developments in distance learning have been made on college campuses, in association offerings, and within corporate training and knowledge management efforts. More adult learners of all kinds have some experience with distance learning or at least in working with collaborative teams at a geographic distance from one another. But there's still a lot of evolution to come: Many distance learning programs are designed and launched without much careful thought as to what their educational role should be—or even whether the students are able to learn in this way. Many organizations have a sense that distance learning can benefit them, but they haven't quite quantified (or even qualified) what that benefit could be. Cost savings is always high on their wish lists, along with the ability to reach a larger audience than with other forms of learning.

On top of the other challenges inherent in any distance learning program then, collaborative development teams face the overall challenge of focusing on a given project and tuning out the noise. A team can become distracted by the next hot thing; there may be external or even internal pressure to go with a solution or move to a distance format because that's the direction in which the lemmings are rushing these days. Or a team can become distracted by the loudest voice in the room, the person who declares that it can't possibly work and that *this* educational problem can only be solved in a traditional learning environment or with a particular distance platform.

The "distance" in distance learning describes geography; it does not require technology to be successful. It does, however, require a process-driven approach, a team of people who are willing and able to pool their collective wisdom and skill, sound instructional design, a method of packaging and delivering content, a student population motivated to learn, and instructors dedicated to connecting with students and establishing a classroom culture of learning. It requires a lot of support and creativity.

It also requires an orientation toward constant improvement. Following any implementation, the team needs to reflect on its successes and on areas in which there can be further improvements. Among the advantages of collaborative development of distance learning, as well as collaborative reflection on its outcomes, is that you always have opportunity, mechanism, and process for improving things. Whatever results you have achieved with a given program can be incrementally better the next time.

Always return to the fundamentals: Interaction with content, instructor, and peers is essential. Everything else is extra credit.

Worksheet 9.2   Worksheet and Discussion Guide: Distance Learning as a
Collaborative Enterprise

Members of the collaborative team should respond privately to these questions
and then share their responses with the rest of the team.

1. Introductions

    Introduce yourself in terms of your role in the distance learning project.

    > Example: My name is Robin, and I am the instructor for this course. My role
    > is to co-create the content for the course and then facilitate the students' learning
    > by helping them interact with the content, each other, and me.

    Does this description of yourself feel strange somehow? Natural?

2. Questions about roles

    What questions, if any, do you have about your role?

    Who might know the answer or be able to help you find it?

3. What are the biggest challenges for you in fulfilling your role?

    Challenges I have control over:

    Challenges I do not have control over:

4. Consider the challenges you have control over. What are two things you could do to
    neutralize them?

5. Consider the challenges you have no control over. What is missing that, if it were present,
    would enable you to overcome these challenges?

6. What are you most excited about in this project or course?

About the Author

Robin Neidorf is currently the director of research for FreePint Ltd., a U.K.-based publisher dedicated to raising the value of information in organizations. FreePint has a global audience of information practitioners who rely on the company's articles and reports to get and deliver professional development, support business decisions around information products and services, and stay ahead of rapid changes in research and information management.

Through FreePint, Robin investigates, comments, speaks, and trains on a number of information-related topics, including content licensing and copyright, mobile technology, communications, and knowledge management. She was responsible for designing and launching the highly successful FreePint Webinar series, which delivers professional development to information professionals at their desktops.

Prior to joining FreePint, Robin ran a research and communications consultancy. In her client work, she often evaluated technical functionality to determine how to use those functions to further business, organizational, or educational goals. In reviewing the various technologies available for distance learning, she helped instructors and organizations understand how to use different functions without getting hung up on particular software packages or technologies that continue to undergo evolution.

Index

BWS (Bennington Writing
   Seminars), 3, 30

C

career development through edu-
   cation/experience, 179
casual learning opportunities,
   182–185
charter, team, 170–173
chat rooms, 25–26, 59, 133, 144
chemistry of classroom, 41–42
class management. *See also*
   communications
   asynchronous classrooms,
      129–133
   culture, creating, 129
   described, 113–114
   dialogue, encouraging, 124
   feedback, delivering, 72, 98,
      125–127, 156–159
   feedback on, 136–137
   guidelines, 138–139
   instructor expectations, 114
   predictability, 114–117
   repetition, 49, 101–102, 125, 166
   responsiveness, 120–121, 122
   student expectations, 114
   traditional classrooms com-
      pared, 113
   when problems occur, 127–129
   worksheets, 138, 139
classroom, defined, 113
collaborative courses, advantages,
   54
collaborative development of
   course, 191–192
collaborative online workspaces,
   22–23
communications
   assessing student, 143
   audience-focus, 41
   encouraging, 122–123, 124

of expectations, 118–119,
   126–127
of grading standards, 157–158
to improve student motivation,
   159
between instructional design
   team, 199–200
with instructor, 126
limiting off-topic, 123
peer, 126
private, 122–123, 166–167
"pull," 18, 120
"push," 18, 118–120
skills required, 11–12
technology difficulties, 130
telephone, 36, 53, 77
variety, 101
video-over-internet, 165
communities of practice, learning
   opportunities, 182–183
community, building, 163, 164,
   165–167
computer simulations, 52, 53, 100
The Conditions of Learning
   (Gagne), 71–72
conferences, benefits of informal
   learning at professional, 189
conferencing, web-based, 26–27,
   28
confidence, building student,
   45–46, 144
conflict, 127–128, 132, 169
consulting companies, training
   from, 180
content, course. *See also* instructional design
   building on previous, 72
   core, 97–98, 99
   determining appropriate
      amount, 69–71
   development worksheets, 111,
      112
   lectures, 88–90
   limiting, 189
   presenting, 72

provided by others, 85
reusable, 105
supplemental materials, 53, 70,
    155
understanding how to create,
    85–86
content management software,
    course content provided by,
    85
continuing education, 179–180
continuous improvement of learn-
    ing program, 201
continuum concept guideline, 32
contribution to group activities,
    lack of, 169
core content, 97–98, 99
corporations, 179–180, 189
correspondence courses, determi-
    nants of success, 163
cost of informal distance learning,
    181
course management systems, 108
culture, creating classroom, 129
curriculum, course. *See* content,
    course

D

definition of key terms, 103
demands on student time, 44, 132
design of distance learning pro-
    grams. *See* instructional
    design
development expert role in course
    design, 195
dialogue. *See* communications
Discover Your Learning Styles—
    Graphically (website), 50, 51
discussion, 98, 130
distance learning
    advantages over traditional
        classes, 6, 7
    challenges, 4–5
    defined, 5

examples, 32–35
future trends, 200
growth, 7
requirements, 201
variety, 6
documents, instructional, 77, 101

E

ease of use, increasing ability, 36
ebooks, instruction via, 6
efficiency of informal distance
    learning, 180
elearning, 22, 52, 77, 105–108
email as instructional tool, 6, 19,
    28–29, 77
email digests, 19. *See also* listservs
emergencies, handling,, 116, 117
emotional responses of teachers,
    141
end-of-class course assessment,
    137–138
English as second language stu-
    dents, 145
errors, responding to procedural,
    121
evaluation
    of learning program, 137–138,
        201
    of student, 174–175
    of student outcomes, 136–137
expectations
    communicating teacher's to
        students, 118–119,
        126–127
    of students, 14, 15–16
experience, student, 43

F

FAQ (Frequently Asked Questions)
    pages, 183–184